MUSICAL PRODIGIES

Also by Renee B. Fisher
Heroes of Music

MUSICAL PRODIGIES

Masters at an Early Age

Renee B. Fisher

ASSOCIATION PRESS / NEW YORK

International Standard Book Number: 0-8096-1854-0

Library of Congress Catalog Card Number: 72-13970

Chapters from this book have appeared previously, in somewhat different form, in *Opera News, Bandwagon,* and *Music Journal* magazines.

Library of Congress Cataloging in Publication Data

Fisher, Renee B
    Musical prodigies.

    Bibliography: p.
    1. Children as musicians. 2. Gifted children.
    3. Musicians—Biography. I. Title.
    ML81.F58   780'.92'2 [B]   72-13970
    ISBN 0-8096-1854-0

Contents

	Foreword by Yehudi Menuhin	7
	Acknowledgments	8
	Introduction: What Is a Musical Prodigy?	9
1	The Prodigy Composers	15
2	How to Succeed as a Child Prodigy	25
3	The Violin Prodigies	35
4	The Piano Prodigies	43
5	Voices That Rang Out Young	57
6	Two Black Prodigies on the Concert Stage	69
7	Podium Precocity—The Conductors	81
8	Two Violinists—A Study in Contrasts	91
9	All Kinds of Prodigies	105
10	The New Generation in the Concert Hall	127
11	Two Prodigies of Early Jazz	135
12	Nonclassical Prodigies—Jazz, Blues, Folk, Rock	147
13	The Role of Heredity	163
14	The Role of Environment	169
15	The Prodigy Personality	179
16	The Crystal Ball	185
	Supplement: Other Musical Prodigies	195
	Select Bibliography	232
	Index of Names	237

5

Foreword

I hope that this book, which deals specifically with the musically gifted child, will convey to the public not the uniqueness of the gifted child (in whatever area of endeavor), so much as the frighteningly rare concurrence of favorable factors—wise and good parents, an encouraging environment, high spiritual and moral standards, enlightenment and humility, self-discipline, sheer good health and vitality, foresight and vision, good luck and good timing—all of which are essential if the gift that resides in every child is to find expression.

It is not only the obvious victims of prejudice such as non-whites, non-Christians, and women who are the real victims of society, for they are still able to raise their voices in protest. It is the children, those living and those yet to be born, who during their first years are sacrificed on the altar of adult vanity, neglect, laziness, cupidity and shortsightedness. Their inquisitive minds are often crammed with the cheap, the false and the trivial, their bodies exploited by the promoters of sweets, soft drinks and food additives. Many of them are kept uneducated by an unequal school system. We wonder at the rebellious assertiveness among many of the young, and at the same time are amazed by the child who excels at the violin, dancing, chess or sports, or by a William Pitt who at the age of 24 became Prime Minister of England. Equally amazing is the present lack of veneration accorded the aged.

Let us, then, forget personal and national grievances and concern ourselves with the well-being of all children everywhere. Let us give them a wholesome environment, inspiration, encouragement, clean air and water, and nutritious food. It was these simple and real things that accounted for the proliferation of so-called "prodigies" in the San Francisco of my youth. These things children need if we truly desire for them peace, happiness and health, as we do for ourselves.

YEHUDI MENUHIN

7

Acknowledgments

This book could not have been written without the generous help and gracious encouragement of many people, including all of the following:

●Louis Armstrong, Louise Behrend, Darius Brubeck, Benny Goodman, John Hammond, Yehudi Menuhin, Mother Morgan, David Putterman, Harry Randall, Ruggiero Ricci, George Schuyler, Ruth Slenczynska, Virgil Thomson, and Jerry Wexler,

●The staffs of the Westport Public Library, the Pequot Library, the Music Reference Room of the Lincoln Center Library of the Performing Arts, the Hansen Library of the University of Bridgeport, and the Sterling Memorial Library of Yale University,

●The following concert managements co-operated by supplying biographical data on their artists: Mariedi Anders Artists Management; Herbert Barrett Management; M. Bichurin Concerts Corporation; Colbert Artists; Columbia Artists Management; Claire Cox; Thea Dispeker; Eastman Boomer Management; Walter Homburger; Hurok Concerts; Judd Concert Artist Bureau; Judson, O'Neill, Beall and Steinway; Albert Kay Associates, Inc.; William Morris; New York Recital Associates, Inc.; Anne J. O'Donnell Management; Pacific World Artists; Benjamin Patterson, Ltd.; Frank E. Salomon; Shaw Concerts, Inc.; Sheldon Soffer Management, Inc.; and Young Concert Artists, Inc.

● In considering the issues of heredity and environment in relation to musical prodigies, I owe a debt of gratitude to Amram Scheinfeld and his enlightening book *Your Heredity and Environment.*

●Milton Fisher, no mere indulgent husband he but a positive inspirational force, a mine of suggestions, and a receptive but critical listener every page of the way.

Introduction:

What Is a Musical Prodigy?

When Bobby Fischer, the new world chess champion, was asked how he had managed to become United States champion at the age of fourteen, he shrugged and said, "I got good." If his modest reply had been "I got great" it would have been closer to the truth. And the world, as it calls anyone who becomes great in a particular field at an early age, dubbed Bobby a "prodigy."

There have been prodigies, by that definition, in dozens of fields from science to sports. The number in music, oddly, exceeds the total for all other fields combined. Strike out the over-three-hundred musical prodigies indexed in this book and there would go most of the recorded history of Western music.

Why has the role of the prodigy in music been the rule more often than the exception? To answer that question requires first of all a definition of the term itself. "Prodigy" did not always refer to people; hurricanes and earthquakes, for example, were called "prodigies of nature" to indicate their extraordinary quality. "Extraordinary" crops up in all the definitions, no matter which dictionary is consulted. The words "wonderful" and "marvelous" are also used freely. But all is not sweetness and light. One definition speaks ominously of "something abnormal or monstrous." And that implication resounds like a jarring discord throughout the critical literature. In 1930 one expert noted: "The thing looks spooky. The idea of a child of ten years or so possessing not only mature technical skill but mature mental and emotional capacities smacks disquietingly of reincarnation."

Harold Schonberg, the New York *Times* music critic, used the

9

same term, "spooky," in referring in 1968 to certain feats of prodigy-musicians, adding, with tongue in cheek, "In a well-regulated society they would have been burned at the stake for being in league with occult powers." The pianist Artur Schnabel once compared prodigies to "five-legged cows seen on exhibition in a circus; when they mature, they generally lose one leg and cease to draw the crowds."

The attitude of many educators is summed up this way in the *Encyclopedia of Modern Education:* "The term 'prodigy' for many years suggested a child who was peculiar, unhealthy, even a freak, and is, for this reason, a term avoided in educational circles today." Instead, a euphemism is used—"gifted children." The word "precocious" is in even worse repute. Literally it means "precooked"; connotatively, it has come to mean "half-baked." In popular terms, one saying has it that "a child prodigy is a youngster who is too young to be as old as he is."

Youth will certainly have to figure in the final definition. A composite definition based on the first listings of all the major dictionaries reads something like this: "Prodigy: a person who shows early signs of extraordinary talent or exceptional ability." One needs definitions only for "early," "signs," "extraordinary," "talent," "exceptional," and "ability" to know exactly what a prodigy is!

For the present, the years under twenty will be considered the "early" ones. It is necessarily an arbitrary decision; no one has as yet put a mathematical limit on youth. It is of course true that twenty was a more mature age, in an economic as well as a professional sense, two hundred years ago than it is today; but, on the other hand, our criteria for extraordinary achievement have risen so sharply that the score probably evens up. Also, there has to be a common chronological base to make comparisons meaningful. All the prodigies to be discussed, therefore—whether in performance or composition—displayed unusual talent and achievement before the age of twenty.

Just why there have been so many prodigies in music is far from clear. There have been enough nonprodigies who made good (Wagner, Paderewski, most singers, etc.) to indicate that you don't *have* to be a prodigy to succeed in later musical life. To separate composing from performing for the moment: music composition, of all the arts, is perhaps the least dependent on worldly experience. Of course its basic raw material comes from the "world" of natural and man-made sounds. But the composing of music is a much more internal process than is either painting or writing, because these feed more directly upon lived experiences filtered through a creative viewpoint.

Given, then, that mysterious keen ear for organizing sounds heard and imagined, and the technical training necessary for putting those musical ideas on paper, the fact that many composers begin writing creditable music in their early teens and even before begins to be understandable. We would not, of course, expect to find in these juvenile efforts that maturity of approach and universality of emotion which mark the greatest musical masterpieces; for those the composer needs the kind of experiences that the first twenty years of life seldom offer. It will be the rare composer, then, who is able to produce any of his *best* work before the age of twenty. Yet even this did happen, as will be shown.

Prodigies of performance are more numerous, more dazzling, and more difficult to comprehend and assess. With all the expertise of modern psychology, personality analysis, biochemistry, etc., at its disposal, the world today is still far from being able to understand how a child of eight or nine is able to compress perhaps ten years' worth of motor skill and memorizing, of musical understanding and even emotional sensitivity, into his short life. Furthermore, he must submit that feat to the gruelling test of public performance. No musical prodigy, it should be realized, can perpetrate the kind of hoax that may occur with literary or art prodigies; there are too many witnesses.

Is it because they feel inadequate in assessing musical ability that behavioral scientists have shied away from intensive investigation of this area? Surely better understanding of the speeded-up learning processes of prodigies (particularly in music, where they are most numerous) could help lay bare the basic principles behind the learning process as a whole. The complete knowledge of how prodigies develop may be as crucial to our understanding of the learning process as the discovery of DNA was to our knowledge of the development of life itself. (Hopefully, today's scientists will not be deterred by the unfortunate experience some years ago of G. Revesz, a Hungarian psychologist who wrote a fine, scholarly book called *An Introduction to the Psychology of Music*. The difficulty was that he attempted to apply his theories by predicting, in another book called *The Psychology of a Musical Prodigy,* a brilliant future as a composer for a young Hungarian boy. The subsequent failure of the boy to live up to the prediction undermined the validity of Revesz's theories. In his overeagerness, this scientist had equated understanding with predictability—something that few today would presume to do.)

Just how reliable are the witnesses of early musical achievement?

Today, with the ready availability of recordings as well as live performances and sophisticated criticism, it is relatively easy to distinguish an extraordinary performer from one of average or merely superior talent. But the evidence of exceptional abilities and achievement becomes more tenuous as we move backward in time. Indeed, testimony is sometimes based on scraps of reminiscences by music-loving dilettantes or on conflicting opinions of often-venal critics of the day; or even on possibly biased, often inexpert, reactions by students, teachers or fellow musicians of the prodigy in question. Only occasionally are there knowledgeable critical judgments expressed by professional composers and musicians like Robert Schumann and Hector Berlioz, who combined musical and literary careers.

Fortunately, many musical prodigies became literate adults with a flair for writing. They have provided us with autobiographies vividly recalling the hazards and rewards of early musical achievement. To cite just a few: How a prodigy fared under the eighteenth-century court patronage system is delightfully portrayed in Karl von Dittersdorf's *Autobiography*. Anton Rubinstein's *Autobiography* shows the tribulations of a Jewish prodigy born in Czarist Russia, who became the intimate of kings and the idol of the masses. Gregor Piatigorsky's *Cello* illustrates how the buffeting of the Russian Revolution spread prodigies throughout the world; and Joseph Szigeti's *With Strings Attached* shows how they made out in the New World.

Harold Bauer: His Book describes the strange transition of Bauer, adolescent violinist, into Bauer, mature pianist. In *Theme and Variations* Bruno Walter gives us a thoughtful, sensitive portrayal of that rarer species, the conductor-prodigy. Among singers, the Russian bass Feodor Chaliapin, in his *Autobiography,* told of his boyhood struggle against all but invincible musical and economic odds. The American Geraldine Farrar's *Such Sweet Compulsion* paints in vivid (and far from modest) colors the traditional pilgrimage of a young American musician to Europe for training and opportunity.

Also, there have been several teachers of musical prodigies who have left valuable recollections of the behavior, reactions, and abilities of their outstanding students. Best among these are violin-teacher Leopold Auer's *My Long Life in Music,* and Mathilde Marchesi's *Marchesi and Music,* which sheds light on the early careers of many famous singers.

The compelling story of how a woman pianist of mixed racial background fared in the largely white world of the concert stage is told in Philippa Schuyler's *Adventure in Black and White.* Perhaps most horrifying of all prodigy autobiographies is pianist Ruth Slenczynska's story, a searing indictment of parental exploitation, called *Forbidden Childhood*.

Among composers there have been, fortunately, some of the most prodigious talents, like Mozart and Mendelssohn, who were also superb letter-writers at an early age; they give us a rare opportunity to learn, in their own words, how they themselves reacted to their extraordinary gifts. Occasionally a particularly doting parent has even written the autobiography his talented offspring never got around to writing, as in *The Memoirs of Mischa Elman's Father*!

In the realm of jazz the hand of the ghost-writer or collaborator lies heavy on most of the prodigy autobiographies. Nevertheless, Louis Armstrong's *Satchmo,* Sidney Bechet's *Treat It Gentle,* Billie Holiday's *Lady Sings the Blues,* Benny Goodman's *The Kingdom of Swing,* and Fats Waller's *Ain't Misbehavin',* among others, provide important insights into the very different problems jazz prodigies have faced, and the varying ways in which they have reacted.

Something new in musical recollections appeared in 1972 when Andrés Segovia narrated the first part of his autobiography on a record called "The Guitar and I." He reminisces about his early youth, his first exposure to music, his adolescent problems both musical and personal. All are narrated in his inimitable English heavy with Spanish overtones. The record gives us valuable clues, with a great sense of immediacy, as to how one prodigy grew to maturity.

The sources of our information on prodigies, then, range from valuable memoirs and letters to more or less authentic evaluations by contemporaries and later chroniclers, along with naive ramblings of dubious relevance. Yet such being the stuff that history is made of, why should the history of musical prodigies be an exception? Much of the bits and pieces of information and opinion that the available sources have yielded is gathered here. It is hoped that they will form a meaningful pattern on a fascinating subject.

In the course of examining the careers, personalities and heritage of these musical prodigies, this book attempts to shed some light on particular aspects of musical and social history. To provide a scientific explanation of the phenomena is beyond our scope and will have to await, as indicated, the intensive microscope of a social scientist applied to these fugitive bits and pieces of evidence. Not that we need to cloak our natural curiosity about musical prodigies in lofty purpose. Their unique abilities have led their lives down strange paths strewn with tragedy, comedy, pathos, irony, and eccentricity; their characters have ranged from admirable to despicable. Their stories are often as fantastic and bizarre as their gifts are incomprehensible.

)

1
The Prodigy Composers

The earliest prodigy composers seemed to be supermen. There was not the specialization of today; most composers started out as performers. As such they were expected to be able to improvise (compose spontaneously at their instruments). Usually they played more than one instrument well enough for public performance.

Johann Sebastian Bach (1685–1750) was born near the end of the seventeenth century. He came from a family of German musicians and composers. In those days it was very exceptional for any Bach *not* to be a musician. Enmeshed for several generations in every facet of musical life in the German province of Thuringia, the very word "Bach" was for a long time synonymous with "musician." The annual gatherings of the Bach clan traditionally featured vocal and instrumental jam sessions.

Although his father taught him to play the violin as early as he could hold one, it was his elder brother who started Sebastian on clavier (an early keyboard instrument) and music theory. He hankered after the organ, however, the way boys today do for the guitar. Once started on it he mastered every page of music put in front of him and longed for more. There is a well-attested story to the effect that his brother doled out the precious hand-copied music as needed, but that Sebastian knew of a particularly choice collection kept in a barred cupboard. In his hunger for new music he forced the rolled-up book through the bars of the cupboard and nightly he laboriously copied it page by page in the moonlight, taking six months to do it, before he was discovered and the book confiscated.

15

Bach was a good all-around student as well. At fifteen he became a scholarship choirboy. When his voice broke a year later he was kept on for his ability as a skilled harpsichordist, organist and violinist. He thought nothing of walking sixty miles to hear a great organist, and once walked one hundred and twenty miles to hear French music in another town. By eighteen, after a short stint as court-violinist, he began the career that occupied him, in various places, for the rest of his life—a career as organist and choirleader. It soon became obvious that his discipline of the boys under him was as bad as the music he wrote for them was good. It was at nineteen that he wrote the two harpsichord pieces still widely played today—"Capriccio," and "Capriccio on the Departure of a Beloved Brother." His early virtuosity and widespread fame, it appears, rested on Bach the organist rather than Bach the composer. Few new organs were installed anywhere in his part of Germany without Bach being sent for to try them out and to play at their dedication.

Bach's place in music history, on the other hand, is as one of the greatest, if not the very greatest, of composers. Masterpieces flowed from his quill in almost every medium of music, whether organ, orchestra, keyboard instruments, violin, cello or choral works. He summed up all that was best from the previous centuries of polyphonic music, and was at the very pinnacle of the baroque period in which he lived.

George Frideric Handel (1685–1759) was born in the same year as Bach, but their careers followed entirely different paths. He was the sole musician on the Handel family tree. There must have been a tremendous inner force that drove him to music—that made him absorb so entirely the musical environment that could only be found outside his home. Three years of ardent but grueling study made the boy expert at the oboe (his favorite instrument), harpsichord, and organ, as well as in counterpoint and composition.

Where did his musical abilities come from? Surely not from his strict father, sixty-two years old at George's birth, who positively forbade music in the home; nor from his timid mother, who dared not rebel against his father's decrees; perhaps from the affectionate aunt who probably smuggled in the portable clavichord on which George practiced secretly in the attic. We only know for certain that he learned to play and to improvise (on organ as well as clavichord) by the age of seven, impressively enough so that the Duke of Saxe-Weissenfels, on hearing him try out the chapel organ, insisted that he be given musical training! Nothing could have shocked the father more, but he didn't dare disobey his most valued patron.

During his earliest years of study George probably wrote over a hundred church services as well as considerable secular music. The earliest surviving example is a set of six trio sonatas written at the age of ten. They are solidly-constructed, typical works of the period.

At the age of eleven he visited Berlin, where the Electress Sophie Charlotte, herself an accomplished musician, tried to assume a music patron role similar to that of Louis XIV in France. Enchanted with Handel's playing, she and her husband offered to take him into their service at court, after first sending him to Italy for further training. His father refused, however, and hastily recalled him home.

Within a year Handel began to play the organ for several local churches, and started a voluntary choir for which he wrote music. At the age of fifteen he was considered a first-rate musician; by the time he was seventeen he had been offered a very important organ post. He went on to become one of the greatest organists of the eighteenth century—a fact often overshadowed by his fame as a composer. At nineteen he was already serving as violinist and part-time conductor at the Hamburg Opera, and managing to find time to write a "Passion" (one of the religious musical forms) as well as his first opera.

A passion of a different sort was involved in an incident of the year before. Buxtehude, the great organist, was about to retire from his church position at Lübeck. Handel, along with his friend and fellow musician, Johann Mattheson, hastily applied to enter the competition for the spot; both retreated even more hastily when they learned that the string attached to the position was marriage to Buxtehude's elderly ugly daughter!

At any rate, Handel remained a bachelor all his life. If he had married, the rest of his days might well have followed Bach's pattern of German church musician. Instead, Handel wrote his first and highly successful opera *Almira* and became a worldly, urbane, internationally famous composer of operas and oratorios whose career was fully launched by the time he was twenty.

Franz Joseph Haydn (1732–1809) is our best example of how well composers could fare under the protection of a royal patron. His childhood, however, was marked by deprivation and neglect. Torn from a culturally meager but happy home at six, he just managed to sustain himself in a cousin's home as a church singer with an exceptional ear and voice. He somehow picked up a working knowledge of clavier, violin and—of all things!—kettledrums, along the way.

At the age of eight he left all semblance of home life and departed for Vienna, where for nine years he sang under Johann Reutter at St. Stephen's Cathedral. Reutter was so unfeeling that he gave no more than two lessons in composition to young Franz, whose insatiable urge to compose was already driving him to write compositional illiteracies on every piece of manuscript paper he could find. Ironically, the vain self-centered Reutter, a successful composer in his day, is remembered solely for his neglect of Haydn.

Haydn was starved physically as well as musically. To complete the shameful picture, it was this same Reutter who tried unsuccessfully to prolong and further exploit Haydn's vocal virtuosity by suggesting, when the boy's voice began to break at the age of thirteen, that as a *castrato* (as the popular castrated artificial sopranos were called) he would enjoy a much longer career.

Franz was dismissed from St. Stephen's at seventeen, on the barest pretext of misconduct—he had clipped the pigtail of a classmate sitting in front of him. He was caned and thrown out into the street with nothing but the clothes he had on his back. From that moment on he carved out his own destiny without the usual starting boost of a patron. Not only did he eventually win widespread fame and recognition in his later years, but his position in music is secure as the father of the symphony in its modern form, and as one of the most prolific and accomplished masters of the classical period in music history.

H. L. Mencken once wrote of Wolfgang Amadeus Mozart (1756–1791), "Like Schubert, he is beyond analysis: he simply happened." But unlike Schubert, Mozart happened in part as a result of a driving, ambitious father who was determined to make a prodigy out of his son.

There is nothing simple about a four-year-old who is able to play many long musical compositions from memory, writing his own short works at five, and by six picking up sufficient virtuosity on the violin to be able to sit in with a grown-up string quartet. In the same year Mozart's violin-playing charmed a customs official out of examining the family luggage. All this on his *second* instrument, since of course it was as a pianist that his father exhibited him up and down the Continent. It was on one of these grand tours, when Mozart was seven, that he spent an hour at the organ in a Heidelberg church; the dean, over-come, ordered an inscription carved on the organ case attesting to the name and age of the boy and the date of the modern miracle he had witnessed.

Picture Wolfgang in clothing of lilac and gold, his older sister Nanette dressed in rose and silver, being fondled and rewarded by kings and queens everywhere. "We could open a shop with all the presents, jewelry, swords and laces, snuffboxes, etc., that are showered on the children," wrote his father. Honor, glory and gifts—but never did Leopold Mozart and his two phenomenal children get what they needed most: enough hard money to live on, and dependable patronage for the future.

When, at the age of eight, Mozart played in London together with Johann Christian Bach (one of Sebastian's many talented children), he was billed as a "Prodigy of Nature." Bach said of his playing "It surpasses all understanding and all imagination." Many musicians refused to accept fees when playing with him; rather, deeming it a privilege. The Philosophical Society investigated his ability the next year, ordering him to play and sing at sight, to compose in particular styles, to play with the piano keys covered, etc. He passed all tests with flying colors. He could undoubtedly read at sight, transpose and improvise superbly before he was ten.

All his gifts as a virtuoso performer would never have saved him from oblivion, however. It is as a composer that Mozart was known as the greatest child prodigy before Schubert and Mendelssohn. He wrote swiftly and surely, with concentration and astonishing maturity from the very start. By the time he was eleven he had composed operettas, sonatas and symphonies as well as a sheaf of shorter works! It is small wonder that at the age of fourteen he was admitted (the youngest in history) to the august Philharmonic Academies of both Bologna and Verona—his three-act opera *Mitridate* had already achieved a great success. At fifteen he wrote to his sister from Milan: "Above us there is a violinist, below us another, next to us a singing master who gives lessons, in the last room opposite us an oboist; that makes it fun to compose, gives me many ideas."

If we no longer hear the masses, trumpet concerto, symphonies, oratorios and other works he had written before the age of seventeen, we still have some idea of his youthful style from the opera "Lucio Silla," which was revived in New York City several seasons ago: "Most of the music is beautiful, sometimes brilliant, sometimes poignant" stated a critic at the time, and concluded, "certainly deserving of occasional production."

The rest of Mozart's life (a scant eighteen years) constitutes a tragic tale—stupendous creative achievement going hand in hand with utter frustration, lack of recognition and physical disintegration. Thus, in heartbreak and sadness at the age of thirty-six, ended the life of the world's outstanding double prodigy in composing and performing. Even a hundredth of the veneration in which Mozart is held today would have been enough to change beyond measure (and probably to have prolonged) his pitiful and brief existence.

If all the composers we now call great had stopped composing at the age of twenty, which would still be called great? Surprisingly few. By and large, the creative gift matures much later than the interpretative one. Mendelssohn or Mozart would probably be in second place on such a list, and Bizet most likely third. Top rank, beyond dispute, would go to Franz Schubert (1797–1828), whose sole virtuosity lay in the music he wrote.

The story of Schubert's first twenty years would be incredible were it not for verified accounts by many of his contemporaries. Born into a schoolmaster's family of musical amateurs (in both senses of the word), he soon absorbed a little violin, viola, piano and organ from his father and older brother. When they played together during Franz's school holidays he early proved to be the most musically sensitive. As his brother wrote: "Whenever a mistake was made, no matter how small, he would look the guilty one in the face. . . . If Papa, who played the cello, was in the wrong . . . he would say quite shyly and smilingly: 'Sir, there must be a mistake somewhere!' and our good father would gladly be taught by him."

Schubert was the least trained of all the great composers. Attending the Choristers School of the Imperial Chapel in Vienna (always with not quite enough to eat and with no money for concerts unless he sold his books) he played violin in the student orchestra. At fourteen he was writing music on hand-ruled scraps of paper until a fellow student, overawed by the compositions Schubert showed him, began to supply him with manuscript paper. It was to this same friend, one von Spaun, that Schubert once said in humble sincerity, "Secretly, in my heart of hearts, I still hope to be able to make something out of myself, but who can do anything after Beethoven?"

Schubert seldom used a piano when composing. Anywhere, with all

kinds of conversation and noise around him, he would sit "bent over
the music paper and a book of poems, bite his pen, drum with his fingers at the same time, trying things out, and continue to write easily
and fluently, without many corrections, as if it had to be like that and
not otherwise."

A friend characterized his rapid and instinctive placement of notes
on paper as "hurling" the notes down. His friends ransacked the entire
German lyric literature to keep ahead of him, and when he was given
a new poem he caught the mood and feeling on a single reading. By
the second reading the notes were already ordered in his mind, so that
the quill had a hard job keeping ahead of the musical thought. How
else could he have written six, seven, and even eight songs a day?
Among the two hundred and fifty songs he wrote in his seventeenth
and eighteenth years were "The Erl King," "Wanderer's Night Song,"
and "Gretchen at the Spinning Wheel." His settings of Goethe's poems
alone were enough to earn him immortality. To list all the musical
works he wrote before he was twenty, including symphonies, operas,
string quartets, masses, etc., in addition to the songs, would take several book pages.

And now the clincher: This enormous and surpassingly beautiful
output from the age of seventeen to twenty was produced in his spare
moments while he held a full-time teaching position!

Schubert's compositions never earned him so much as a thousand
dollars during his entire lifetime. A devoted band of friends gave him
food, lodging, admiration and the only audience he ever had. With
neither royal patronage nor public concerts to sustain him, he still
managed to write over six hundred songs (including the "Serenade,"
"Hark, Hark the Lark," and "Who Is Sylvia?"). In addition he gave
to the world many immortal masterpieces in other fields such as symphonies and chamber music. He died very young, at thirty-one, never
dreaming that his works would earn for him a shining immortality as
the greatest of all melodists, and would serve as direct inspiration for
every song composer from his day to ours.

All the prodigy composers mentioned so far have been German or
Austrian; later there were the French Georges Bizet and Camille
Saint-Saëns, the English John Field, the Rumanian Georges Enesco,
among many others. Americans are conspicuously missing, and with
good reason: For most of the nineteenth century it was extremely difficult for would-be composers and performers born in the United

States to get proper training and to start careers in their native land. Most virtuoso performers in the United States were Europeans who had ventured the hazardous trip across the ocean in order to reap the large fees paid for appearances in the entertainment-hungry cities of the New World. Not until well toward the end of the 1800's were there enough trained musicians settled permanently in the United States to make the founding of music conservatories possible.

Even without the facilities for proper training, the very first American composer to achieve an international reputation was a prodigy. Louis Gottschalk (1829–1869) grew up in New Orleans, which was a kind of European and African outpost right in the swampy heart of America—a crossroads at which many cultures met. The son of well-to-do English-Creole parents, from early childhood Louis was exposed to the strong French influence of the early New Orleans society (still strong today). The city was a center for performances of French operas. Spain also had had its turn at ruling New Orleans, and there was a strong Spanish influence from Caribbean islanders who had settled in the gay, cosmopolitan city. Also from the Caribbean had come Afro-Cubans, with their own exciting musical culture. And New Orleans attracted a great many freedmen (black slaves who had been set free), who brought to the city their plantation songs and remnants of African musical traditions.

It was this heady mixture of musical currents that later made New Orleans the natural birthplace of jazz; and these surroundings stimulated powerfully the keen musical imagination of little Louis Gottschalk, who watched and listened with fascination to the ritual African dances in the Place Congo as well as to the popular syncopated beats of the Afro-Cuban bands. Meanwhile he was studying the piano (and improvising on his own); at the age of ten he succeeded in dazzling musically knowledgeable New Orleans with his public debut. By the time he was twelve it was obvious that only in Europe could his exuberant talent be developed further. He sailed for Paris after a farewell concert that amounted to a city-wide ovation.

The head of the Paris Conservatoire wouldn't even listen to Louis' playing. "Americans are not musicians—they build railroads," he said contemptuously. But after four years of private study Gottschalk was ready. He had not only put the finishing touches on his playing, but had also acquired all the airs and accomplishments of a Parisian gentleman. He had been welcomed in the most exclusive aristocratic salons where high society mingled with its favorite artists, musicians and writers.

Gottschalk gave his first Paris concert when he was sixteen and every musician of note attended. He played a concerto by Chopin (who was in the audience), and the composer was so impressed that he predicted to Gottschalk after the concert: "You will be the king of pianists." Berlioz arranged follow-up appearances, Liszt championed him from the start. But what really swept the jaded Parisians off their feet, even more than the brilliance of his playing, were the original compositions he played.

Gottschalk came from the country that the Europeans pictured as the land of noble savages. As one Parisian newspaper exclaimed: "An American composer?—good God!" The music itself amazed them, for in his earliest works Gottschalk already drew on what to European ears were the utterly exotic musical elements he had absorbed back in New Orleans. Within a short time after his first concert a newspaper commented: "Who does not know the 'Bamboula'?" Not only the "Bamboula," which had spicy cakewalk rhythms, but the African beat of "The Banana Tree," and his free arrangements of old Creole melodies all proved utterly irresistible. Every concert pianist played them; the piano-playing public made the publisher of the latest Gottschalk pieces rich by buying copies by the thousands, almost as fast as they could be printed.

After several triumphant years in France, Switzerland and Spain, Gottschalk returned to the United States in 1853, when he was twenty-four. For the remaining years of his life he toured the States, the West Indies and South America, giving thousands of concerts, arranging elaborate music festivals in Brazil and elsewhere. His Creole background gave him a special fondness for Latin-American people, and this feeling was reciprocated. The circumstances of his death at the age of forty had all the drama of an old-fashioned movie scenario: he collapsed on stage while playing an original piece entitled "She Is Dead!" Within hours, he himself was dead.

During those last thirteen years of hard touring he kept a kind of journal, published in 1964 as *Notes of a Pianist,* which offers keen insights into the life of a traveling virtuoso, the personalities he encountered, the social and economic conditions of the United States before, during and after the Civil War—all observed with intelligence, sensitivity and a touch of cynicism. For Gottschalk was fully aware of his limitations, which were largely self-imposed. He catered to his audiences, which expected their pianists to be entertainers above all. He managed in the process to raise the level of piano playing and programming on the American continent, but he didn't attempt to play the great music of the European master composers; rather his programs consisted almost entirely of his own works—not only the charming folk-based pieces which he continued to produce, but also sentimental sure-fire stuff like "The Dying Poet" and "The Last Hope,"—pieces which no audience would ever leave the concert hall without hearing.

The popularity these pieces achieved is beyond our understanding, but when Gottschalk's music underwent a considerable revival in 1969, the hundredth anniversary of his death, the American public showed itself ready to appreciate many of his other works which they had the opportunity to hear for the first time. He was the first well-known American pianist as well as composer, and the first to mine the rich vein of native American musical idioms. His music deserves its renaissance.

2
How to Succeed as a Child Prodigy

Did success spoil Felix Mendelssohn? That it didn't seems almost miraculous; the silver spoon he was born with stayed with him until his death, since he passed away, at the early age of thirty-eight, at the peak of an over-demanding acclaim. But it is the early successes that concern us here. There was every reason for him to succeed; his was a most unusual head start in life, unmatched by any other composer.

Felix Mendelssohn (1809–1847) was born at Hamburg in Germany. His grandfather was Moses Mendelssohn, the great Jewish philosopher who was known as "the German Socrates." His father's business acumen was sufficient to permit the family to live in affluence. So well educated was his mother that she had to conceal her unfashionable ability to read Greek! Also, she was able to start the children's musical instruction. Taken together it was quite a heritage.

Although the children were early baptized into the Protestant faith, there seems to have been some reluctance on the part of the parents to take the step, since they put off their own conversion for some time. A strong Jewish ethic pervaded the Mendelssohn family life—love of learning and emphasis on high goals and achievement, along with severe personal discipline and devotion to duty. In the family itself there was a great feeling of solidarity—a strong patriarchal orientation blended with deep maternal influence.

The spacious Mendelssohn home in Berlin was, from 1811 on, in a happy state of more-or-less-perpetual open house. Artists and musicians, diplomats and intellectuals—all sooner or later found their way to the Mendelssohn home for good conversation, good food and gen-

25

eral *gemütlichkeit*. Of the three (later four) handsome Mendelssohn children, the most striking was Felix, with his sturdy, healthy body, curly hair, flashing dark eyes, great animation and sensitivity, along with early aplomb. Even the slight lisp, which he never altogether lost, was appealing. His piano lessons started out of sibling rivalry. Fanny, his eight-year-old sister, was already on her way to becoming an accomplished pianist when Felix was four. At his insistence their mother started him out with simple five-minute lessons which gradually increased in time and scope. After three years, when there was nothing more she could teach him, he studied piano very briefly in France.

Meanwhile, one of the frequent visitors to the Mendelssohn home was Wilhelm von Humboldt, the Prussian minister of education, who had strong leanings toward the ancient Greek culture. Perhaps that explains the rigorous, curriculum Abraham Mendelssohn imposed on his son. It sounds straight out of Plato. There were private lessons not only for the usual three *R*'s, but also in Latin, Greek, gymnastics, landscape painting, piano, violin, and music theory. To fit it all in meant rising at five o'clock daily, six days a week, over a period of many years.

By the age of eight, when he began to study composition with Karl Friedrich Zelter (who was to exert an enormous influence on him) Felix was able to play most of the Beethoven symphonies by heart. So it is not too surprising to hear that he made his public debut at nine, appearing in a trio with two adult horn players.

The next year, during which his father became a member of the Berlin City Council, Felix began attending singing classes at the Berlin Singakademie and started writing music. He wrote a number of pieces for the chorus in which he sang, such as a setting of the Nineteenth Psalm which was performed in September of 1819. He also wrote piano duets to play with his sister Fanny at Zelter's informal Friday night musicales. (Fanny, too, did a considerable amount of composing.)

Sometimes part-songs were sung around the dining-room table, with Felix playing and directing from the piano.

The boy looked forward most to Sunday mornings, however, and not alone because of the chance they offered to sleep a little longer. At the age of eleven, instead of the usual toys of childhood, he had a live "orchestra" to play with, to conduct, and to write for. His younger sister Rebekah sang, young Paul played his half-size cello, Fanny or Felix played the piano, except when he mounted a small stool to conduct, baton in hand, spotting errors with an incredibly sensitive ear. Local amateur and professional musicians joined in every week, forming a kind of permanent floating musical ensemble eager to play music conducted by Felix, who presided happily in his tight-sleeved short jacket and balloon trousers. This was the training ground that made him one of the great early-nineteenth-century conductors of both choral and instrumental music.

He thus had what so many composers have lacked—ready-made groups to write for. And write he certainly did. By twelve his output included piano trios, a violin and piano sonata, string quartets, piano pieces, fugues, part-songs, motets, symphonies, operettas and a cantata. It was at this time that he began giving musical presents—for his birthday Paul would get a special cello piece, or Rebekah a song, or Fanny a fugue. (She was a superb Bach player.) Or he would set to music a humorous skit written by the family doctor.

There was nothing childish or scrawling about the way he wrote out these manuscripts, eventually filling forty-four volumes. From the very first he wrote with the most extraordinary neatness and finish, evidently thinking out his musical solutions in his head before notating them, since there are very few corrections or changes. Furthermore, he kept up this prolific rate for at least the four following years. Works from his twelfth year on are still in the active repertory.

Hardly a musician of any importance passing through Berlin failed to attend these Sunday morning music sessions. One of the visitors was sixteen-year-old Julius Benedict, pupil and protegé of Carl Maria von Weber. Benedict later told of playing the principal tunes from Weber's just-written *Der Freischütz* for the excited twelve-year old. Felix played them back for him a few days later—an unusual feat of memory and re-creation. This was immediately followed by the more usual forms of boyish fun, for they both went out to romp in the park, jumping hedges and climbing trees for a change of pace.

Felix, around this time, had begun trying to compose directly at the piano—extemporizing. Within a year or so he became the youngest inheritor of the mantle of great improvisers, in a direct line from Bach, Mozart and Beethoven.

It was also in his twelfth year that Felix visited Goethe for two weeks, the event having been arranged by Zelter. Before the visit there were impassioned family conferences full of admonitions on thinking before talking, speaking clearly, using good table manners, and, above all, being sure to record every utterance of the great man. Johann

Wolfgang von Goethe, then seventy-three, was a legend in his time. He was attracted to music but had at best only a superficial knowledge of it.

By piecing together the boy's letters and Goethe's comments we have a vivid idea of this remarkable encounter. Felix had a way with words even at twelve, and showed acute perception in his description of Goethe: "It does not strike me that the old gentleman's figure is imposing. He is not much taller than Father; but his look, his language, his name—*they* are imposing. His hair is not yet white, his step is firm, his manner is mild. But the amount of sound in his voice is wonderful, and he can shout like 10,000 warriors."

On the very first evening he played the piano for over two hours, impressing Goethe considerably with his improvisations and some Bach fugues. Thereafter he was asked to play every day. "I have not heard you yet today. Now make a little noise for me," Goethe would say. The noises must have pleased him, for Felix put in four to eight hours every day at the piano.

At first Goethe must have been a bit skeptical of the boy's genius, for he arranged a series of testing situations, such as the presentation of a scrawled, unpublished musical manuscript for sight reading. It turned out to be by Mozart, and gave Felix no trouble. Another manuscript was so full of erasures, blots and cross-outs as to be almost illegible. It took several minutes of puzzling out before Felix was able to toss it off brilliantly. It was, characteristically, a Beethoven score.

One day, from among the steady stream of guests Goethe had invited, the Grand Duke and his family appeared. Felix wrote, "I played from eleven in the morning till ten in the evening, with only two hours' interruption, finishing with the Hummel 'Fantasia.' "

The relationship between the old man and Felix soon took on an intimate quality. They played poetry games together; Goethe called him "my little David who plays to me, his grouchy old Saul, whenever I am weary with the world." He kissed Felix after every session at the piano, and before Felix returned home he presented him with a silver medallion portrait as a memento of his visit.

Goethe's own words describe the daily music sessions thus: "His coming did me a great deal of good, for my feelings about music are changed; I hear it with pleasure, interest and affection. I love its history. . . . It is a great thing that Felix fully recognizes the value of going through its successive stages, and happily his memory is so good as to furnish him with any number of examples of all kinds. From the

Bach period downward he has brought Haydn, Mozart and Gluck to life for me, has given me clear ideas of the great modern masters of technique, and, lastly, has made me understand his own productions and given me plenty to think about in himself. He took away with him my warmest blessing." In earlier days Goethe had heard Mozart as a child prodigy. He now told Zelter: "What your pupil has already accomplished is to the Mozart of that time as the conversation of an adult is to the talk of a child."

During the next two years Felix appeared several times in public, playing his own works or having them performed, all to very kind words from the critics. A trip to Switzerland inspired not only a new wave of compositions but also a quite remarkable series of landscape watercolors and sketches. As always, no vacation was complete without three or four tutors along to stimulate his intellect at the same time! No wonder his good friend Edouard Devrient later said, "His brain had from childhood been taxed excessively."

With Fanny, he revisited Goethe in 1825. On the trip they came across two other well-known prodigies of the day, Ferdinand David, the twelve-year-old violinist, and Ferdinand Hiller, the eleven-year-old pianist. Much impressed with Felix's latest piano quartet, young Hiller showed him a new violin and piano sonata by his teacher. They read it together, Felix playing the violin (his second instrument) and managing to fake those parts which were technically beyond him. But this was unusual for the musical perfectionist Zelter had made of him. (When he was supposed to play a Mozart concerto with a local orchestra in Silesia, he found the playing to be so bad that he persuaded the sponsors to let him play a solo piano program instead.)

His grandmother, for his fourteenth birthday, gave him a beautiful copy of the almost unknown *Passion According to St. Matthew* by Bach, a gift whose full significance would not be realized for several years to come.

During the next year he resumed violin study, visited a Baltic resort which later inspired his "Calm Sea and Prosperous Voyage" Overture, completed his thirteenth symphony (now called Symphony No. 1) and many other works. After a concert by Ignaz Moscheles, that famous virtuoso, along with Johann Hummel, played at the Mendelssohn home. Felix, awed, was for once too overcome to consent to follow their acts. The next morning Mrs. Mendelssohn wrote Moscheles, the "Prince of Pianists," asking him to give lessons to Felix and Fanny. Moscheles was much impressed with Fanny's musicianship, especially her playing of Bach. Felix amazed him. He said, "If he wishes to take a hint from me, as to anything new to him, he can easily do so; but he stands in no need of lessons." For a few weeks they spent hours together daily at the piano. Moscheles wrote later: "Even then I was always conscious that the boy who sat beside me was not a pupil, but a master."

A rehearsal of one of Felix's operettas, *The Two Nephews,* fell on his fifteenth birthday celebration. Zelter, in toasting the composer-conductor, parodied the Masonic ritual, saying: "My dear boy, from this day you are no longer an apprentice but an independent member of the brotherhood of musicians. This I proclaim in the name of Mozart, of Haydn and of old Father Bach!"

The year of 1825 appears to have been a turning point in Felix's life in many ways. He was now, in the words of a friend, "of middle height, slender frame, and of uncommon muscular power, a capital gymnast, swimmer, walker, rider and dancer. . . ." It was also the year of decision. He was a mature composer, but not as yet committed to music as a profession. In the family tradition he had been expected to go into banking, business or law.

His parents well knew how the face of Europe was strewn with the gaunt, sorrowful wrecks of overworked prodigies and the broken hearts and dreams of their parents. They were aware of the pitfalls, hardships, rivalries, exorbitant physical demands of the professional musician's life. And the nagging question remained—was Felix good enough to overcome the objections, did his talent warrant the sacrifices involved? Music could always be a delightful avocation. This was not an easy decision, especially with an influential uncle lined up on the negative side.

His father and mother agreed to abide by the decision of Luigi Cherubini, the monarch of matters musical in Europe, the head of the Paris Conservatory, and known to be sharp of tongue, blunt and forthright. Felix was shocked, maybe even a little ostentatiously self-righteous, about the low taste and frivolous musical attitude of the French. He met all the outstanding musicians of the day, but was infuriated by one who knew not a single note of *Fidelio.* He also complained, "They think of Bach as a wig stuffed with learning."

Then came the great day when he performed in his own piano quartet for Cherubini. The old man was kindness itself, saying: "This young man will do well . . . already he has come a long way . . . but he gives too much of himself." Felix later described him thus: "He is like a dead volcano, now and then rumbling, but all covered with ashes and stones."

Cherubini asked Felix to write a *Kyrie* (a brief church petition "Lord, have mercy . . ."), for five voices and full orchestra. As a delicate tribute, Felix wrote it à la Cherubini. The manuscript has been lost, but it must have been impressive. Cherubini begged him in vain to remain in Paris as his special private pupil. In any case, the question of whether or not to turn professional was settled once and for all in the affirmative.

For Felix Mendelssohn this was a turning point in composition as well. The year produced his first major composing disaster, his opera *The Wedding of Camacho,* of which more later, and a work which would have marked him as a great composer at *any* age, the "Octet for Strings." As one critic has said "Not even Mozart or Schubert accomplished at the age of sixteen anything quite as astonishing as this major work of chamber music. . . ." The freshness and lightness of its scherzo, the individuality of its style, its fugal finale, foreshadowed the quality of the still greater work which was to come the following year.

This was also the year when Felix probably sowed the seeds of that envy and jealousy among the professional Berlin musicians which plagued him in later life. When he was asked to give for the orchestra musicians and a number of music lovers a piano preview of Beethoven's just-completed Ninth Symphony, he was able not only to read the complex score, but analyzed it and imitated the orchestral effects on the piano, as well as giving valuable suggestions on how this strange, bewildering work should be performed. Quite a bitter pill for the great Gasparo Spontini, musical director of the Berlin Opera, to swallow from the hands of someone not yet seventeen!

But the most significant change of 1825 was one of geography. The Mendelssohn family moved to a magnificent estate in another part of Berlin; the main house was in later years to be used as one of the chambers of the Prussian Parliament. One room, with a raised stage area, was large enough to be used for concerts and plays. Set in the midst of ten acres of beautiful lawn, shrubbery and trees was a garden house, with a music room that could seat several hundred people. Life took on a new and joyous dimension as young people swarmed about, riding, swimming, bowling, dancing, playing chess and billiards, making up imaginative games and entertainments—what one writer has called "an uninterrupted carnival of poetry, music, charades, masquerades and improvised plays." All their creative juices were stimulated by each other and by both the serious and light reading they did together. Their new ideas were recorded in a common journal to capture the witty, the amusing, the poetical. They called it *The Garden Times;* the winter sequel was called *The Tea and Snow Times.*

Felix was in his element, winning games, excelling in sports, painting, acting, writing, revelling in the natural beauty which surrounded them. During this period they read a new translation of Shakespeare's *Midsummer Night's Dream.* Imagining how very like a wooded area near Athens in Greece the Mendelssohn garden must have seemed, we begin to understand how an inspired seventeen-year-old could write the masterpiece that the "Midsummer Night's Dream" Overture unquestionably is. The piece has the inevitability of greatness about it. Felix himself, for once, felt it to be perfect, expressing the eerie, elfin quality of the play's setting. His scoring has served future generations as a model of how to achieve maximum effect with minimal means. The sheer charm, airy grace and youthful élan of the piece elude imitation. It may very well be the best thing he ever wrote. If it is, then Mendelssohn is the only great composer who wrote his best work before he was twenty.

Even in piano duet form the work captivated audiences; for orchestra it was overwhelmingly successful. With it he left his lessons with Zelter behind, enrolling instead for some courses in literature, philosophy and geography at the University of Berlin. This brought him into contact with the finest minds and all the swirling doctrines of German romanticism.

Intellectually and musically he was now miles ahead of the opera *The Wedding of Camacho,* which he had written two years earlier. When it was finally produced in 1827, despite rather obvious roadblocks from Spontini, the audience received it well, but Felix himself left the hall early so as not to have to take a bow. He was too honest with himself, too high in his standards to consider it good enough, and he refused to agree to a requested second performance. There was only one bad review, but it affected him greatly. He had blithely shrugged off criticism before, when he felt it wasn't justified, but this time, the one critic who agreed with his own harsh judgment of *Camacho* must have introduced the first glimmer of self-doubt that life had ever given him. It took him several months to throw off the resulting deep physical and spiritual malaise.

There are many who feel that the mammoth enterprise Felix undertook in his nineteenth year of getting the Berlin Singakademie to give a public performance of Bach's *Passion According to St. Matthew,* under his direction, with a chorus of between three and four hundred voices, was his crowning achievement and the one that earns him the highest niche in music history.

Among the musical treasures which he had pored over, studied, and memorized in the course of his teens had been the score of Bach's *St. Matthew Passion,* which his grandmother had given him on his fourteenth birthday. For some time a group of sixteen singers had been meeting at the Mendelssohn home on Saturday evenings to try out little-known choral works for their own pleasure. Felix had been rehearsing the group in this work for months, filling in missing vocal parts, playing the accompaniment, gradually arousing in them the same feelings of reverence and love for this music that he himself felt.

His friend Devrient, who acted and sang the role of Christ, was especially sensitive to its beauty and depth, considering it one of the gems of German music, although never sung or heard, and known by only a few people. He was certain of its universal appeal, and he worked on Felix to try to get it performed properly—and with Felix himself conducting it.

Felix was overwhelmed at the magnitude and daring of the idea. Several hundred musicians and a big hall would be needed, and there was no assurance of public interest or even any purchase of tickets. Zelter, at the Singakademie, had long insisted that the music was too difficult for singers and for the public. Bach's works, except for a few minor pieces, were performed very rarely, and most of his more important scores were still unpublished. Now dead for eighty years, Bach was considered even more antique than the years indicated.

The scheme finally concocted by Felix and Devrient was brilliantly simple—and it worked! They approached Zelter, asking simply for the use of the hall of the Singakademie for a charity concert. Only incidentally did they mention that they had the *St. Matthew Passion* in mind.

Rehearsals got under way. The chorus was amazed at Felix's ability to conduct without a score. Gradually everyone concerned caught the Bach fever; so did the listeners at the rehearsals, who spread their enthusiastic news by word of mouth. Felix was mature in his handling of the several hundred people involved, many twice his age. His poise, musicianship, tact and energy were tremendously impressive.

At concert time, on March 11, 1829, not a ticket was left. Fully a thousand people were turned away. Almost single-handed, with only an assist from his devoted friend, Felix had revived Bach and altered the course of musical taste and knowledge for generations to come. In one of his rare references to his religious origin he later commented with some irony: "It was an actor and a Jew who restored this great Christian work to the people."

As Mendelssohn's teens were coming to a close, he and his father planned carefully the next phase of his career. It was to start with a journey during which he was "closely to examine the various countries, and fix on one in which to live and work; to make his name and abilities known, . . . and to employ his good fortune in life, and the liberality of his father, in preparing the ground for future efforts." That was pretty much the way it worked out, although no one anticipated that his life had already passed its halfway mark when he left for England at the age of twenty. There, his influence on England's music was incalculable. His magnificent oratorios made that the dominant form of English composition for a hundred years to follow. Most English music of the nineteenth century was utterly Mendelssohnian, just as in the eighteenth century it was largely Handelian.

And in the midst of an incredible output of choral works, symphonies, chamber works, piano pieces and songs Mendelssohn also managed to change the face of music and music education in Germany. He did this by rebuilding the Leipzig Gewandhaus Orchestra to his own lofty expectations. Of even more significance, he founded and then administered through its first turbulent years the Leipzig Conservatory —to this day a fountainhead of German and international musicianship. His death in mid-course, at the age of thirty-eight, put all of musical Europe into deep mourning.

3

The Violin Prodigies

The violin was perfected in the late sixteenth century, and great performers were not long in appearing on the scene. But written records about instrumental prodigies of the seventeenth century are spotty, at best. We can only guess how Jean-Baptiste Lully (1632–1687), whose antecedents and training are unknown, picked up enough knowledge of the violin to play with roving groups in Florence at carnival time. At any rate, he was "talent-scouted" there by a friend of Mlle. de Montpensier when he was twelve years old; after a stint as kitchen scullion he finally joined her "band" at fifteen. He must have been pretty high-spirited as well as talented, however, for soon thereafter he wrote a satirical song about his benefactress which quickly led to his dismissal. King Louis XIV snapped him up, however, for the choice group called "The Twenty-Four Violins," which Lully was soon conducting and also composing for.

A suave and wily courtier, Lully quickly rose to the position of Music Master to the Royal Family, and began, with Molière, to write comedy-ballets which led to the first French operas. Lully eventually became virtual czar over all operatic production in France, controlling its artistic direction, and raising the standards of performance in the process. He not only established the French National Opera, but brought it out of the court atmosphere, making it a popular new art-form for all levels of French society. When he died at the age of fifty-five there was no figure richer, more famous, or more powerful in all of French music.

The first example of a girl prodigy violinist was Gertrude Mara (1749–1833). She had more than the usual three strikes against her. Brought up without a mother, by a father who barely earned enough for food by repairing musical instruments, she spent her first few years tied to a chair whenever her father went to work. Permanently crippled as a result, she underwent partially successful surgery in her teens.

It was when she was about five years old that she first playfully drew a bow across a violin in her father's workshop, producing a surprisingly good tone. Within a year her father had taught her enough so that he could carry her to one provincial stage after another in their native Cassell, Germany, and surrounding towns, so that she became the major breadwinner of the family. Rescue from that particular form of eventual musical oblivion appeared in the admiration of an anonymous music lover who sensed the deep musicianship of the exploited child, and subsidized several years of legitimate music study for her. She continued to appear in public, in Frankfort and Vienna, and was much admired for her youth, beauty and musical accomplishments in those discriminating cities.

A blow to her violinistic ambitions came on a trip to England when she was about eleven. Her newly-acquired English patrons, including the Queen, persuaded her that the violin was not a feminine instrument, and suggested that she switch to singing! She had a bright, clear voice, but of course totally untrained. Nothing daunted, she attempted to sing at the Prussian court. Then came a new stumbling block—even the musically enlightened Frederick the Great couldn't conceive of, and wouldn't listen to, a singer who was not Italian. "A German singer! I should as soon expect to get pleasure from the neighing of my horse," he said.

Despite this discouragement, it took just a few years of study at Leipzig to turn Gertrude into a remarkable singer, as outstanding for her knowledge of music and brilliant sense of style as for the unusual range and quality of her voice. Now, Frederick capitulated gracefully as soon as he heard her, giving her a court appointment for life.

Gertrude subsequently achieved enormous professional success along with disastrous personal unhappiness in the course of a long life full of drama. We will never know whether or not the prejudices of her day, in forcing Gertrude Mara to abandon the violin for the voice, didn't deprive the world of one of its potentially greatest violinists.

The first well-known concert prodigy of black origin was the violinist George Bridgetower (1780?–1860). His tall, striking African father, nicknamed "the Abyssinian Prince," accompanied George in London during his early stage triumphs at the age of ten or eleven, where the Prince of Wales became his patron. It was in Vienna, where he played a concert after visiting his mother in Germany, that he played Beethoven's "Kreutzer" Sonata with the composer at the piano. Beethoven admired George's playing very much; it is too bad that a personal quarrel between the two led Beethoven to change the dedication of that work, which otherwise would now be known as the "Bridgetower" Sonata.

A pall fell over violin playing in the early days of the nineteenth century. It grew out of the despair of violinists unable to follow in the footsteps of Niccolò Paganini (1782–1840). And well might they despair, for he was unquestionably the greatest virtuoso, on any instrument, that ever lived.

Paganini had the misfortune to be born twenty-six years after Mozart, when the remembrance of that amazing prodigy's feats was still fresh in everyone's mind. Between his mother's dream in which an angel told her that little Niccolò would become the greatest violinist in the world, and his amateur musician of a father who was determined to mold his son into a Mozart of the violin, he had little choice as to his future. He was harshly treated in his youth, which undoubtedly undermined his frail body. But the beatings and starvation to which he was subjected, the ten hours' daily practice in a locked room, were not in themselves what made him great. There was in him a fierce inner compulsion to succeed—not merely in conquering existing difficulties, but in exploring new problems. His earliest teachers were upset by his extraordinary, precocious technique. He insisted on working things out in his own unorthodox ways.

Niccolò Paganini wrote his first sonata at eight, and when he made his debut at the age of nine he played his own variations on a French air. He soon outgrew all that the local teachers had to offer. One sweltering July day in 1795 the following advertisement, along with a program, appeared in the local newspaper: "Niccolò Paganini of Genoa, a boy already known to his country for his skill in handling the violin, having determined to study at Parma to improve his talents under the direction of the renowned Signor [Alessandro] Rolla, but lacking the means to do so, has adopted this plan, and has taken courage to beg his compatriots to contribute towards this object, inviting them to come to this entertainment for his benefit." The proceeds of the concert more than paid for the trip for Niccolò and his father.

On this first visit, Paganini found Rolla ill and surly. In his own words: "His wife showed us into a room adjoining the bedroom, till she had spoken to the sick man. Finding on a table a violin and the music of Rolla's latest concerto, I took up the instrument and played the piece at sight. Astonished at what he had heard, the composer asked for the name of the player, and could not believe it was only a young boy till he had seen for himself. He then told me that he had nothing to teach me, and advised me to go to [Ferdinando] Paer for study in composition."

Paganini's tour of Italy when he was thirteen caused a sensation in every town in which he appeared. This was also a period of rigid self-discipline on his part: he would compose music too difficult for him (or anyone else) to play, and then invent means of getting around each difficulty, trying a passage in hundreds of different ways if necessary. The rapture with which he was received in public was intoxicating. It also taught him cynicism—he played the tricky effects which won the most applause, reserving for himself the pleasures of playing better music to satisfy his own taste.

By the time he was seventeen he ran away from home, a finished virtuoso, ready to make his way by himself with his violin. His discipline in music didn't carry over into his private life, for now began a period of wild adventure. His early addiction to gambling often completely wiped out the considerable sums he earned by his public performances. More than once he had to pawn everything he owned, including his violin. Once, when this happened right before a concert, a wealthy music lover loaned him a beautiful Guarnerius violin. The owner was so overcome by Niccolò's playing that at the end of the concert he jumped onto the platform, embraced the violinist, and said "The Guarneri is yours—provided it is never played by anyone but Paganini!" Paganini later acquired a Stradivarius as a result of a bet on his sight-reading ability, but the Guarnerius remained his favorite violin.

Constant dissipation combined with hectic concert schedules gave Paganini a peculiar gaunt, waxy look which, to the feverish imagination of the romantic period in which he lived, surrounded him with an aura of the mysterious, even the supernatural. A contemporary described him thus: "He is so thin that one could hardly be thinner; he has a pale yellow complexion, the nose of an eagle, and long bony fingers. He looks as if he were barely held together by his clothes." Another described his flexible fingers as making his hand look like "a handkerchief tied to the end of a stick." With the deadly paleness, the deep-set brilliant black eyes, the long curling black hair, and the scornful, sometimes sinister smile added to the fantastic skill of his playing, many thought him to be quite literally in league with the devil. Rumors were rife—he had been in prison for murder, he had led a bunch of brigands, and so on. Crowds followed his strange figure through the streets; in Vienna there was a Paganini craze after his first appearance there, with Paganini hats, Paganini gloves, snuffboxes, canes, even Paganini-engraved coins attesting to the astonishment and admiration he engendered.

The spell he seemed to cast over his audiences included the critics as well. One critic said: "He plays the most difficult passages on one string alone, at the same time playing an accompaniment on the other strings. . . . One often finds it difficult to believe that one is not listening to several instruments." Another wrote: "The crowd in the opera house was wild with excitement. He had to play nearly everything twice over."

There is no question that Paganini was a great showman, who would stop at nothing that would increase receipts. He didn't bother for twenty years to refute the charge that he had been imprisoned for murder; even his deserved reputation for avarice and downright greed, for cruelty and eccentricity, added interest to his public image. He thought nothing of putting on a circus act, imitating birds, cats and dogs, or placing the violin on his head, or back, or hip, or knee, in front of him or behind him—playing, in these ridiculous positions, the most formidably difficult music—music that was the despair of violinists who held the violin in the conventional way. Either accidentally or on purpose, one time when a string snapped he continued playing the same music on the remaining three strings. So successful was this with the public that he would often play entire selections on one string alone, and was sometimes called the "one-string fiddler."

Was he then nothing but a charlatan, as some violinists accused him of being? Or was the very elongation of his body and fingers, his early rhythmic grasp and mechanical fluency, when added to incredible study and deep musical intelligence, responsible for his being the finest violinist in a serious sense? Some of the critical comments at the time give us clues: "His fingers attain a rapidity, his notes a velocity, which neither the ear nor the eye can follow." Another critic wrote: "There is no trickery in Paganini's performance, and if there is, the sooner our violinists learn some of his tricks the better—for then they will play in time and in tune, with expression and power." As for the richness of his tone, another said: "He knows how to impart to his violin the divine quality of the human voice."

Paganini claimed to have a magic formula, a secret devised by himself, which would enable violinists to attain in three years a fluency that usually required ten years. If he had such a secret, it died with him. Paganini was a loner. He never settled in one place, almost never took pupils, was never heard to practice after the age of twenty, would not permit his music to be printed the way he played it, and never allowed anyone to see how he tuned his instrument.

But enough was discovered or surmised by contemporary violinists to give some insights into his technical contributions to violin playing, and they were many. He used specially-made thin strings; he revived the old art of variable tunings; he added a whole new dimension to the range of the instrument with new harmonics, he developed the art of playing on one string to new heights, along with writing many special works for one string alone; he invented many new bowing techniques, all of which eventually became standard; he systematized the throbbing "vibrato" effect which humanized and "emotionalized" the violin's tone; and he was the first and greatest improviser on the instrument.

In addition to technical innovations, Paganini also greatly enriched the violin repertory with his original compositions. The "Caprices" which he wrote at nineteen, would have been masterpieces at any age. They were perhaps a hundred years ahead of the violin music of their time. Among others, Johannes Brahms admired them greatly, saying, "His genius for composition was fully equal to his genius for his instrument, and if he had not allowed his flair for virtuosity to gain the upper hand, in later years he would have been a great composer." He then paid Paganini homage by writing a set of variations on one of the caprice themes. Chopin, Mendelssohn, Schumann, Schubert, Meyerbeer and Berlioz are but a few of the serious composers who had the greatest respect for him. Rossini wrote: "I have wept but three times in my life: the first, on the failure of my earliest opera; the second time, when, in a boat with some friends, a turkey stuffed with truffles fell overboard; and thirdly, when I heard Paganini play for the first time."

Liszt transcribed five of the caprices for the piano. His tribute at the time of Paganini's death was as follows: "The unexcelled, unapproachable grandeur of his genius awes even those who attempt to emulate his example. No other will succeed him, no other will share his fame. . . . The violinists went to inconceivable lengths trying to discover his secret. In the sweat of their brows they toiled at difficulties which he had created with ease; but the public had naught for them but a pitying smile. Thus did Paganini enjoy the rare good fortune of wandering alone on unapproachable heights. . . . I say it without hesitation: There will be no second Paganini."

To date his prediction has been quite accurate; there never has been a second Paganini, perhaps there never can be. For he was very much a product of the romantic age in which he lived. There have been many fine violin prodigies since then—Fritz Kreisler, Mischa Elman and, among the still living, David Oistrakh, Joseph Szigeti, Nathan Milstein, Erica Morini, Isaac Stern and Jascha Heifetz (the latter certainly something of a legend in his own lifetime). And there is a younger generation of fine violin prodigies in addition to Yehudi Menuhin and Ruggiero Ricci, who are discussed in a later chapter. These include, among others, Michael Rabin, Jaime Laredo, Erick Friedman, Itzchak Perlman, Pinchas Zukerman, James Buswell III, and a talented group of Korean and Japanese violinists. But the era of the swashbuckling personality, the cult of the eccentric, the gullible openmouthed acceptance of fantastic rumor, the indulgence of an artist's tampering with the sacred written notes—all this is gone, and probably forever.

4

The Piano Prodigies

When, at the age of nineteen, he first heard Paganini play the violin, Franz Liszt (1811–1886) was already a famous prodigy pianist and composer, yet that event changed his life.

As a small and sickly child in Hungary, Franz had been given a good musical education by his father, who was a fine amateur pianist. The boy's formal schooling was meager. A priest taught him the rudiments of reading, writing and arithmetic, and that was all. Franz felt the lack of formal education all his life, and never stopped educating himself through voracious reading.

At nine, a thin but handsome blond blue-eyed youngster, Franz Liszt made his debut. Six Hungarian noblemen, all of whom were musicians or music lovers, were sufficiently impressed by his ability to organize a fund which enabled Franz to go to Vienna, with his parents, for further study and for exposure to the great musical minds who converged on that city.

There he studied with Carl Czerny, a famous teacher who had been Beethoven's favorite pupil and who later said of young Liszt: "It was evident that nature had intended him for a pianist." Franz made his Vienna debut at the age of eleven. At the rehearsal, while the orchestra was tuning, he said "See what I can do!" and began turning cartwheels in front of the piano. His father was greatly upset about possible injury to the boy's fingers, but the musicians were delighted with the pianist who was a virtuoso at the keyboard but a little boy at heart. As was usual at the time, his improvisation was a brilliantly executed hodge-podge based on themes from Beethoven symphonies and Rossini operas. Liszt later claimed that Beethoven was present and kissed him after the performance.

Franz soon captivated the knowledgeable Viennese audiences, and within a year his composing abilities were recognized as well. The music publisher Anton Diabelli asked every well-known Viennese composer to write a variation on a given melody as a publishing stunt and invited Franz also to contribute.

In his twelfth year Franz set out for Paris with his father. There he encountered envy and jealousy on all sides. Not only was he refused admittance to the Paris Conservatory, but production of his opera *Don Sancho,* which he had been asked to write by the director of the opera house, was delayed for almost two years by the intrigues of Parisian rivals. When he was fourteen years old it was finally produced, and while not particularly successful, it did add a great deal to his reputation.

Piano manufacturers were key figures in the careers of pianists of that time. The firm of Erard, which had just perfected an enlarged, more powerful, seven-octave piano, sponsored Franz's London debut so that he could introduce the new instrument there. Despite success in London, Franz still longed to be a composer rather than a pianist. That hope was shattered for the time being by his father's death when Franz was sixteen. Back in Paris, he continued giving concerts, although for financial reasons he had to start taking pupils. He was a popular teacher despite his unorganized and unreliable nature. Undoubtedly his tall and striking figure, long hair, graceful ease and personal magnetism had much to do with his appeal to the daughters of the aristocracy who flocked to him for piano lessons.

During this time he went through a period of extreme melancholy. For a year and a half he withdrew entirely from social and musical life; he alternated periods of utter apathy with periods of religious fervor, during which he considered becoming a monk. He verged at times on the brink of suicide. And then, in 1831, he heard Niccolò Paganini play the violin. It was a shattering experience. It punctured his hardy ego, making him humble for perhaps the first time in his life. Instead of despair, however, it left him with the determination to become the Paganini of the piano, to push the bounds of that instrument far beyond the capabilities that had been realized so far.

Franz went into utter seclusion with his piano. By the age of twenty-two, when he emerged, he was the greatest pianist in the world, as well as the handsomest; he was quickly idolized, painted, and sculpted

—in short, he became the ideal romantic hero of his romantic age. His mobile face, deep-set eyes, superbly confident manner, his very arrogance and capriciousness were as important as his piano playing to his success. The Don Juan of his day, he ran off with married titled women on more than one occasion, and flirted with dozens more. His popularity verged on the ludicrous, what with jewels being flung on stage as if they were flowers. Shrieks of ecstasy and fainting were a common occurrence among members of his female following. Wildly rushing to the stage, women fought to capture his broken piano strings (and there were many) as sacred relics; kneeling, they begged to kiss his fingertips; they kept his cigar butts, even the leaves of his tea, as souvenirs.

For many years this "indefatigable vagabond" toured triumphantly throughout Europe. A dandy in his dress, he carried 360 cravats with him on one trip to Russia. All the while he was composing incessantly. In all he wrote almost eight hundred works. He played, for the most part, his own works and those of a very few other favorite composers. The Studies he wrote to parallel Paganini's caprices did indeed represent the ultimate (even today) of the piano's technical possibilities, the peak of piano power. In them, and through his brilliant transcriptions and variations for piano of operatic and symphonic themes, he can truly be said to have created modern piano playing.

He exploited all the possibilities of the new full-sized piano, explored and combined its extremely high and low ranges, invented new fingering techniques, and made the piano orchestral with new dimensions of sonority. In the process of converting a simple Schubert melody into a Liszt fantasy, all kinds of frills and ornaments were added, the tempo and rhythms often distorted. The end result was often bad Schubert but dazzling Liszt. The intensity and power of his playing carried one critic to these lyrical heights: "After the concert Liszt stands there like a victor on the battlefield, like a hero at a tournament. Daunted pianos lie around him; torn strings wave like flags of truce; frightened instruments flee into distant corners; the listeners look at each other as after a cataclysm of nature that has just passed by."

Liszt was also one of the first pianists to play entirely from memory. He set the concave side of the piano to the audience, as it has been ever since (of course there were those who claimed this was prompted simply by the desire to show his fine profile while playing). And only once before had any musician dared to fill an entire evening by himself as a solo performer. Before this time several musicians—perhaps a pianist, violinist and singer—would share a program sometimes interspersed with orchestral selections.

What of the long list of original works for piano, orchestra, voice, chorus, and so on? Much of it is bad, suffering from the same traits that marred Liszt's personality. It is often shoddy, showy, tinselly, sometimes pompous and lacking in sincerity. But a few of his works are very good, almost first-rate, such as his Piano Sonata and the Faust Symphony. He pioneered in using literary sources for musical inspiration, inventing the form called "symphonic poem." His later works have a disquieting bareness, and a harmonic daring and experimentation which had a real influence on other composers much greater than he, such as Richard Wagner, Richard Strauss, Johannes Brahms, and Claude Debussy. In his exciting, vivid "Hungarian Rhapsodies" he was among the first of the nationalists to make all Europe aware of the unique folk aspects of his country's music.

In the twelve years he spent as Chapel Master to the Grand Duke of Weimar, Liszt made his greatest contribution by championing unselfishly the new music of young contemporary composers. He had the courage and generosity to promote actively the performance of their works at a time when their music was fiercely unpopular elsewhere. As he wrote to a friend: "There is without doubt nothing better than to respect, admire, and study the illustrious dead; but why not also sometimes live with the living? We have tried this plan with Wagner, Berlioz, Schumann [his contemporaries]. . . ." He revived and popularized works by Beethoven which had been long neglected. And he encouraged, even started on their careers, such composers as Edvard Grieg, Bedrich Smetana, Nicolai Rimsky-Korsakoff, Edward Mac-Dowell and Johannes Brahms.

After Liszt left Weimar, his piano classes, which he conducted for the last twenty years of his long life, attracted pupils from all over the world. Fortunately, some of his American students returned to the United States and headed up piano departments in various conservatories. In this way the great Liszt tradition has continued down to the present day.

Anton Rubinstein (1829–1894) made his debut at nine, complete with frilled blouse and high-buttoned boots, in an outdoor park concert in Moscow. Three years later, when he appeared in Paris, Liszt was enchanted with his playing. He lifted Anton up onto a table and declared melodramatically, "On these shoulders my mantle will fall." The prediction turned out to be true. With his perfect pianist's hands, amazing musical memory and incredible power, Anton, who idolized Liszt, played in the grand manner from the very beginning. The French composer Camille Saint-Saëns once compared the two: "Liszt was an eagle, Rubinstein a lion. Those who saw his fierce velvety paws lay their powerful caress upon the keyboard will never forget it."

Anton imitated all of Liszt's gestures, right down to the way he held his hands and the way he tossed his huge head of hair. Unlike Liszt, however, he played entirely spontaneously, unpredictably, and according to his mood of the moment. When the mood was stormy he could pulverize the piano with his fury, but the resultant wrong notes and broken strings were accepted as part of the total devastating Rubinstein experience. Hans von Bülow, a fine contemporary pianist, said "I would rather listen to his wrong notes than to my own correct playing." The Steinway Piano Company, which provided the stronger piano he played on, made it a practice to have a spare piano on stage at all his American concerts, just in case!

Anton's tone was as notable as his temperament. Edward Hanslick, an outstanding and very severe nineteenth-century critic, summed up the source of Anton's appeal as follows: "His youthful and untiring vigor, his incomparable power of bringing out the melody, his perfection of touch in the stormy torrents of passion, as well as in the tender long-drawn notes of pathos, his wonderful memory, and his energy that knows no fatigue . . ."

In his youth Anton endured anti-Semitism and experienced periods of extreme poverty. Among his many adventures he was once stopped at the Russian border at the time of the European uprisings of 1848, suspected of being a spy. His music manuscripts were thought to be an elaborate code containing military secrets. Only by playing the piano for the customs officials did he convince them otherwise. It was in his native Russia that Anton later won his greatest (and deserved) adulation. He forced the recognition of music as a profession by founding the St. Petersburg Conservatory of Music and putting his brother Nicolas, also a brilliant musician, in charge of the Moscow Conservatory, thus bringing Russia into the nineteenth-century world of music almost single-handedly. Like Liszt, Anton would have given all his pianistic fame for recognition as a great composer, but very few of his hundreds of works (all strangely conservative and all widely performed during his lifetime) are still played.

Towards the end of his life this great pianist and disappointed composer said, "All that I care that men should remember me by is my conservatory." That much of his dream did come true. The still flourishing St. Petersburg and Moscow Conservatories, twin hearts of Russia's great musical culture, survived the Russian Revolution and are today a living tribute to Anton Rubinstein's vision.

The Liszt tradition was also upheld by a great woman pianist, the Venezuelan Teresa Carreño (1853–1917). Even from the tender age of eight, when she made her debut, her strong and fiery playing was considered "masculine." Her tempestuous career included an unexpected detour of several years as an opera singer, starting at the age of nineteen, and she even conducted a Venezuelan opera company for a time. Gottschalk, Liszt, Rubinstein—all admired her as a person as well as pianist because of her unusual combination of talent, verve, charm and beauty. She played before Abraham Lincoln in the White House, and is revered as a national heroine of Venezuela.

Today the Lisztian aura is still alive and flourishing in the person of the Polish-born Artur Rubinstein (1887–   )(no relation to Anton). In 1972 a headline read: "AT EIGHTY-FIVE; STILL A FRESH OUTLOOK." He is still the American piano idol, whether performing live or recorded. How can a man who has appeared in public for more than seventy years still be in the very forefront of his profession? Only with the help of these several factors: superb physical endowment and stamina; a remarkable precocity which developed, with intelligent self-awareness, into flexible maturity, and a nineteenth-century romantic personality and showmanship which is utterly refreshing in the mid-twentieth-century era of artistic restraint.

There also was a distinct revolt against Liszt and the personality cult he stood for. It started early in his own life and has continued down to the present day, perhaps stronger now than ever before. Clara Wieck (1819–1896), better known in adult life as Clara Schumann after her marriage to composer Robert Schumann (1810–1856), was the very feminine and yet very persuasive head of the anti-Liszt movement. There was nothing personal about Clara's antipathy to his style of pianism. She was herself a champion of Romantic music, particularly that of her husband, along with Chopin and Brahms. And certainly nothing in musical history is more romantic than the details of her personal life—the infatuation of eighteen-year-old Robert with the nine-year-old prodigy daughter of his piano teacher; his patient wait for her to grow up; her father's implacable opposition, which resulted in several years of painful wrangling in the law courts before they could marry; their brief, intense years of happiness crowned by Clara's concert successes and Robert's inspired composing, and ending with the sudden onslaught of his insanity and his early death. Clara spent the remaining forty years of her life giving concerts to support their children, meanwhile spreading her husband's music and fame to every corner of Europe. The story sounds like a movie script, and indeed became one in 1947 when Katharine Hepburn played Clara in the movie *Song of Love.*

The quiet revolution which Clara began was not against Romanticism as such but against its excesses, against the atrocities committed upon great music by less-than-great pianists for the sake of the dazzling virtuosity which electrified the new concert audiences. In a book of musical proverbs which she studied as a serious little girl being coached by her even more serious father was a proverb that read: "Skill is a tool, never an aim." She learned that lesson well. With her great naturalness and poise, and her thorough systematic training behind her, she strove to express the finer shades of feeling, to reveal the melodic and harmonic beauties of such neglected composers as Bach, Mozart and Beethoven, as well as the great new Romantic music she forced Europe to notice. Not for her the endless glittering transcriptions and arrangements from operas and symphonies, the waltzes and fantasias. Those glib concoctions, she decided (and later generations have concurred), were musical trash unworthy of a true artist. In refusing to tamper with the (to her) sacred notes of the great composers she went against the mainstream of the showy salon tradition of her time with its artificial playing mannerisms and eccentric, exaggerated gestures and musical effects.

At the age of twelve, when she had first heard Liszt and other salon pianists in Paris, she had noted their "unmusical desire to attract attention by circus tricks." Not only were her standards very high, but she was also her own severest critic. Despite a tremendous ovation after a concert she once played in her early teens, she burst into tears and refused to acknowledge the applause, saying, "I have not played as I should." Later in life she said of Liszt that "he had the downfall of piano playing on his conscience," and she was among the group of serious dedicated musicians who signed an anti-Liszt manifesto in 1860.

By the time she died in 1896 the tide of educated musical taste had
swung to her side.

In the history of performance there has surely never been a prodigy
with a more adventurous and fascinating early life than that of Isaac
Albeniz (1860–1909). From his first public performance as a pianist
at the age of four his parents insisted that he appear in a Napoleonic
costume, complete with sword, at his concerts. After two years of sensational appearances in his native Spain, he was taken to Paris for several months of study, to culminate in an audition for entrance into the
Paris Conservatory. There he thwarted for the first, but far from the
last time, his parents' plans for him. About to be admitted by an astonished faculty at the unprecedented age of six, he suddenly took a
ball from his pocket and threw it at a large mirror, smashing it to bits.
Needless to say, he was hastily despatched back to Spain to grow up a
bit before re-applying (which he never did).

In Spain he continued to play before amazed audiences. He had little general schooling and minimal piano instruction. Perhaps it was his
avid reading of Jules Verne's adventure stories that made him restless.
For whatever reason, he began running away from home, over and
over again, exploring every corner of Spain in the process. Penniless,
he would board a train in his Napoleonic costume, inveigle some pas-
senger into paying his fare, get off at a good-sized town and arrange
an impromptu concert to raise money. Sooner or later, however, someone would put him back on a train for home, and then the whole pattern would be repeated.

He intermittently wandered this way until he was twelve. Then,
when the Governor of Cadiz, on the Mediterranean coast, threatened
to arrest him and have him forcibly returned to his parents, he stowed
away on a ship in the harbor bound for Puerto Rico. After a concert
on shipboard, the passengers quickly took up a collection for the boy's
fare, but the amount only covered his passage as far as Buenos Aires.
After landing there hungry and tired, he was reduced to begging in the
streets and sleeping in churches before he finally found a job playing
in a café. A Spaniard who heard him helped to arrange a concert tour
of South America; by the time he sailed for Cuba a year later he had
amassed ten thousand francs, a tremendous sum in those days.

Now occurred one of those strange coincidences with which history
abounds. Isaac's father, a tax officer, had in the meantime been assigned to one of Spain's outposts—Havana, Cuba. Hearing of his son's

arrival, he had the police take Isaac into custody. It must have been quite a confrontation—the outraged father on one hand, the self-assured professional pianist of thirteen on the other. If his home had not been able to hold Isaac at the age of eight, his five years of wandering made that less likely than ever now; reluctantly, the father permitted the independent Isaac to go his own way, which led to New York.

There, as in Buenos Aires, he had to rely at first on odd jobs, including stevedoring on the New York docks, before approaching music once again through the back door of waterfront saloons, where he played with his back turned to the piano keyboard as a novelty act. Before long he had again worked his way onto the concert stage, playing across the entire continent to San Francisco and back. This time he earned more than enough to pay his own fare back to Europe.

After successful appearances in various European cities Isaac decided, at fourteen, to perfect his technique with a short period of study at the Leipzig Conservatory. His native country then received him with open arms, and the patronage of a Spanish nobleman and music lover named Count Morphy enabled him to study briefly at the Brussels Conservatory. For all his musical virtuosity Isaac still revelled in adolescent fun and practical jokes. Not until he was eighteen and had decided to seek out his idol, Franz Liszt, for lessons were there about him the first signs of maturity. Soon after this he began to figure as one of the great pianists of his day.

It wasn't until Albeniz's marriage at twenty-three that he began to reduce his concert schedule and to devote himself more and more to his true vocation—composition. Perhaps it was the irregularity of his early life, or the pressures of achievement in two different careers, but whatever the cause, Albeniz died at forty-nine just when he was at the height of his productive life. In the history of music he is known not as a pianist but as one of the great national composers of Spain. "Iberia," a four-part series of piano pieces considered to be his masterpiece, was written in the last three years of his life.

If only the father of Ruth Slenczynska (1925–   ) had modelled himself on Frederick Wieck, Clara Schumann's father, life would certainly have been better for her. But when Ruth was born, her father, an embittered failure as a professional violinist, determined to realize his success through her at no matter what cost. The family was then living in San Francisco, where only a few years before Yehudi Menuhin and Ruggiero Ricci had achieved fame as violin prodigies.

From the time she was two years old, Ruth's musicianship was obvious. She hummed in the correct key every piece her father taught his pupils and then picked each one out on the piano. When her father gave her a miniature violin, she dashed it to pieces in a rage, insisting she wanted to play only the piano. He began to teach her, and when she was four, tiny and chubby, she played an entire program in public, all from memory. Newspaper feature writers speculated that she must be a reincarnation of Mozart, perhaps, or Chopin. Some claimed she was playing in a hypnotic trance, under some sort of spell. One music critic said: "They tell us she is four; she does not look a day over three, nor does her playing sound as if she were a day under sixteen . . ."

At her Berlin debut, the German critics mounted the platform to examine the full-sized piano on which the legs and pedal mechanisms had been shortened to enable her to play. They were seeking some sort of concealed mechanism or wires to account for the undersized six-year-old's ability to produce the sounds she had just drawn from the instrument. Apologizing for their disbelief, they departed just as dumbfounded as the rest of the frenzied audience. At another time, in Copenhagen, a doctor was sent to examine her in order to ascertain if she were a midget. "Gentlemen of the press," he announced after the examination, "this is a genuine child."

Not until Ruth in later years wrote her poignant book *Forbidden Childhood* could her achievement be understood, along with all the misery that underlay it. When we read of the regimen to which she was subjected we can sympathize with, even if we don't quite agree with, her later disclaimer of any extraordinary gifts. "I was merely doing what I was taught very rigorously to do. The results were dearly won by a driving, incessant process of teaching and learning," she said.

In his determination to make her the finest pianist in the world, her father woke her at six o'clock every morning of her childhood years, to begin practice in her nightgown, in often icy-cold temperatures and before breakfast. Gradually giving up all his other pupils, he increased her practicing period until it added up to nine hours a day. His discipline was very simple: every mistake earned a slap across her cheek. More serious infractions or signs of rebellion were punished by denied meals. Each meal she ate was treated as a reward. Until she reached her teens Ruth practiced in her petticoat, no matter who might be present, so as not to spoil her dresses with perspiration.

First place among the pieces that earned her the greatest punishment was a certain Haydn sonata. Before she mastered it to the fanatical perfection her father demanded, she sustained a record number of slaps, had her ears boxed, was sworn at in five languages, and was pushed violently off the piano bench. Not a moment of her life was permitted to be "wasted" in playing with dolls, skipping rope, going to a movie, riding a tricycle, or playing with other children. "Stay away from those kids and their stupid games," her father commanded. Not even a doll handed up to her on the Berlin stage was she permitted to keep. Her father snatched it from her arms and threw it back, saying "Away with the doll!"

Intellectually Ruth was brilliant. During her brief stays in school she always earned a place far ahead of her age group. Only sporadically did she study with several of the great pianists, including Artur Schnabel, Alfred Cortot and Egon Petri. By the time she was eight she had three completely different full concert programs, each running over an hour, which she could play by heart.

In her short white dress with red velvet bows, the petite eight-year-old taxed the vocabulary of the critics trying to do justice to her New York debut. One found her even more amazing than Yehudi Menuhin had been at the same age. She was called "electrifying." One review began with "Not since Mozart. . . ." She was said to show "the temperament, the brilliance and the confidence of a born virtuoso." Only one person, the dean of the New York critics, W. J. Henderson, sounded a note of warning by saying she should have been kept at her studies until she was sixteen, not eight. This judgment infuriated her father, but it was confirmed later by the great pianist and composer Sergei Rachmaninoff, who tested her privately and concluded she needed better teaching. "She is all talent . . . the greatest talent I have ever heard," he said. "If she gets first-class training, by the time she is fifteen she will play so well that other pianists hearing her will give up the piano in despair."

Rachmaninoff utterly disapproved of her wasting precious time in concerts. But the huge sums she earned were too important to her father to allow for any interruption of her heavy concert schedule. Not only did he keep every penny she earned but he also confiscated or pawned every gift she received. Occasionally he had to pay small fines when a local child labor board would try halfheartedly to enforce the laws against child exploitation.

Josef Slenczynski took full credit for Ruth's achievements. "You wouldn't be playing the way you are if it weren't for me," he would say. But he considered her failures entirely her own responsibility. When she didn't sight-read particularly well in an informal chamber music session he called her an idiot, an imbecile, a dumbbell. "You've disgraced me! That wants to be a musician! Why, you're a thing, not a person. A person has brains. You're no good for anything."

He ruled out marriage for her—that was something only for ordinary girls. Ruth summed him up as an arrogant, grasping, bitter, ruthless man, disappointed in his own career and in having a daughter instead of a son, a pianist instead of a violinist, with a wife he considered not good enough for him. No wonder she often dreamt of a substitute father—for example, the conductor Eugene Ormandy. But it was not until "immaturity," the same word that had haunted Ruggiero Ricci, crept into her reviews that Ruth started to lose faith in her father as a musician. She realized that she was playing works whose musical and emotional implications eluded her, simply because people would pay to hear her play them. Only as her musical faith wavered did she begin to face conflict within herself, and the doubts as to her own ability. For the first time she began to dread concerts, even music itself. She feared going before the public, but couldn't bear the void of living without music.

There was public debate about her, with other musicians and critics taking sides. Josef Hofmann, who had himself been a prodigy, bitterly resented the action of the Society for the Prevention of Cruelty to Children which had forced his retirement from the stage for several teenage years and therefore sided with her father. Prodigies needed the constant stimulation of public appearances in order to grow, he said, citing Menuhin as an example. Critic Olin Downes saw her as a glaring example of child exploitation. Neither had any knowledge of the inhuman routine to which she was being subjected.

Inevitably several fiascos brought her career to a halt. Ruth, whom countless parents had used as an example for their hapless musical children to emulate, was a "burned-out candle" at fifteen, a has-been. She broke completely with her father and with music. She never again became reconciled with him, but gradually, over a period of years, while attending college and afterwards, she normalized her life socially, marrying a man who turned out to be, unfortunately, all too like her father. As soon as Ruth began exploring the piano again, this time following her own ideas for the first time, he pushed her prematurely back onto the concert stage. Her book ends with her divorce, but with these prophetic words, "My future was in my hands."

It has turned into a bright future after all. At the ripe old age of twenty-nine, when Ruth made her comeback, she was hailed with the words: "She has matured into a pianist of keen taste, thought and personality." She has since remarried, and has arrived at a happy equilibrium she describes as follows: "Every three years I play internationally—between fifty and sixty concerts. Every year I play between twenty-five and thirty concerts and workshops all over the United States. At this university I teach performance piano between concerts . . . and write on musical subjects for various magazines."

5

Voices That Rang Out Young

Vocal prodigies? We usually don't think of singers as early bloomers in the way that Josef Hofmann or Yehudi Menuhin was. So it's rather surprising to find that a number of the greatest singers made their official debuts and started on flourishing careers before the age of twenty, some even in their early teens.

As long as virtuosity has reigned there have been prodigies. Only the paucity of written records prevents us from citing names from as far back as ancient Egypt and Greece, where virtuosi were heaped with honors and riches. By the seventeenth century, when we begin to be able to identify individual singers by name, virtuosity was respected both in the church and at royal private concerts and opera houses.

Consider the role of the *castrati,* who dominated the vocal scene for the two hundred years from about 1600 to 1800. Here was a "prodigy" situation in reverse. Instead of attempting to speed up their performing skill in a race against age, these talented youngsters were castrated to preserve their beautiful boyish voices despite an increase in years. Some of the best known appear to have been true prodigies, singing for several years in church before making their operatic debuts at about fifteen (usually in female roles).

By the eighteenth century, when Farinelli (1705–1762) reigned supreme, it was not unusual for these artificial sopranos (and sometimes contraltos) to earn for one performance ten times the sum paid a composer for writing an entire opera. This led directly, one suspects, to the rash of castration "accidents" all over Italy, which swelled the number of *castrati* to thousands. The singer was indeed supreme; he was expected to embellish the music to his greatest vocal advantage. With fully developed "masculine" lung capacity added to "feminine" agility and brilliance, their voices were truly exceptional both in range and power. They often stayed on stage after their arias were over, ignoring the actions and singing of the lesser performers. The audience did the same, talking, playing cards, drinking—giving its undivided attention only to the special big arias.

This was the star system at its worst. At its best it produced singers like Farinelli (his real name was Carlo Broschi), considered by some music historians to have been the greatest who ever lived. He made his operatic debut and thenceforth fought to keep himself at the top against a series of challengers in much the same way a boxing champion does today. He was both idol and dictator, financially and artistically, of any operatic enterprise in which he took part.

One of his first competitive encounters, when he was seventeen, was reported thus by a contemporary: "During the run of an opera there was a struggle every night between Farinelli and a famous player on the trumpet in a song. . . . This, at first, seemed amicable and merely sportive, till the audience began to interest themselves in the contest, and to take different sides. After severally swelling a note in which each manifested the power of his lungs and tried to rival the other in brilliancy and force, they had both a swell and shake together, by thirds, which was continued so long while the audience eagerly waited the event, that both seemed exhausted; and in fact the trumpeter, wholly spent, gave up, thinking, however, his antagonist as much tired as himself, and that it would be a drawn battle; when Farinelli, with a smile on his countenance, showing he had only been sporting with him all that time, broke out all at once in the same breath, with fresh vigor, and not only swelled and shook the note, but ran the most rapid and difficult divisions and was at last silenced only by the acclamation of the audience." As long as the vogue for Italian operas which featured their voices lasted, the *castrati* were an artistic necessity.

In the Jewish synagogue, by contrast, to be the "cantor" (or chanter) of the service was, and is, considered a sacred calling second only to that of the rabbi. The boy singers in the supporting choirs of the great cantors underwent rigorous training. Occasionally, among them, an obviously gifted youngster, soprano or alto, was permitted to act as cantor.

One such famous prodigy cantor of the twentieth century is David Putterman (1903–   ). Considered the best of alto soloists while he was serving as choirboy from the age of eight years on, he was much sought after by well-known visiting European cantors, such as Josef

Rosenblatt, when they were to make guest appearances in temples or in concerts in New York City. From the age of eleven to fourteen David chanted complete services in one of the largest temples, attracting hundreds of auditors. As was customary, he stopped singing completely and concentrated on other intensive musical studies at the onset of puberty. At eighteen, when his voice changed to adult tenor, he became a full-fledged cantor. As late as 1972 he was still active as cantor of the Park Avenue Synagogue, where he had served continuously since 1933.

Only occasionally has an outstanding boy soprano remained outstanding as a mature male singer. One who did and who became the greatest bass in history, equally superb as musician and actor, was the Russian Feodor Chaliapin (1873–1938). Chaliapin's childhood was one long struggle to evade the merciless beatings of his usually drunken father, to say nothing of the bitter poverty and a series of menial jobs that permitted little regular schooling. Few musicians ever have been raised in such a vehemently anti-musical atmosphere. When he won an antique harpsichord in a lottery it was kept locked up. He was permitted to sleep on it but not to play it. Eventually it was sold before he ever touched a single note.

A clown at a local fair fired Chaliapin's imagination by introducing him to the magic of the theater. A kind choirmaster taught him how to read music and let him earn some money by singing in the choir and occasionally at weddings and funerals. His various apprenticeships—to a furrier, a tinker, a cobbler, and so on—sometimes stretched out to twenty hours of work a day and entailed as many beatings as he had formerly gotten at home. He must have had an iron resistance and inborn stamina, for from a painfully thin, undernourished adolescent he became a giant of a man, very tall, robust and striking in appearance.

When Feodor was twelve his first visit to a theater had left him bewitched—in a spell from which he never quite recovered, for he remained theatrical on stage and off for the rest of his life. His sporadic stints at school ended forever when he was thirteen. The obsession with theater drove him to become an occasional extra in the local theater, although odd jobs still sustained him.

At sixteen, when his voice changed to bass-baritone, Chaliapin passed himself off as nineteen and wangled his way into a small provincial opera company as a chorister. After a month of severe stagefright in awkward, ill-fitting costumes the magic of actually being on stage at last took effect. In this period an emergency arose and he learned a major opera part (as an elderly father) overnight, having stayed awake all night to learn it. During the performance he clumsily missed a chair and landed on the floor, but somehow survived the incident, to receive considerable applause for his voice (and perhaps for his mishap). Such was his professional debut.

Chaliapin first played with small opera companies for short seasons, sometimes sleeping on park benches between engagements. At one time, unable to bear the pangs of four days' starvation, he contemplated suicide. It was while at this low ebb that a former artist of the Imperial Theatre, having heard of him, auditioned him, and offered Feodor free coaching lessons, also helping him to earn some money. Now, for the first time, he learned operatic roles in their entirety, and by twenty years of age he was a full-fledged operatic bass, singing in both opera houses and concert halls with a growing recognition of his genius.

By the time he was twenty-five the Russian critics were astounded at his dramatic and musical portrayals of old men as well as young— portrayals containing a vividness, a fluidity of movement, and an extraordinary grasp and projection of every variety of mood, emotion and situation. Soon he became world-famous, introducing Russian opera to all the great musical centers of Europe and America. His long rich life in music and theater also encompassed a great flair for art and sculpture. He was a most unusual man, always in the center of a swirling controversy about his art, his life, and his outspoken views on everything and everyone.

In the first golden age of vocal art, the period of *bel canto* (meaning "beautiful singing"), the preference for high voices was marked. Women singers were therefore more highly prized than men, and the outstanding ones were greeted with the kind of fervor and clamor we now associate with the avid followers of popular rock groups. The childhood of Jenny Lind (1820–1887) was thoroughly immersed in the theater during this era. She appeared regularly as singer or actress in Stockholm from the time she was thirteen. Over the next few years she abused her voice by the strain of too many performances and too many different roles. At eighteen she made her operatic debut. After a vocal crisis at the age of twenty, she recovered her voice under the expert guidance of the finest vocal teacher in Europe, Manuel Garcia, Jr. Known as the "Swedish Nightingale," she carried her sensational European career to the United States, where P. T. Barnum, of later circus fame, carefully built her up, through his flamboyant showmanship, into an act that brought waves of delirious excitement at her every appearance, enriching her and himself in the process.

Another of the great singing soprano prodigies of the nineteenth century was Adelina Patti, whose story will be told later.

Parallel with the predominantly high-voiced singers was a line of singers who combined superb acting with their purely vocal gifts. Among these were several prodigies. Most remarkable were the two Garcia sisters, Maria Malibran (1808–1836) and Pauline Viardot-Garcia (1821–1910) (their married names, which they used professionally). They were the daughters of Manuel García, once a famous tenor, who also had been well-known as a composer, actor and conductor by the time he was seventeen. He was the first to sing the role of Count Almaviva in Rossini's *Barber of Seville*.

García trained his wife and all three of their children to become professional singers—it was his son, Manuel Jr., who turned to teaching and restored Jenny Lind's voice. The elder Manuel's most remarkable results were with Maria and Pauline.

The beautiful Maria inherited her father's wilfulness, audacity, and temper, along with his extraordinary energy. Pauline, lacking beauty, had unusual intelligence, ambition, and perseverance, along with a magnetic personality. The two girls required very different kinds of training. As the father himself said, "Pauline can be guided by a thread of silk, but Maria needs a hand of iron."

It was magnificent training rather than a great voice that led to Maria's brilliant debut at sixteen. Only a year later the father brought the "García Troupe," consisting almost entirely of his own family, to New York, giving that city its first taste of Italian opera sung in Italian, with Maria as the major attraction. From the beginning she had an uncanny knack for musical embellishment (a freedom singers were allowed then, but which they often abused) and an intuitive genius for dramatic projection of her roles. Her rise was meteoric, and her sudden death as the result of an accident at the early age of twenty-eight left all of Europe stunned and grief-stricken.

Pauline played a quite different musical role. Intellectually brilliant, she far surpassed her sister in musicianship and in depth of understanding and interpretation of every role. She could make the audience shiver, shudder or cry, at will, so great was her acting ability and her

command of her voice. She was a double prodigy. Franz Liszt, her
teacher, had predicted a brilliant future for her as a pianist before
Maria's death. But that event persuaded her to follow in her sister's
footsteps and led to an early vocal debut.

When she was still in her late teens, such composers as Chopin and
Liszt, and later Berlioz, Brahms, Gounod and Wagner sought her musical opinions and advice. Pauline herself wrote charming operettas as
well as extremely difficult cadenzas for her operatic appearances. Her
home became a gathering-place for most of the great musicians, artists
and writers of France. After her retirement from the stage she continued the García tradition of vocal teaching. Among her pupils and
her brother's were some whose students in turn are considered the finest
operatic performers today, including Beverly Sills.

Most phenomenal of all during this time was the career of vocal
prodigy Adelina Patti (1843–1919). Almost from the very beginning
of a musical career that lasted from seven to seventy, she exemplified
the classic pattern of the prima donna, and it was typical of her that
she came close to being born on stage. Her parents, both singers, barely had time to reach their rooms after singing one evening at the Madrid Opera House before Adelina made her appearance in the world.
The family went to New York when she was three, where her father
was to manage the Italian Opera Company. Her sister and half-broth-
er were singers, her brother Carlo a violinist. From her earliest years
(in her own words) she "sat in the opera house every evening when
my mother sang; every melody, every gesture, was impressed on me
indelibly. When the performance was over and I had been taken home
and put to bed, I got up again stealthily, and by the light of the night
lamp played over all the scenes I had seen; thus I acted, danced, twit-
tered through all the operas."

A gift for mimicry and a good natural ear enabled her to memorize
arias and getures and absorb vocal technique. Add to that a remark-
ably mature voice and the sudden need for money when the Italian Opera Company failed, and it is small wonder that at the age of seven
Adelina stood upon a table for visibility, doll in hand, and sang a concert of difficult coloratura arias. The wonder is not that she did it at
all, but that she sang so well, with such natural mastery and such an
almost-complete vocal technique that the family was soon able to begin redeeming its pawned goods on the strength of her stage appearances.

Guiding her career through these and subsequent years was her brother-in-law, the expert impresario Maurice Strakosch. Under his management, while between the ages of seven and nine, she sang about 300 times, in the United States, Cuba and Mexico. An eyewitness to her earliest tour described her as "a somewhat delicate, pale-faced, dark-browed child, with thick glossy hair hanging in two long braids down her back, dressed in rose-colored silk, pink stockings, and pantalettes." Audiences were amazed at her ease and confidence. For only two years was she kept off the stage during intensive voice training and coaching in operatic roles.

By the time Adelina made her formal debut at sixteen in *Lucia di Lammermoor* she was a veteran of seven years' stage experience. Her poise, her iron nerves stood her in good stead at that debut, during which a loaded gun accidentally went off. As she later recalled: "For an instant everyone on the stage stopped still; then we just went ahead again." She made a profound impression. In that same year she sang fourteen different operatic roles—a remarkable memorizing achievement for a sixteen-year-old—and became famous for her beauty as well as for the unusually rich, pure, haunting yet warm quality of her voice.

Her success, among the longest in vocal history (lasting as it did for almost sixty years), went to Adelina's head. She was undoubtedly the most spoiled, most egotistical, most selfish, and most grasping of all the singers of her time. A hard-headed businesswoman, she told one harassed manager who pointed out that she was asking much more than the President of the United States was given for his services, "Very well, get the President to sing for you." Rumor had it that her pet parrot was trained to say "Cash! Cash!" whenever a manager entered her dressing room.

On one occasion, when she insisted as usual on full payment in advance of her very high fee ($5,000 for a single opera performance), the manager was only able to scrape together $4,000 before curtain time. After consultation with Adelina, her agent informed him that the prima donna would most certainly be ready to go on stage, fully costumed, but without her shoes. Frantic, the manager cleaned out the last-minute box-office receipts, which totalled $800. Patti thereupon consented to put on one shoe. Not until the last $200 was delivered did she don the other shoe and sally forth resplendently on stage for another triumph.

She travelled luxuriously, crossing the United States in a special private train car costing $30,000, which was lavishly furnished in pink satin as a kind of boudoir on wheels. In Europe the horses of her carriage were frequently unharnessed by adoring male admirers so that they could draw it personally to the opera house and back to her hotel. When she reappeared in New York at the age of forty her boat was greeted by a clamorous throng, the playing of several bands, and a twenty-one gun salute.

How did Patti achieve such prolonged success? Her beauty, for one thing, was very durable. In her mature years she always looked twenty years younger than her age; she dared to play the teen-age role of Rosina in *The Barber of Seville* when she was sixty-one. "Her eternal youth borders on the miraculous," wrote one infatuated critic.

That her voice was equally durable was no doubt due to the extreme care she gave it. "If I did not feel well, I did not sing," she said, "but went to bed and said there was no one in." She took only roles that were absolutely suited to her voice. Furthermore, in her entire long career she never sang more than three times a week. Her contracts stipulated that she was not required to attend rehearsals, only performances. Her manager more than once took her place on stage at rehearsals for the sake of the action. She even arranged for other singers to take the high notes in ensembles at the end of acts, where chorus, orchestra and soloists all sing together!

Another singer once said that the reason Patti never had a vocal crisis was that she avoided acting and forceful or emotional singing. "She never acted, and she never, never felt!" Acting certainly was not her strong point. Playwright and onetime music critic George Bernard Shaw said of her: "She seldom even pretends to play any other part than that of Adelina, the spoiled child with the adorable voice; and I believe she would be rather hurt than otherwise if you for a moment lost sight of Patti in your preoccupation with Zerlina, or Aida, or Caterina."

Patti had little real respect for, or understanding of, the music she sang, treating it, rather, as a vehicle to display her glorious voice. She added rhythmic changes, trills, runs and other decorations that showed her voice at its best, no matter how these distorted the composer's intentions. Exasperated with her musical liberties in an oratorio performance, conductor Theodore Thomas once said to her, "Excuse me, madam, but here *I* am the prima donna." And composer Rossini, on hearing her for the first time, when she sang an aria from one of his own operas, asked coldly afterwards, "Who wrote that aria you just sang?"

She was intellectually lazy, never reading for background or studying the implications of the roles she sang; she didn't move people emotionally, and showed little feeling or temperament in her singing. Only the sheer beauty, the incomparable quality, of her voice made for her success. Listening to the strangely mellow, penetrating tone, the ease and agility of its production, compensated for everything else. In the perfection of her vocal mechanism and the way she used it, she deserved the title once given her—"The Paganini of Vocal Virtuosity."

But Patti didn't know when to quit. After her operatic career was over, the United States became disenchanted first with her hackneyed concert programs and exorbitant admission fees; in England nostalgia kept her old admirers still revering the echo of her past glories. Each of her American visits was announced as a "farewell." One critic wrote: "Future historians will be obliged to record the fact that toward the end of the nineteenth century some genius invented the Patti farewell. . . ." He then speculated that she had picked up the practice from early appearances with the violinist Ole Bull, who began "his dangerous practice of farewelling. It rapidly grew into a habit, and at last he could not shake it off. He gave plain farewells, 'grand' farewells, 'last' farewells, 'absolutely last' farewells, 'positively last' farewells for over a quarter of a century. Patti caught the infection and gave us many farewells . . . but she was always forgiven."

But by 1903 the tone was hardly forgiving. "Over twenty years ago 'Patti's farewell' was already a joke in New York. At present it is a rather pathetic reality. . . . Adelina Patti is a dreary exhibition. Magnetic, well-preserved and willing to sing out of tune for $5,000, she triumphs," wrote a New York critic.

From her earliest years Patti had been accumulating wealth; she earned in all the sum (incredible for those days) of about five million dollars entirely through personal appearances. When she finally retired, her beauty as well as her voice gone, it was to live like royalty with her third husband in a castle in Wales which she had bought. They entertained as many as eighty guests for weeks at a time; her private theater was equipped with one hundred and twenty-six stage settings; many rooms were filled entirely with trophies—jewels and gifts from the crowned heads of Europe. Singer Lillian Nordica once said: "A prima donna dies three deaths . . . when her beauty fades; when her voice fails, and when the breath leaves her." Throughout her career Patti had fought all three as if she could outwit them.

It wasn't until the second half of the nineteenth century that native American singers began to appear as prodigies. The reason is obvious. There was no opportunity for superior vocal training and little opportunity for even the most gifted to be appreciated and rewarded, since there were so few opera companies or concert halls. So important was a foreign (preferably Italian) name and background for a singer who hoped to succeed in the United States that one adopted the name of the city of Albany, in which she had spent her childhood. Under the name of Emma Albani she received European and American recognition. Lillian Norton became famous as Lillian Nordica. To be acceptably exotic an American violinist named Harkness spelled her name backwards as "Senkrah" before launching her concert career.

Geraldine Farrar (1882–1967) was the nearest American counterpart and successor to the phenomenon of Jenny Lind. Born in Boston, she was the daughter of a major-league baseball player. Both parents, however, loved music and sang in church choirs. Geraldine, even as a child, showed the imagination, the obstinacy and individuality which marked her entire career. As a youngster, for example, she was asked to do an impersonation of Jenny Lind singing her sentimental hit *Home, Sweet Home*. Geraldine sang it, but only as an encore after bluffing her way through a difficult operatic aria in self-taught Italian.

Upon reaching New York in her early teens for study with Nellie Melba, the Metropolitan Opera star, she went to the opera as often as possible. Able to afford only standing room, she later remembered "clinging to the familiar old railing, always in a joyous daze." Both she and her mother agreed to reject various offers for public appearances, including a child role at the Metropolitan. Once the Metropolitan manager offered her a chance to sing in a Sunday night concert there. Upon her refusal, he urged "But it might be valuable to you to have your name on the billboards of the Metropolitan Opera House." "You will see it there some day," she replied confidently—a daring prediction at a time when only one American singer (Lillian Nordica) had broken the Metropolitan's tradition of employing only foreign singers with European reputations.

When she was seventeen, Geraldine and her parents left by cattle-boat for Europe, moving into the Parisian home of a lady who had agreed to underwrite the cost of the girl's European study. Besides the vibrant, thrilling quality of her voice, Geraldine had beauty, with her lustrous black hair, dark blue eyes and slim figure—the latter a great rarity among prima donnas of the day. She also had plenty of temperament, that electric stage presence which is now called "charisma," and the ambition and intelligence to apply her own interpretation to every role she studied.

From her earliest studies in Europe Geraldine worked at becoming what she later described as: "An actress who happens to be appearing in grand opera." The great singer Lilli Lehmann, her vocal teacher in Europe, taught her how to achieve the remarkable mobility of facial expression for which Geraldine became famous. She would tie the girl's hands behind her to prevent the exaggerated motions then prevalent in operatic acting, and say, "Now express your feelings."

At the age of nineteen Geraldine made her debut in an atmosphere which opened an era called, in musical circles, the "Farrar Furore." Never before had an American singer been permitted to sing in Italian (while the rest of the cast sang in German), design her own costumes, ignore the stage prompter and devise her own stage movements, and interpret the role her own way—all this on the august stage of the Berlin Royal Opera House. Perhaps the presence of the Crown Prince among her many admirers helped make her flamboyance possible. At any rate, her singing and acting captivated the sophisticated audience and the even more demanding critics. As she wrote in her autobiography, she was quite a novelty after the usual "stout ladies who waddle about protesting their operatic fate to spectators who find it difficult to believe in their cruel lot and youthful innocence."

Geraldine Farrar didn't have to change her name to Farrarini to appear at the Metropolitan Opera House in New York, either. After several years of triumph in Europe she portrayed, at her Metropolitan debut, the fourteen-year-old-Juliet in Gounod's *Romeo and Juliet,* with what was described as "a woman's voice in a girlish body." From that moment on she ruled operatic New York, in the words of one critic, as "Queen Bee." The "Farrar Furore" grew more hysterical, giving rise to a newly-coined word for her shrill, squealing, devoted women admirers—"Gerry-flappers."

Farrar carefully limited her roles to those she could do most effectively. Her Carmen was described as intense, passionate and vividly Mediterranean. Besides whistling, and rocking her hips, another critic said, "she projected into her Carmen one of the swiftest one-round fights ever seen in grand opera." She threw herself into the role so completely that on one memorable occasion she overreacted in flinging a rose back to Don José (played by the great tenor Enrico Caruso), following through with a smack on his cheek that was heard all over the opera house. Her match in temperament, he, in turn, overreacted in the last act by "accidentally" flinging her violently to the floor.

Geraldine played Carmen in a silent film version, among a dozen films she made in all. Of it a reviewer said "Into her whole body and being she can concentrate Carmen's elation . . . or her utter weariness and detachment, or her gay abandon with the pleasures of the tavern, her camaraderie, her flashes of anger, her forebodings of tragedy."

Her glamorous marriage to Lou Tellegen, the most famous actor of pre-World War I days, added to the romantic aura and interest in her private as well as her public life during the two stormy years before the marriage ended in divorce. During World War I she was one of the most effective fund raisers for wartime charities, using all her ingenuity, talent and influence in the process.

Geraldine had said she would retire at forty, since she felt her credibility in the young roles in which she specialized would be over by then. At forty her voice was as magnificent as ever; no one really believed she would quit, but she did. No farewell tours for her à la Patti. Her last appearance at the Metropolitan, however, was an event of such magnitude as to fill the front pages of every newspaper, something like the stir Charles Lindbergh caused when he returned from his solo flight across the Atlantic a few years later. At the end of the first act of the now-forgotten opera *Zaza* paper stars inscribed G. F., along with balloons and bouquets were thrown from the upper boxes. After the second act a large silk banner inscribed "None but you. Gerryflappers" was drawn across the stage, and Geraldine was presented with a crown and scepter. At the opera's end, more than three hundred bouquets blanketed the stage; a rope carrying a banner was suspended across the hall from one side balcony to the opposite one. The banner spelled out the message "Farrar, Hurrah!!! Hurrah, Farrar!" There were tears, screams, and frantic waving of Farrar pennants as the adoring stagehands carried her off to her waiting car. One headline the following day read: "CHEERING THOUSANDS OVERWHELM POLICE AT METROPOLITAN."

Geraldine kept in close touch with many of the most devoted Gerry-flappers during her retirement. When she died in 1967 at the age of eighty-five, she had been off the stage for many years, but she remained a vivid presence among the thousands who bought her numerous recordings that today are collector's items.

6

Two Black Prodigies on the Concert Stage

Helen Keller had Annie Sullivan who single-handedly turned her from a presumed idiot into a remarkable, accomplished human being. "Blind Tom" (1849–1908) was not as fortunate. The tag of "idiot" stuck with him throughout his life, although his basic gifts and what he did with them were as incredible as Helen Keller's.

The twenty-first child of a slave, so unpromising was the blind baby that he was "thrown in to the bargain" when his mother was put on the slave auction block. At their new place, he was confined to the slave house and small yard. Playing mostly by himself, he very early showed signs of extreme sensitivity to sounds, whether of nature or people. His physical reactions were extraordinary—he would caper joyfully when sounds pleased him, or bang his head against the object, roll his sightless eyes, mark time bodily with a heard rhythm.

Before he was two he imitated vocally the cries of animals, the sounds of storms or clocks—in fact, every sound he heard. They included the singing of the slave owner's young daughters. Not only did he join accurately in their singing; they soon reported that he harmonized as well.

Around the time he was five, a piano was brought into the master's house. Tom listened avidly, whirling and dancing outside the parlor window while the girls practiced. Late at night he would evade his mother's eye and steal into the big house to pick out sounds on the piano. The entire family surprised him very early one morning playing with considerable accuracy every piece in the girls' repertoire. Given free access to the piano he spent hours at it every day, hours broken only by brief spurts of physical activity out of doors. Soon he began devising pieces based on natural sounds. "This is what the wind said to me," or the birds, or the trees, he would explain.

Gradually it became obvious that here was a most valuable property. Colonel Bethune, his owner, began exhibiting Tom throughout Georgia when he was eight years old and had in his repertoire an impressive number of original as well as composed pieces. Meanwhile Tom had been exposed to all kinds of new sounds which soon became grist for his own compositions. His programs began to feature imitations of bagpipes, stump orators, music boxes, and so on. Somewhere along the line (certainly not in school, which he never attended) he learned the names of the music notes—no more. Technically, he seems to have been entirely self-taught.

People up and down the Eastern Seaboard were soon talking in extravagant terms of this marvelous prodigy who not only had an amazing repertoire of his own songs but could also reproduce immediately, upon a single hearing, anything played on the piano, no matter how complex. He could also name any notes that someone else played, and could improvise on a theme suggested by a member of the audience. Further, as an Albany newspaper reported, "With his right hand he plays *Yankee Doodle* in B flat. With his left hand he performs *Fisher's Hornpipe* in C. At the same time he sings *Tramp, Tramp* in another key—maintaining three distinct processes in that discord, and apparently without any effort whatever."

As was inevitable, the musical establishment raised the question of possible charlatanism. John Dwight, the distinguished Bostonian and editor of the *Journal of Music* fired the first blast in 1866 when Tom was only seventeen and earning vast sums of money for Colonel Bethune. As part of the arrangements for a European tour that year, the Colonel felt it was time to submit Tom to testing by the outstanding European musicians of the day. But first he gave the more sophisticated English and Scottish newspapers a chance to react to Tom's musical exhibitions or "entertainments" as they were billed.

One reviewer said: "You turn away convinced, surfeited with marvels, satisfied that you have witnessed one of the most incomprehensible facts of the time." Another mentioned that blind people often developed acute ears and retentive memories, but "in no case have we ever heard or known of one with auditory nerves so fine, or with memory so powerful, as Blind Tom." He went on to compare Tom with Mozart who also, as a child, had an amazing ear, and could reproduce music on a first hearing. Another critic referred to "this extraordinary musical prodigy [for which] history affords no parallel. His ability would be marvellous even if he had his eyesight."

A particularly interesting comment was that "his ability is a singular confutation of the theories of Hunt and Blake about the inferiority of the negro; for we may challenge any white man to compete with him, in perfect safety." One music journal columnist speculated in all seriousness that Tom's powers were proof that he was a reincarnation of some great musical intelligence of the past.

Ignaz Moscheles was one of the outstanding pianists, composers and teachers of the nineteenth century. His confrontation with Blind Tom, in a special interview, resulted in the following "testimonial" letter he wrote in 1866: "I think him marvelously gifted by nature. . . . I then went so far as to play him that part of my *Recollections of Ireland* in which three melodies are blended, and even that he imitated with most of its intricacies and changes. . . . I next put my hands on the keys at random, and was surprised to hear him name every note of such flagrant discord. Tom's technical acquirements are very remarkable . . . ."

Sir Charles Hallé, himself a piano and conducting prodigy, was the undisputed dean of English musical circles, and later became head of the Royal Academy of Music. This is what he wrote on hearing Tom for the first time: "I was very much astonished and pleased by his performance. His natural gifts seem to me quite marvelous, and the manner in which he repeated several pieces I played to him, which he had evidently never heard before, was most remarkable. Perhaps the most striking feature was the extraordinary quickness with which he named any notes struck by me on the piano, either single or simultaneously; however discordant they might be. I also named to him several notes, choosing the most difficult and perplexing intervals; these he instantly sang with perfect truth of intonation, although they might have puzzled a well-educated musician. Altogether Blind Tom seems to be a most singular and inexplicable phenomenon."

The story of how Daniel Auber, the most popular French opera composer of the day, was utterly chagrined by Tom is recounted in the memoirs of a singer in 1867: "The impresario came forward, saying, 'I am told that Monsieur Auber is in the audience. May I dare to ask him to come up and play something?' Auber said he thought he should die of fright. We all urged him, for the curiosity of the thing, to play something of his new opera, which no one as yet had heard; therefore no one could have known it. Auber mounted the platform amid the enthusiastic applause of the audience and performed his solo. Then Blind Tom sat down and played it after him so accurately, with the same staccato, old-fashioned touch of Auber, that no one could have told whether Auber was still at the piano! Auber returned and bowed to the wildly excited public and to us. He said 'This is my first appearance as a pianist and my last.' "

Despite this repeated corroboration of his remarkable abilities, every article about Blind Tom harped on his being an idiot. "Idiot" indeed! Perhaps, as some have suggested, instead of the usual boyish outlets of a normal childhood, he concentrated all his physical energies on his response to music. Surely his manager would not rechannel his reactions into more socially acceptable patterns when the "idiot" actions were so profitable. It was considered particularly significant that he cheerfully applauded himself along with the audience when he finished performing. Wouldn't applause be part of that whole spectrum of human sounds that he naturally imitated? Who would have explained to him that it was just not done?

Might Tom have become, in another day, and with other sponsorship, a great pianist or a great composer? James Trotter, a contemporary, wrote: "Who ever heard of an idiot possessing such memory, such fineness of musical sensibility, such order, such method as he displays? Let us call it the embodiment, the soul of music, and there rest our investigations."

Tom toured Europe throughout the Civil War, occasionally returning, however, to continue appearances in the States. He was in and out of court as various people laid claim to the valuable position of being his guardian. His repertoire was improbably put at between five thousand and seven thousand memorized pieces. His programs, typically, were a hodgepodge of straight classical selections, fantasias on popular operas, his own piano works, improvisations, vocal and piano imitations, the singing of popular ballads, and even recitations in Greek, Latin and German.

All together, he appeared successfully on concert and vaudeville stages for about thirty years. When he died in 1908 one of his own marches was played. Then—at last—he was taken seriously.

Philippa Schuyler's background, on the other hand, made the strongest possible contrast with the background of Blind Tom. Her parents were a mixed couple long before the word *integration* (in a racial sense) was invented. Her father, George Schuyler, a novelist whose autobiography is entitled *Black and Conservative,* was still, in 1972, doing free-lance political and literary writing for *American Opinion,* the *National Review,* and the *Manchester Union Leader,* among other newspapers and periodicals. White-haired and white-mustached, he moves slowly, wistfully, proudly through the cluttered rooms of his apartment in Harlem's once-famed Sugar Hill, displaying and explaining with great fluency touched with pathos the souvenirs and memorabilia of the short life of his daughter Philippa.

The pictures of his wife Josephine, who died in 1969, show the early loveliness that made a blue-eyed Mack Sennett beauty of this Texas heiress. A journalist as well as a poet and painter, she had strong views on many subjects; among which, interracial marriage for love was only one. She had her own theory of dreams (later writing a book with Philippa on the subject): She believed (forty years before any uproar over cigarettes or cyclamates) in putting only what was pure and close to its natural state into the mouth; both her husband and daughter learned to eat food almost entirely raw—even potatoes; only meats were subjected to minimal cooking.

Above all, she felt that environment was everything. Stating the same theme a little differently later, she maintained, "Genius is only an overdose of energy." Neither Josephine nor George Schuyler was musical in any way, nor could they recall any particularly musical forbears.

When their only child was born on August 2, 1931, the *Amsterdam News* announcement said in part "This baby, who may in time be a columnist and novelist, has been named Philippa." Not only was Philippa a much wanted and deeply cherished child, but she was to be the proving ground for her mother's theories. The journals relating her development from month to month, from year to year, are loving in tone, clinical in detail, vivid with sketches and photographs. Philippa's physical achievements were normal, her ear for sounds keen, her responses to an unusually rich environment were gratifying.

Mrs. Schuyler reserved her deepest scorn for the then popular John Dewey "learn by doing" school of educational thought. She ridiculed it in verse, exaggerating to suit her purpose, as follows:

> There's not the slightest doubt—
> For children under ten,
> The alphabet is out
> And finger-painting's in.

Only in the last few years have experts on all sides begun advocating teaching very young children to read. Philippa knew all four alphabets (printed and written—capital and small) and the numerals as well, by the time she was eighteeen months old. Not long afterwards a writer for the *New York Herald Tribune* devoted two columns to her achievements, headlining his story "NEGRO BABY 2½ READS, WRITES, SPELLS AND QUOTES OMAR KHAYYAM." Her spelling vocabulary of several hundred words included such choice tidbits as *Constantinople* and *rhinoceros*. Though full of childish sparkle, gayety and restless energy, she could also locate the Mississippi River on the globe as well as do cartwheels.

Philippa started fooling with the family piano early. Soon after her third birthday she began lessons; within three months she also started composing little pieces at the piano. At the age of four she played ten of these original compositions to the astonishment of the National Piano Teachers' Guild and reporters from various newspapers and magazines. Shortly afterwards she played coast-to-coast over the NBC radio stations. (She continued to do so intermittently for the next five years.)

The same interviewer who saw Philippa at 2½ visited her again when she was five. She could now add, subtract, multiply, divide, and so on; but she could also discuss such things as cosmic rays, and the difference between war and revolution. In between she dashed to the piano, playing, singing, doing dance steps while the adults talked. Her compositions ran the gamut from "Nigerian Dance" to settings of nursery rhymes and fairy tales to "Vegetable Dance," replete with the pathos of the malodorous onion's loneliness until befriended by a potato. Never, explained Mrs. Schuyler privately, was Philippa allowed access to the newspaper publicity stirred by her precocity; and it was made very clear that the word *prodigy* was forbidden in the Schuyler home.

Philippa finished grammar school when she was ten, even though she had spent part of each year giving solo piano recitals (mostly for charity) all over the country. Deems Taylor, who had interviewed her reluctantly on radio when she was six, discussed music gravely with her between her selections, coming to the startling conclusion: "This is no infant. This is a born musician." He could also easily believe that her I.Q. score was indeed 185 (well in the "genius" category) as tested at New York University.

Mayor Fiorella LaGuardia, as well known for his amateur conducting as for his fireman's hat, was one of Philippa's early patrons. It was no doubt partly his doing that June 19, 1940, was declared Philippa Schuyler Day at the New York World's Fair. She played two programs that day—one in the morning for about 40,000 schoolchildren, included works by Bach, Daquin, Schumann, Ibert, and so on, plus several of the sixty-odd works she herself had composed. One of the latter, written while she was studying harmony at the Pius X School of Music, was called "Cockroach Ballet." Asked by Mother Stevens with some concern why she didn't write about angels instead, she had answered, "But, dear Mother, I've never seen an angel, and I've seen lots of cockroaches."

When Philippa began composing an opera the following year, a visitor said, "Oh, how charming and childlike this is." She immediately put it away, saying, "I don't want to write childlike music." She credited her unusual ambidextrous strength of touch to her teacher, Paul Wittgenstein, famous one-handed pianist who had lost his right hand in the First World War, but played brilliantly nevertheless. Besides the piano, she studied harmony, sight-singing, counterpoint, and orchestration, partly with private teachers and partly at the Pius X School. She was tutored at home rather than attending high school. Her taste in reading kept pace with her intelligence, and her keen ear enabled her to pick up languages easily.

It was while visiting Mexico with her mother during her twelfth year that she experienced a wave of homesickness which found its outlet in a composition called *Manhattan Nocturne*. She arranged it for 100-piece orchestra, but played a piano version for friends at her thirteenth birthday party. Her modesty, among other things, impressed an interviewer at that time—she managed adroitly to turn the conversation away from herself. The reporter summed it up this way: "She has been a student of the classics since she was five. . . . She excels in mathematics, she paints, she writes poetry, and she knows more about current events than the average well informed adult. But her principal love is music, and she thinks that working at it is so much fun that there ought to be another name for it besides work."

She had other interests too. Her reading ran to Flaubert and Dostoievsky, she "dug" the drumming of Gene Krupa and loved to jitterbug. When a skeptical reporter asked her how she could play chess against herself, she said, "Maybe I'm a schizophrenic."

At fourteen she had decided for herself to become a Catholic. She continued throughout her teens to feel a deep attachment for the Pius

X school (which later became part of Manhattanville College of the Sacret Heart)—giving annual concerts there from the time she had started studying harmony. Mother Morgan, her harmony teacher, found her hard to contain musically. "She was such an independent and gifted child, so charming, so full of fun, so bouncy and clever that the discipline of harmonic rules was hard for her to stick to—she knew what she wanted to write and we could only help by giving her the tools to do so."

Philippa became the youngest member ever elected to the National Association of Composers and Arrangers as a result of the *Manhattan Nocturne* and another composition called *Rumpelstiltskin*. This came about when she was fourteen and had submitted both works in a contest for young composers held in Detroit. From among a hundred entries, those two works were found to display the most originality and technical skill; they were awarded first and second prizes. Philippa was present when seven thousand Detroit children heard the *Nocturne* performed right after Mozart's First Symphony (written when he was eight) by the Detroit Symphony Orchestra. A critic commented, "Neither score was great, but both showed great promise."

Did the child ever resent the energy-plus-work formula? It seems not. Years later she wrote: "I am not sorry that I was a child prodigy. There is so much to learn and so little time in which to learn it. . . . It is a shame to waste one's early years, for the memory then is most retentive. Childhood now is too often considered just the period for 'having fun'. There is nothing to challenge the spirit when everything is made too easy. Youth is brave and wants to battle."

She was petite, pretty, with glowing eyes, exuberant vitality, unusual poise and charm when she made her double debut as composer and pianist in New York at the age of fifteen with the New York Philharmonic before an audience of twelve thousand at the Lewisohn Stadium. *Rumpelstiltskin* was described as an "adroitly scored and active piece in gnomish vein . . . [revealing] imagination in tonal handling." The *New York Times* critic declared it was "expertly written, with a broad melodic core that has genuine charm." Her playing of the Saint-Saëns G Minor Concerto indicated "ebullient musicality. . . It was bright and interesting." The reviewer noted with surprise the very resonant, rich and singing tone he had hardly expected from her delicate appearance. He called her a "pianist of extraordinary natural talent."

At nineteen Philippa first went abroad by herself, to play a program for the inauguration, in Haiti, of President Paul Magloire. She had been offered a tour as a night-club performer—for which she certainly had the looks as well as talent—but turned it down. With the acclaim and decorations of that first foreign appearance Philippa's life took a completely different turn from that of the usual concert artist.

Within the next ten years she visited over fifty countries on four continents; in many of the African countries she was the first American artist, black or white, ever to appear. She was heaped with medals and costly gifts, besides being summoned to command performances by the Queen of Belgium and the Emperor of Ethiopia. She once described her life during those years as similar to that of the jongleurs, the wandering musicians of the Middle Ages, but with infinitely more problems because of the complexities of modern life.

Some of her tours were sponsored by the U.S. State Department. When Josephine Baker, the expatriate American Negro singer, told an Argentinian audience that the United States was dedicated to "constant persecution of the Negro," Phillippa was sent on a South American tour as an antidote; the most hostile anti-American audiences were captivated by her personal charm, intelligence and musical ability. It is small wonder that the monograph her mother wrote about her after her death was called "Philippa, the Beautiful American."

She was much more than a purely musical ambassador. Her command of many languages and her continued interest in world politics and social problems, in addition to her personal attributes, gave her access to the heads of state and most influential people in the government and the arts in every country she visited. And her extraordinary insights into, and sympathy with, the problems of common people enabled her to come away with balanced views about the true state of affairs behind official propaganda. Before long she began acting as roving foreign correspondent for United Press International and various magazines in addition to giving concerts. Over the years she sent back more than two hundred closely reasoned, perceptive reports—those from the new African countries she visited both before and after they achieved independence were especially valuable.

She had a delightful sense of humor as well as a way with words. Both are evident in her several books, particularly in *Adventure in Black and White,* which describes some of her travels, her musical and human encounters, her personal life in the course of playing from the frozen wastes of Iceland to the ant-infested jungles of Ruanda. Her word portraits of some of her local managers, various suitors, and such

famous individuals as Albert Schweitzer and Pope Paul are unforgettable. *Adventure* is the word for it: traveling by Jeep, airplane, camel
and rickshaw, beset by tropical diseases, con men, kidnappers, bigots,
playing in quonset huts and under thatched roofs. Then there were the
many compensations, such as visiting and playing for thousands of delighted children in hundreds of missions.

"It was my good fortune to discover that I had a real love for people and places. It's a great joy to go into a strange land, to make
friends, and to give, in return for freely bestowed kindness, the universal beauty of great music," she said.

She influenced African thinking on the role of women in society.
Once she was told: "Do you know, it has been very important, your
coming? Now, all the Baganda are saying, 'Is wonderful, Miss Philippa. Can a young girl do all that, achieve so many things? Perhaps
then, we should not despise our girls? Perhaps a girl can learn as can a
man, and then should we not teach our girls?' "

The pianos she encountered form a tragi-comic story of their own.
One which had a number of missing keys she described as "a gnarled,
bowed upright, half-toothless." In Lagos flashlights had been kept in
the grand piano during the rainy season, and water dishes during the
dry season. Nothing had helped. "The sounding board had an immense crack which closed up during the rainy season, opened in the
dry. Now it was gigantic. Finally it was tuned by the area's sole musician, an ancient Englishman who had not tuned a piano in forty-six
years."

Only once did she voice any doubts about her ability to meet her
schedule. "As the plane settled at last on Roberts Field in Liberia I
thought to myself 'How can I stand this? It's hell playing classic music
in soggy, damp tropical heat. It's been too fast—Accra concerts on the
26th and 28th, Kumasi recital on the 27th, that twenty-four hour trip
to Abidjan on the 29th, the Abidjan concert on the 30th—and now
concerts in Monrovia on the 31st (tonight) and February 1st, in Da-
kar on the 4th and 5th, and Morocco on the 7th and 8th! It will kill
me!" But it didn't. Even when, in Cuba, a television camera tube ex-
ploded on stage and showered sparks on her nylon dress, the camera-
man stamped out the fiery remains while she went on, without interruption, playing Bach to an audience of seven thousand.

She kept her cool through hundreds of appearances in the most sophisticated cities of the world, including several concerts in New York.
The reviews were all she could ask for. In the middle nineteen sixties

she continued with her double role as entertainer and news correspondent in Viet Nam.

It was while on a voluntary errand of mercy there that she met her death at the early age of thirty-five. Philippa was one of the founders of the Amerasian Foundation to aid the mothers of illegitimate children fathered by American soldiers in Viet Nam. Hearing that some orphans were caught in a wave of violence near Hue, she prolonged her stay in order to carry out a rescue mission. There were three crewmen, Philippa, and eight Vietnamese children in the helicopter when it plunged into Danang Bay. Only Philippa and the child in her lap were killed.

Several thousand people lined the streets to pay their respects at her funeral procession in New York, in which six Harlem boys played the muffled drums and six sailors served as pallbearers. Mayor Lindsay attended her memorial service and President Johnson sent flowers.

In her writings Philippa had been outspoken against oppression and injustice. "We cannot uphold liberty and equality while permitting racial segregation and discrimination here," she said. The concluding words of *Adventure in Black and White* summarize her life well: "I admire the people who are doing their best to shape a new world. I think there is great hope for the human race, and I feel a deep warmth of affection for all peoples, everywhere." As things turned out she not only lived for these ideas but also died for them.

7

Podium Precocity—The Conductors

We tend to think, and rightly so, that conducting, of all branches of music, requires the most developed musicianship as well as great personal maturity needed to handle a hundred or more musicians replete with talent and temperament. It is surprising, therefore, to find a small number of hardy souls who made their way to the podium before the age of twenty—some with marked success, some with spectacular failure. Not included are composers or instrumentalists, such as Mendelssohn, who conducted in the course of otherwise distinguished adolescent careers. Also excluded are conductors who were prodigies in other areas first, such as Serge Koussevitzky on the double bass and Eugene Ormandy on the violin. The conductors to be discussed in this chapter are those who made their mark only in conducting before they were twenty years old.

The art of conducting (by our modern definition) is not much more than a hundred years old. It had a long and fascinating prehistory of leadership divided between two people; at first, a harpsichordist and the first violinist; later a time beater and the concertmaster. Only gradually did the complexity of the texture of orchestral music make a single leader necessary. Even more gradually did the idea take hold that the conductor should interpret as well as keep time. Eventually, however, clapping and stamping of feet came to a halt; the stick came to be replaced by a roll of paper or leather, a violin bow, and, finally, a baton. The conductor began to face the orchestra instead of the audience, and his role was finally crystallized into its present-day mold.

Detailed records of youthful conductors from the early nineteenth century are scant. We do know, however, that a Master Joseph Burke was an "immense favorite" with London audiences around 1830, when he was eleven. He led the orchestra, played the violin, and acted, and it is impossible to tell in which of these triple capacities he won such favor. Arthur Napoleon (1843–1925) at nine years of age conducted well enough to win the praise of Hector Berlioz, himself a superb conductor and critic whose opinion cannot be lightly dismissed; but there are no further references to show what happened to young Arthur.

It was only in the late 1800's that names we recognize began to appear among conducting prodigies. Arturo Toscanini (1867–1957), for one, became a prodigy conductor by accident. A penniless cello student at the Parma Conservatory in Italy, he supported himself by copying scores at night, ruining his eyesight in the process. He must in his early teens have shown strong leadership, and even dictatorial, qualities, for the schoolboy nicknames bestowed on him—"Napoleon" and "Little Genius"—were enough to send him into a towering rage of the kind that later became part of the Toscanini legend.

By the age of seventeen Toscanini had graduated with the highest possible scores in both cello and composition, and had made his cello debut before a private audience at the conservatory. The program included a number of his own works—in fact, some of his professors had urged him to go further into the field of composition. No prodigy as yet, he joined a touring opera company as second cellist, highly respected by his fellow musicians for his score-reading ability and stupendous memory.

A South American tour brought the company to Rio de Janeiro and into a crisis. The Brazilian conductor, in a fit of pique, refused at the last moment to mount the podium for the scheduled performance of *Aida*. The concertmaster, who tried to fill in, was hissed off by the noisy, hostile audience, as was the chorus master. The Italian women in the chorus were in tears at the prospect of being stranded in this alien land without pay, and it was one of them who urged that the baton be handed to the second cellist: "He will save us!"

Toscanini took the baton, mounted the podium as to the manner born, and before the end of the first act the hostility had subsided. The curiosity of the audience soon turned into enthusiasm that became sheer pandemonium by the end of the evening. The seventeen-year-old Toscanini, the score still open at page one, had conducted the magnificent performance entirely from memory!

In a number of performances on that South American tour he conducted several other operas before the troupe returned to Italy. There he went back to his cellist seat, but not for long. Members of the chorus spread word of his skill, and he was soon conducting in opera houses up and down the Italian boot. His cello-playing days were over.

Thus, from his first conducting stint and due in part to his poor eyesight, Toscanini started the vogue of conducting from memory. For many it became a stunt, but its inevitable side effect was a closer study and deeper understanding of the score. Every conductor since has had to be a scholar as well as a musician. In the course of almost seventy years on the podium, Toscanini set new standards for conductors, reversing the trend toward arbitrary distortion and over-romanticizing. He raised the standards of orchestral players as well by making seemingly impossible demands on them and insisting on the results he wanted. To the end the famous memory persisted. He was far from young when a worried bass player confessed anxiously during an intermission that he had broken his E string and had no spare with him. Toscanini stared into space for a few moments before reassuring the musician: "Don't worry. You won't need it." He was, as usual, correct.

Years later, someone reminded him about that first evening in Rio de Janeiro, and mentioned the perfection of the first performance. The characteristic Toscanini response was "Ah, but you are wrong. I made two mistakes, one in the first act, and one in the third."

George Szell (1897–1970), who in his last years conducted the very fine Cleveland Orchestra, was a triple prodigy as pianist, composer and conductor. Soon after his piano debut when eleven years old he had been widely hailed as "the new Mozart." His special affinity for Mozart's music indeed carried over to our own days, during which his recordings and interpretations of that composer are considered definitive.

The debut (with the Vienna Symphony) had included his own Overture and also his Rondo for Piano and Orchestra. The Variations for Orchestra which he wrote at fifteen remained a part of the repertory of the German orchestras for many years. There is a story that just a few days before Szell's sixteenth birthday a fellow prodigy named Rudolf Serkin, who was then twelve and who greatly admired Szell's compositions, learned a few of them to perform in honor of the occasion. Szell's reaction is said to have been expressed in the question: "Serkin! How can you play such trash?"

The following summer the Vienna Philharmonic visited the spa where the Szell family was vacationing, and George watched and questioned the conductor for weeks on end. When the conductor injured his hand, the seventeen-year-old George was given his first opportunity to wield a baton. His formal debut as a conductor came shortly afterward when, still seventeen, he appeared in three capacities with the Berlin Philharmonic: as soloist, conductor, and composer (he played Beethoven's "Emperor Concerto," conducting it from the piano, and also conducted his own Symphony No. 1, which, he said years later in an interview, "is now happily forgotten.")

We will never know whether George Szell might, in maturity, have become a great pianist or composer. We do know that in his chosen branch of music, conducting, he reached the heights, in both opera and symphony. At the time of his death he was considered to be among the half-dozen greatest conductors in the world.

The first dawning ambition to conduct often stems from adolescent hero worship of a successful conductor. When Bruno Walter (1876–1962) studied at the Berlin Singakademie he was able by the age of twelve to earn money by accompanying singers at the piano. In that year, he heard a concert conducted by Hans von Bülow that changed the course of his life. From then on he took every opportunity to conduct the Berlin Conservatory orchestra.

By the age of seventeen, when he made his debut conducting an opera by Lortzing after a stint as vocal coach at the Cologne Opera House, he knew he was in the right calling. He wrote a friend: "I felt no uncertainty whatever and was not worried . . . my hand automatically knew what to do; it had the ability to hold the orchestra together and keep the soloists and chorus in harmony with it. . . . The general effect of my first performance was the encouraging feeling of having stood in the place for which I had been destined."

Walter was a very literate and thoughtful man. On the fiftieth anniversary of his conducting debut he commented wryly: "It is only later in life that a conductor learns how much there is to worry about. At seventeen I had no worries. I had conducted at the Conservatory since the age of eleven, so of course I knew all about it."

These men were exceptional. Most of the other great conductors, such as Ernst Ansermet, Willem Furtwängler, Herbert von Karajan, Erich Leinsdorf, Gustav Mahler, Dmitri Mitropoulos, Charles Munch, Fritz Reiner, Artur Rodzinski and William Steinberg followed the more traditional route. They started as virtuosi on some instrument, or as vocal coaches in small opera companies, eventually working their way up within the hierarchy as operatic assistant conductors, operatic conductors, symphonic assistant conductors, and finally symphonic conductors; eventually, via recordings, they became artists of the world. All of this takes time, which is why so few famous conductors have become known before the age of twenty-five or thirty.

There is a brilliant group of "youngsters" on the conducting scene today, but to acquire the musicianship and personal maturity needed they all were at least in their middle twenties before making their first impact. These younger stars include, among others, such conductors as Thomas Schippers, Zubin Mehta, Seiji Ozawa, Claude Abbado, Istvan Kertesz and Michael Tilson Thomas.

An outstanding musical prodigy came on the scene in 1930 when Lorin Maazel was born. Music was in Lorin's blood. His grandfather was a brilliant violinist, his uncle and his father were singers, his mother was an accomplished pianist with absolute pitch. When Lorin was born his father was a singing teacher in Los Angeles. Music was part of the daily life, as was concert-going.

At an early age Lorin began music study on the piano, and followed it with the violin; but it was while playing a simplified piano version of Haydn's Surprise Symphony one day that his imagination was stirred toward becoming a conductor. He began conducting to records, using props and family members as orchestra sections so that he could practice cueing. Vladimir Bakaleinikoff, associate conductor of the Los Angeles Philharmonic, was approached to give him lessons. Bakaleinikoff was rather dubious about teaching a child, but one interview changed his mind. He taught Lorin for nothing.

Two summers at the famous National Music Camp in Interlochen, Michigan, gave Lorin his break, putting him in the national spotlight. He conducted the camp's National Youth Orchestra at the New York World's Fair. This led to a guest appearance with Leopold Stokowski and the Los Angeles Philharmonic in Hollywood Bowl. At this time the Maazel family moved to Pittsburgh, where Dr. Bakaleinikoff had become associate conductor of the Pittsburgh Orchestra.

It was shortly after this move that Toscanini invited Lorin to conduct the NBC Symphony. At the first rehearsal the orchestra, outraged at what they considered an affront to their dignity and musicianship, stared at him in open defiance, all the while sucking on lollipops to emphasize their scorn. Lorin faced them down, and coolly began to rehearse. At the very first purposely wrong note, he stopped to correct the player in such a way that it became obvious he had the whole score in his head. From then on, even more remarkable than his completely mature approach to the works, was his ability to get along with the musicians at rehearsal; he treated them as colleagues, and his brisk efficiency and courtesy made them forget his age and respect him on personal as well as musical terms. He also broke the "black velvet" precedent in attire. The public and the critics received him with acclaim.

But the most important part of the story is yet to come. This early success could have frozen him into a pattern of exploitation that would have stunted his personal and musical growth. Instead, wisely, he was brought up normally, as any boy, attending public schools and the University of Pittsburgh, playing violin in the Pittsburgh Symphony, conducting only a few concerts each year. By the time he was twenty-one Serge Koussevitzky had invited him to conduct the Boston Symphony at Tanglewood, and he had received a Fulbright scholarship. Now, as general director of the Opera in West Berlin and conductor of the Berlin Radio Symphony, he also makes important guest appearances and recordings. Recently appointed Music Director of the Cleveland Orchestra, Lorin is spending half the year guest conducting in the United States.

There is a good deal more to Lorin's story, however, than these bald facts about his career reveal. Maazel himself gave a series of somewhat different insights in an interview several years ago. He claimed with some truth that despite his proven capabilities at an early age there was no place for him as a conductor on the American scene between the ages of fifteen and twenty-one. "I lost my market value as soon as I ceased to be a monstrosity," he said. There was some irony in the fact that after having already conducted major orchestras for several years he was appointed "Apprentice Conductor" at Pittsburgh; a highly successful appearance at Tanglewood led nowhere; the Fulbright grant simply exiled him to a life of scholarship in Europe.

As things developed, Europe turned out to be the scene of his success, beginning with an emergency debut when a local conductor became ill. From then on he triumphed, appearing with thirty major European orchestras in ten years, on a continent that had never known him as a child prodigy. He became the youngest conductor and the first American ever to conduct at Bayreuth, the Wagnerian shrine. He is no longer essentially a European conductor since he returned triumphantly to the States at thirty-two. "THE FORMER PRODIGY IS STILL PRODIGIOUS," headlined one reviewer.

His personal reaction to his child-prodigy experiences is not bitter. He does feel, however, that a child should not be subjected to performing before "a bunch of gushing adults," adding that "a mathematical prodigy doesn't have to get up in front of audiences and do sums, or something—why should a music prodigy?" And when asked the hypothetical question if he would allow any gifted child of his own to appear in public at an early age, his answer was an unequivocal "No." Lorin has two children (aged ten and five) from his first marriage, both artistically gifted but not specifically for music. He and his second wife, Israela Margalit, a well-known concert pianist, have one child, who is still too young to have shown any artistic proclivities.

Outwardly it would seem that any musically precocious child could be taught to go through the motions, to acquire the stage presence, to learn a few scores, with nothing like the comparable virtuosity of sheer technique needed by prodigies on piano or violin. Critics, as a matter of fact, usually have treated these appearances in gingerly fashion. There is often no telling which will turn out to be the real thing and which the flash-in-the-pan.

A picture story in *Life* Magazine in 1947 featured Pierino Gamba, (1937–   ) who at nine had already conducted concerts in Rome, Milan, Zurich and Paris, where the critics had called him a "pocket Toscanini" and the audience had cheered him for twenty minutes. The boy evidently had a remarkable memory and considerable musical intelligence. One London critic appraised his performance on purely musical grounds as follows: "One sensed the child mind in all its logic and ruthlessness. Beethoven was viewed in a clear morning light, everything in its place and sharply defined. Pierino does not smear Beethoven intrusively with his own personality, perhaps because he hasn't yet developed a personality that will smear . . . and all the more superficial tricks are there." Now in his late thirties, Gamba's name is missing from among the musical luminaries of today.

Of Ferruccio Burco (1939–1965) we can speak with finality, since he died at twenty-six. His conducting career began in 1947 when, at the age of eight, he conducted a concert in Paris entirely from memory, dressed in the "uniform" of child prodigies—black bolero jacket, short pants, Eton collar, and the requisite curly hair. He was quite obviously talented, not merely physically appealing, and possessed a good memory, ear and sense of rhythm. Nevertheless a critic at the time suspected him of bluffing. He summed up his reactions in this expressive sentence: "The spectacle of this child on the podium is both adorable and sickening."

Sir Thomas Beecham, the British conductor, exclaimed when he heard of Ferruccio's projected tour of the United States; "Who is responsible for this outrage? The child should be in a kindergarten, sucking a lollipop." Nevertheless, the boy conducted triumphantly at Carnegie Hall. A group of backers, following this debut, sent him on a tour that covered Philadelphia, Detroit, Boston, Chicago, Los Angeles, and San Francisco.

Even at the first concert, however, there were some suspicions of high-powered public-relations methods being used. It was even harder to take seriously his second New York appearance, this time around Mother's Day, when his mother was the featured soloist in several operatic arias. In the words of a review of the day: "The boy knew when to quiet the orchestra, slow down the tempo, and give his mother the right of way in the big dramatic moments. . . . Mother and child were doing as well as expected in Carnegie Hall last night." At the time of his death, Ferruccio was still conducting—a small, traveling, provincial Italian band.

There must have been something in the air of the late thirties conducive to child conducting prodigies. It produced not only Gamba and Burco, but also Robert Benzi (1939–   ), who made his debut in 1949 at the age of ten. Two critics—one French, one English—noted his successes were due to a high degree of co-operation from the orchestra. As one critic said, "He gesticulates so skillfully before eighty good, complaisant craftsmen." There was also skepticism about his choosing works the orchestra knew almost by heart; and the implication was that only in new works could the true degree of talent of a conductor be tested adequately. The prognosis was guarded: "Nothing proves that these minute jockeys who wield the whip so well will one day become real circus riders." Robert Benzi later made a successful conducting comeback. In 1972 he conducted at both the Paris Opera and the Metropolitan Opera in New York.

Conducting, of all musical fields, has been the most difficult for a woman to enter. That didn't stop six-year-old Gianella de Marco (1945?–   ) from going in where grownups seldom tread. Having conducted in Italy from the age of four, she made her Paris debut at six to uniformly bad reviews which found her showmanship to be far more precocious than her musicianship. Terms like "ridiculous," "piti-ful," "humiliating to a fine orchestra" were hurled about. Nevertheless, she did go on to triumph, two years later, in Manchester and London, where an Albert Hall audience of six thousand stood and cheered her program. The critics grudgingly gave in, saying things like "really good performances, a credit to conductress and players alike," and cited her "genuine, albeit immature musicianship." One wonders whatever happened to little Gianella. Wherever she is, she isn't on any orchestral podium that we know of.

Lorin Maazel had been hailed as the most successful child conductor since Mendelssohn. But there is a new contender on the scene. In April of 1968, Oliver Knussen (1953–   ), whose father is principal double bassist with the London Symphony, conducted that group in his own First Symphony. He was fifteen at the time, and had already written about sixty works. He was then just finishing his Second Symphony. In an interview he said "I don't like all this prodigy rubbish. I just started early." He must have started growing early too, for at fifteen he was six feet three inches tall and weighed 225 pounds.

Critical opinion of the Knussen symphony was mixed. One British critic said that it contained no definite hint of unusual gifts; another described the finale, a set of variations, as "a serious and gifted young person's guide to the orchestra." It was very well received in the United States, including the rather sophisticated fun it poked at the composers Gustav Mahler and Oliver Messiaen who, in Knussen's words "use the cymbal, bass and drum in a vulgar way." The conductor André Previn (himself a prodigy composer-pianist-conductor) found it amazing and frightening that a lad not yet fifteen could have written it. The audience applauded it tumultuously for ten minutes.

But it is of course because of his conducting rather than his composing that Knussen belongs in this chapter. Irving Kolodin, a critic not easily moved to superlatives, called his possibilities as a conductor "awesome." Kolodin went on to call attention to his technical skill in terms of reflexes, coordination and authority, summing up with the accolade: "a rare order of aptitude." Now it remains to be seen if Knussen's family and teachers can enable him to grow to a musical stature to match his physical development.

8

Two Violinists—A Study
in Contrasts

The history of prodigies seldom has provided so clear-cut a contrast in development as that between the two violinists, Yehudi Menuhin and Ruggiero Ricci. Both were phenomenally talented at the same age, at almost the same time, and both studied with the same teacher. The contrast lies in the way they became prodigies and the subsequent effect on their personal and professional lives.

Yehudi Menuhin (1916–   ) was born to well-educated, music-loving immigrant parents who had come penniless to the United States. No one could possibly have predicted his remarkable gifts nor, for that matter, that his two younger sisters would become outstanding concert pianists. True, his parents took him to concerts of the San Francisco Symphony before he was two years old, baby-sitters being an impossible luxury. He took particular delight in the sound of the violins, singling out Louis Persinger, the concertmaster, who occasionally played solo.

When he was four Yehudi asked for a violin and lessons with Persinger. Instead he was given a toy violin, which he promptly smashed, saying: "It won't sing!" His grandmother, who lived in Palestine, sent a few dollars for the purchase of a real one, and Yehudi started lessons at the age of five. Two years later he played for Persinger, who sensed in his playing a "potentiality for greatness" besides an acute ear and extraordinary rhythmic sense. Persinger proved to be a great teacher, but Yehudi's phenomenal debut at seven years old was surely

91

as much a product of his own personality and his home environment as of Persinger's teaching.

Yehudi's very name is a clue to the independence of his parents' thinking. Both were strongly Jewish; they had met in Palestine, and both taught in a Hebrew school on arriving in this country. The name "Yehudi" means "Jew" in Hebrew, and was decided on as the result of an anti-Semitic slur made to his mother shortly before he was born. The mother dominated the strictly-routined household from the beginning. Yehudi at first spoke in Hebrew; by the time he was four his mother had taught him to read and write in that language and how to read music notes; she had also started him and his two sisters on English, German, Italian, Russian and Spanish.

Music, however, was entirely his own domain. His father once noted that the boy's very personality changed in the presence of his violin. Ordinarily a calm, even-tempered cheerful and sunny child, the violin aroused him to a frenzied inner drive for perfection. At his San Francisco debut the playing of the chubby youngster, who was totally unruffled by the heady atmosphere of the concert stage and the wildly cheering audience, impelled that city's chief music critic to write, "This is not talent; it is genius!" Every music store and pawnshop was sold out of violins within a week, as eager parents determined to make a Yehudi of their offspring.

Yehudi's New York debut a year later was another story, in that it outlined the need for proper publicity in order for even the greatest talent to be recognized. Promotion was poorly handled and the concert went almost unnoticed, although the audience was enchanted. The tone of the third-string music critics sent to cover it was friendly but wary.

Nothing daunted, Yehudi, blue-eyed, red-cheeked, blonde, made his symphonic debut with the San Francisco Symphony two months later. The San Francisco *Chronicle* reviewer wrote: "What built the world in six days is what contrived the genius of Yehudi. He walks on the waves." But almost more important was the interest this concert aroused in Mr. Sidney Ehrman, a native of the city. The Menuhins had consistently refused to have Yehudi play at the homes of prospective patrons—the time-honored road to success for poor prodigies. His mother was reluctant even about his few public appearances at so tender an age and would not permit any separation from the close-knit family, or any training that would run counter to her own strong ideas on behavior and education. The offer to underwrite Yehudi's study in

Europe which was finally accepted was generous enough to enable the entire family to go together.

The touching letter of farewell to Persinger from Yehudi was couched in somewhat flowery English. It read in part: "You are my father of music. Wherever life brings me . . . I will always hear your sweet voice, that voice which ofttimes corrected me, and if I would be without it, only God would know the kind of life I would lead."

Going abroad was a gamble. Even in his state of childish innocence Yehudi was well aware that the fortunes of the family now rested on him, on whether Georges Enesco, the great violinist, composer and teacher (who had himself been a prodigy) would accept him as a pupil, and whether his eventual Paris debut would turn out to be the great breakthrough of his career. As it turned out, Enesco not only accepted him with an awed sense of his musical destiny but also became the single most important influence in his musical life. From Enesco he learned not so much violin-playing as a craft but a philosophy of performance. The performer's role was to express the intent of the composer, never to act merely as a vehicle for display of virtuosity. To this end they studied the violin repertoire together, with emphasis on the composers, their lives, their times, their musical problems and styles, and how best to share their music with listeners.

From the moment of arrival in Paris the Menuhins' family life was organized around the children's education, most of which the parents carried out themselves. There were, however, regular outside lessons in French and history. Just as Yehudi had taken along his violin for practice when they had gone on short vacation trips in California, even a two-day train trip to join Enesco in Rumania didn't break up the routine of practice and other lessons. For exercise Yehudi and his sisters ran up and down the train corridors a prescribed number of times.

It was on this trip that Yehudi's parents refused to let him perform at the royal castle, as requested by Queen Marie of Rumania. Instead she listened to his lesson from another room. Sturdily unself-conscious, he shook hands with her afterward instead of kissing her hand in the expected way. She said: "This is probably the first time that you have met a real queen"; he responded by saying: "Oh, no, in America every woman is a queen." So well had the eleven-year-old learned his democratic lessons from his thoroughly Americanized parents.

Yehudi's Paris debut in 1927 fulfilled all expectations, making him a celebrity overnight. He was billed as being ten years old instead of his true age, almost eleven. Yehudi himself exposed his true age some years later. But ten or eleven, the audience marvelled at the poised yet childlike and placid youngster, whose muscles were not strong enough to tune his own three-quarter-size violin. Yet when he attacked the Symphonie Espagnole by Lalo, with the Lamoureux Orchestra, in the words of one writer the "sonority, rhythm, technique, and maturity of style exceeded anything one could have imagined."

Concert offers poured in from all over but were turned down for further study with Enesco. Only an invitation from Fritz Busch, the conductor, to play a Mozart concerto with the New York Symphony Orchestra was accepted. Yehudi had his heart set on playing instead the crowning glory of the violin repertoire, the Beethoven violin concerto, and he said so. When one realizes that Jackie Coogan was a child actor at the time it is possible to appreciate the outraged telegram which Busch sent on hearing of this proposal: "One does not allow Jackie Coogan to play Hamlet!"

Busch, in his autobiography later, described Yehudi at his first meeting with him, in a hotel room: "A healthy, sturdy lad with a fine sense of humor and with beautiful eyes, very calm and measured in his movements." It took but one movement of the Beethoven concerto, played gloriously, before Busch, throwing his arms around Yehudi, exclaimed, "You can play anything with me, anytime, anywhere!" As a foretaste of things to come, the orchestra's musicians gave him a standing ovation at the first rehearsal.

Dressed in the uniform of child prodigies, white silk blouse and black velvet knee pants, Yehudi appeared at Carnegie Hall on November 15 1927. The audience could not contain its enthusiasm, all but stopping the performance by its unprecedented applause even before the first movement ended. When the concert was over, the audience wouldn't let him go, even after twelve recalls. Only then did he show a certain childish uncertainty about coping with the situation. He finally dragged his teacher onto the stage. The audience, thinking it was his father, kept applauding and cheering lustily. Only when Yehudi appeared in his overcoat and cap did the audience acknowledge that the experience was over, and even then they stampeded his dressing room.

Olin Downes, dean of the New York music critics and a determined foe of the very idea of child prodigies, later admitted that he had intended to leave after the first movement, but simply could not tear himself away. Three times he rewrote his review, afraid its extravagant tone would make him a laughing stock among his fellow critics. The review said, in part: "It seems ridiculous to say that he showed a mature conception of Beethoven's concerto, but that is the fact . . . a boy of eleven proved conclusively his right to be ranked with the outstanding interpreters of this music." If anything, the other critics outdid him in their praise.

Again, offers for appearances came from every great orchestra and music management. All but ten or twelve engagements a year were refused. The rest of the boy's time was given over to study and recreation at home. The Menuhin home was now a school and musical conservatory for the three brilliant children. There were seven private tutors in addition to the parents. The rigorous daily routine included 2½ to 3 hours of music practice, recorded music played during breakfast and dinner, regulated table conversation on many topics at lunch, at which time family letters received were read aloud, attendance at every worthwhile musical event in San Francisco, and extensive reading in several languages. There were definite periods for outdoor play. Swimming, tennis and running were the only sports allowed. Only secretly did Yehudi later learn to ride a bicycle, much against the wishes of his parents because of their fear of the possible effects of a fall.

Isolation from the world outside was nearly complete. Yehudi's father censored the daily newspapers (mainly to insulate him from reviews of his concerts), clipping out the articles he thought were worth discussion. Never was there talk in the home of numbers of tickets sold, reaction of critics, or money arrangements. When soprano Elizabeth Rethberg, in Yehudi's presence, was asked about her fee, she explained that it depended on the size of the hall and the audience. When she in turn asked Yehudi how much he had received for one of his major concert appearances he replied, "An ice cream cone. Strawberry is my favorite."

Naive and modest as he was, he greatly impressed the occasional interviewer with his surprising dignity, his formal, old-fashioned English, his keen intelligence and humor, and his breadth of knowledge on many subjects. Scientific inventions and mechanical gadgets were among his many interests.

If his mother made all the private family decisions, it was his father who handled the public career. There was hardly a moment unaccounted for—in terms of work, play, sleep or study. The musical core of his life thrived on the regimen. His musical taste was fastidious from the beginning. He never indulged in the empty "fireworks" display pieces so prevalent in violin programs at the time. Playing on his newly acquired Khevenhueller Stradivarius 1733 given him by a blind admirer, Henry

Goldman, his debut before a cold, distrustful, musically blasé Berlin audience came to be known as the night of the "three B's."

For this great audience Yehudi played, at thirteen, no less than three concertos—by Bach, Beethoven and Brahms. Yehudi had been mocked in the newspapers in advance as "the latest American freak." Bruno Walter, who conducted the concert, recalled years later: "He was a child and yet he was a man, a man and a great artist. The astonishing thing was not that he had mastered the music technically, but that there was a spiritual mastery, a maturity. Therein lay the miracle." The great scientist Albert Einstein was part of the audience rush backstage which had to be quelled by police. When he reached the artist's room Einstein lifted Yehudi and kissed him, saying, "Now I know there is a God in Heaven!"

Yehudi's London debut brought out the firemen to prevent a riot. His European reputation, prizes and honors, as well as his recordings, were spreading his fame to the United States, where numerous articles appeared bearing such headlines as "AMERICA'S PRIDE," "THE VIOLINIST OF THE CENTURY," and "MENUHIN THE GREAT."

On one of the family's annual ship crossings to America, in 1932, Arturo Toscanini, conductor of the New York Philharmonic Symphony, happened to be aboard. To Toscanini's delight, Yehudi played for him several hours every day. The boy begged Toscanini for suggestions or corrections. Toscanini's reply was, "You don't know how to make a mistake! Just go on playing!" This from the most feared conductor of the period, who had cut down many a famous performer with a look or a word. Later, when the two were rehearsing in Toscanini's hotel room before the all-Beethoven concert they were to share, the telephone rang during Yehudi's playing of the slow movement. Toscanini, with controlled rage, got up, walked over and tore the telephone from the wall. Then he returned solemnly to the piano to continue the sublime music. W. J. Henderson, the noted critic, wrote of Yehudi's performance at the concert: "The boy projected his spiritual immersion in the music with an art that defied analysis . . . violin playing of the first order, ranking with anything the present recorder had ever heard in his long years of listening."

When their family was living in New York, author Willa Cather spent much time with the three children as a close friend. She reveled in their unspoiled, loving quality, their strange blend of traveled sophistication wedded to inner simplicity. Nevertheless Yehudi's progress was not a smooth uninterrupted pathway to growing success.

The dutiful boy had to become the no less dutiful but self-assured adult—and the search for truth, beauty and perfection based as much on deep personal convictions as on universal principles wasn't achieved without inner questioning and outer penalties. When he was twenty, his parents insisted on a period of retirement at home which came to be known as "Mother's Year." This gave the three children a chance for the first time to be with young people of their own age in the beautiful setting of Los Gatos, California.

Technically, Yehudi was now of age, controlling his own money, free to read reviews of his concerts, to live anywhere he pleased and to choose his own friends. But the habits of his prolonged childhood hadn't trained him for independence. Marriage seemed a likely solution, but it didn't work out well, and soon ended in divorce. Significantly, all three Menuhin children had unsuccessful first marriages. His sister Hephzibah, expressing the problem poignantly in a letter, said their lives, so sheltered from everyday troubles, made them incapable of facing common life situations like most people. Other people had never been factors in their lives. They had never had to adjust to the standards of others, and had no experience with, or precedents for, solving people-related problems. Still, musically, "Mother's Year" accomplished much. During this period Yehudi realized that his success had been based on instinct and an inborn flair for the instrument; now he began to re-examine his playing minutely for technical flaws, emerging with greater mastery than before.

Telescoping the early years of his adulthood—Yehudi eventually became his own man, outliving the prodigy label, making a triumphant comeback and remaining a great artist; turning down a two-million-dollar Hollywood contract; remarrying after his divorce and finally establishing his own home; playing all through World War II for the troops and for wartime charities; being the first great artist to play in the liberated cities of Europe; living through a postwar crisis in his playing; having music composed specially for him by such outstanding composers as Béla Bartók, Ernest Bloch, Georges Enesco and William Walton; expressing outspoken if sometimes unpopular political opinions; promoting interest in the music of India and personally adopting many aspects of Eastern philosophy and life; aligning himself with humanitarian causes of every description. He has been described aptly in recent years as an energetic true "Citizen of the World."

Musically Yehudi Menuhin's development also has been extraordinary in scope. While still maintaining a busy violin concert schedule, he also conducts extensively, both in live appearances and on recordings. On the side he somehow found time to open a natural food shop in London and in 1963 he started a school for musically gifted children, presumably to capture for others the best of his own training. At the age of fifty this remarkable man was called a "virtuoso-philosopher." Today, at fifty-six, an eager involvement with life on many levels still gives Menuhin a look that can only be called "boyish."

There is nothing boyish (and almost never has been) about Ruggiero Ricci (1918–   ). He was born in San Francisco just two years later than Menuhin. But whereas Yehudi's parents emphasized his background in naming him, Ricci's poor Italian immigrant parents sought to hide their son's lineage by naming him "Woodrow Wilson Rich." Ironically, when it became obvious that music would be his destiny, his violin teacher urged a return to his real name as better suited to a career in music.

Ruggiero's father was a struggling musician, barely able to support his large musical family. Each of the children learned to play a different instrument; sometimes they appeared as a group, occasionally even getting paid, much to their father's satisfaction. One of them, he was determined, must become a prodigy. If Yehudi Menuhin, only three years earlier, was able to make it, then so could one of his children. Struggles with poverty from the time he came penniless to America perhaps accounted for the father's impatience, temper, and unbending drive to produce a prodigy. "Be a fiddler or a garbage man!" he would shout when the boy balked at six hours of daily violin practice. The mother, loving but timid, played an utterly submissive role in relation to the overbearing father.

Papa Ricci himself taught his son, getting him to play a set of variations on *The Blue Bells of Scotland* sufficiently well to impress Louis Persinger, the same teacher who had worked with Yehudi Menuhin. But the noise, confusion, and tyrannical discipline of his home, plus the pressure of attending public school and daily practicing for so many hours didn't help Ruggiero's remarkable natural ability to flower —and his progress failed to match Yehudi's. He seemed, however, to respond well to Elizabeth Lackey, Persinger's assistant. Weekends with her soon stretched into weeks. As he spent more and more time with her the change of scene and personality seemed to help him. He saw no other children now, and didn't go to school. He visited his family every other Sunday. His entire days were spent in and out of his teacher's house. As he once described those days: "I practiced four hours every morning—with a fifteen-minute play period, like a coffee break, at eleven o'clock. In the afternoon, I studied with a tutor for three hours. After the session with the tutor, I practiced two more hours, ate dinner, did my homework, then went to bed."

Ruggiero's violin became for him the be-all and end-all of his existence, and his great musical gifts—a wonderful ear, fine sense of rhythm and amazing technical skill—now began to mesh into a coherent whole. Above all he wanted to play as well as his idol, Yehudi, whose concerts he attended "with lips tight and hands clenched." He was eleven (the publicity releases said he was nine) when he made his formal debut, playing the Mendelssohn Concerto (on a three-quarter-size violin) with the San Francisco Symphony Orchestra. The critics called his performance "fantastic"; they were awed at what could only be an instinctive sensing and projection of the emotional tone of the work, aside from its purely technical requirements.

When Ruggiero played the same work in New York a few months later, his tone was judged, even on his undersized violin, to have "a hundred shades of color"; when the orchestra threatened to run away with the tempo of the last movement "it was the boy who steadied the orchestra, and not the orchestra which steadied the boy." After commenting that "Master Ricci's performance revealed a technical mastery of the violin and a genius for interpretation that places him in a class with the handful of great living violinists," one critic went on to compare him with Yehudi: "He has a surer bow arm and a cleaner finger technique. . . . Ricci stands head and shoulders over his rival through possession of a temperament that burns unceasingly, a burning vitality that makes every note he plays momentous." His career was launched brilliantly.

Ruggiero's sole companion during those early training years had been his younger brother Georgio, also studying violin (later cello) and also living with Miss Lackey, who had, in the meantime, become the legal guardian of both boys. It was not a playful childhood. That is perhaps why at his Chicago recital the next year the frenzied applause mattered less to Ruggiero than the electric airplane one of his admirers handed up to him on the stage. Yet completely unchildish was his singleness of purpose, that urge to become Yehudi's equal which made him ruthless in his self-criticism. One discerning critic had already remarked, however, that Ruggiero looked as if he "had not received his share of fun." He noted that Ruggiero was not so robust as

Yehudi, and appeared high-strung. He suspected, (correctly) that Ruggiero was being "forced past the normal and happy growth of a child."

In 1930 began a series of events of such significance for Ruggiero that they almost certainly changed the course of his musical and personal life. His father, after a separation of sixteen months from Ruggiero and Giorgio, assailed Miss Lackey's guardianship, claiming that it was exploitation and alleging that the two boys were now "forcibly and wrongfully detained and deprived of their liberty." Thus began a highly publicized child custody battle, with Ruggiero as the very valuable prize. Were the previous contracts valid? Were the parents repentant for what appeared to be their previous neglect or merely greedy now that their son was a confirmed money-maker? Was there really child exploitation? (The Children's Aid Society attended the hearings to help settle that issue.) The two boys laughed when their father protested that their health was being impaired. To his plea, "My boys' life comes before art," Ruggiero answered, "Papa, you know you gave me away and I can prove it." He branded his father's words as outright lies.

Frederick H. Bartlett, a wealthy oil man who had subsidized Ruggiero's studies, sided with the father in claiming financial and physical exploitation. A neurologist testified that the mental strain of playing the projected ten concerts in ten cities in ten weeks would indeed be excessive. "A boy who neglects play, social relations and companionship does not lead a normal life," he asserted. Other physicians argued otherwise, however. Miss Lackey's attorney cited such prodigies and former prodigies as Menuhin, Kreisler, Heifetz and Hofmann to counteract the idea that there is an inherent danger in youthful appearances in public. A music critic testified that genius like Ruggiero's needed public appearances, that lack of them would harm him. Mixed in with musical and financial charges was mention of kidnap threats, as well as new offers of patronage.

The California court dismissed the parents' appeal for custody, upholding Miss Lackey's guardianship. The New York court, however, gave the parents custody—but not until after the completion of the ten scheduled concerts. The judge's opinion specifically credited Miss Lackey with "splendid work" in bringing out Ruggiero's ability. "She is entitled to the additional prestige which may come to her by reason of the wider public acclaim from his prospective artistic successes during the year." Just in case, however, the New York Society for the

58206

Prevention of Cruelty to Children was to keep a watchful eye on the boy during his tour.

The tour started triumphantly enough; one audience was even "moved to tears." But in October the parents prevailed on Mayor James (Jimmy) Walker to refuse to sign a permit required by law for his New York City concert. Two thousand disappointed fans were turned away, and the whole legal haggle over possession opened again, with the mayors and governors of those cities and states where Ruggiero was to appear caught up in the controversy. The reviews, when he was finally permitted to perform in New York again, were extraordinary. Not only was he called "fully as significant a talent as Yehudi Menuhin" but he was unequivocally described as a "boy player of genius." "The playing was so fresh, normal, natural and unforced in character. . . . The foundation of Ricci's later career seems to have been laid so wisely and well."

The immediate future, however, saw the two boys, now in New York City, run away from Miss Lackey's apartment. They returned to their parents' temporary New York household and the court agreed temporarily to leave them there. It was an embittered Miss Lackey indeed who wrote to the *New York Times:* "I wish to disclaim any further personal responsibility for the musical guidance of Ruggiero Ricci. . . . Any sense of gratitude or intelligent appreciation for having developed Ruggiero's gifts during these past years to the artistic niveau displayed that evening one cannot hope for, under the circumstances."

It was on the last day of the year 1930 that the New York Supreme Court finally decreed that the parents were to have complete custody of Ruggiero. The judge lauded the two teachers, Louis Persinger and Elizabeth Lackey, urging that the parents as well as the boy should be deeply grateful for their vital role in his development. The total of forty-one hearings, which lasted seven months, had their demoralizing effect on Ruggiero and the tabloid style of publicity had been sordid and degrading. As one observer noted: "The general apathy of public opinion and studied silence of the musical fraternity all tend to justify the European conception that we are, after all, a people of little culture and less courage."

Nowadays this kind of litigation would be carried on in private. The only good that came out of it was a series of state laws curbing exploitation of children. But its effects on Ruggiero were devastating. He later recalled feeling that he was a pawn caught between overwhelming powers, rejected as a person and robbed of his childhood in the process. "Youth," as he later expressed it, "is too precious a quality to snatch away like that."

Despite their protestations, his parents' custody brought little change in Ruggiero's concert schedule. Now, stage-fright sometimes set in, along with a certain loss of self-confidence. At a New York recital shortly after the hearings a critic wrote: "Master Ricci has, in some ways, retrograded as a performer since he made his New York debut two years ago." He felt like a has-been at the age of thirteen.

On the European tour that followed, the reviews were good, but his spirits were not. He was lonely, spending hours alone in hotel rooms, knowing not a soul in the cities where he played, self-conscious about being short and about having a prodigy-bobbed haircut. He realized one day, on reading old newspaper notices, how good he had once been, and he determined to make the long, hard climb back to the top. For the next few years he gave about twenty-five performances a year, spending the rest of the time in intensive study.

Ruggiero enlisted in the Army during World War II, and soon felt he was an oddball having nothing in common with his contemporaries, never having been to a regular school or even to a ball game. Fortunately he was assigned to Army Special Services and toured Army camps giving violin recitals. In so doing he was often forced by inadequate pianos and mediocre accompanists to concentrate on heavy doses of unaccompanied music. It was owing to this unique necessity that Ruggiero made himself into such a superb interpreter of Bach's unaccompanied Sonatas and Suites, as well as Paganini's fiendishly difficult unaccompanied Caprices.

When he returned to civilian life, Ricci started slowly once again to build his concert reputation. In 1946 he played unaccompanied at Carnegie Hall. His playing was called "exemplary of the finest, most sensitive and most beautiful manipulation of the violin you may expect to hear anywhere." In 1964 he played a spectacular cycle of concerts which covered twelve of the greatest concertos. Over the years he has been sent as musical good-will ambassador by the U.S. State Department to many countries, and has also made many outstanding recordings.

The spirit of flamboyance and dazzle that marked Ruggiero Ricci's New York debut is still there. As a critic said in 1967: "Not many violinists in this world of ours can generate his excitement . . . born of a genuine thrusting musicianship, combined with a technique so assured, so totally without effort." Another critic spoke of a "perform-ance of diabolical brilliance. The big, silky tone encompasses technical fireworks."

Whereas Menuhin's musical horizons have stretched in wide direc-tions, toward discovery of unknown violin works, exploring Eastern music, conducting, and so on, Ricci's have been bounded by the violin itself, which he has explored to the fullest extent, playing rare old in-struments as well as his own priceless violin. Contented in his mar-riage, fully appreciated in the musical world, Ruggiero Ricci is, and has been for some years, a happy man.

9

All Kinds of Prodigies

There have been prodigies on instruments other than the violin, piano and voice, but much more rarely. The cello, for example, is too large to be attempted seriously by a four- or five-year-old. Yet the greatest living cellist, Pablo Casals (1876–   ) was a prodigy, as were several other cellists.

In 1970 Casals, then ninety-four, was the first musical performer ever to receive (amidst a standing ovation) the United Nations Peace Medal. During the same year a hundred of the world's outstanding cellists gathered to do him honor by forming a "Salute to Casals" orchestra which he conducted. Casals is a double symbol—of greatness in music and in humanity. He has championed freedom by word and deed all his life, refusing to play wherever tyranny existed, and using his music to aid the oppressed. Of conscience he once said, "Its importance is eternal, like love."

Pablo Casals' father was the musician in the poverty-stricken family and taught his son to play several instruments, but it was the mother's iron resolve that made him a musician, despite all odds. Pablo heard a cello for the first time, as part of a trio, when he was eleven years old. Overwhelmed by the sound, he told his father at once, "That is what I want to play!" But it was his mother who insisted that only in the big city of Barcelona would he find expert instruction. It was she who later joined him in Madrid when he went there for further study and playing experience. She took the two younger children along, leaving the father to fend for himself. Pablo was nineteen when he and his mother traveled to Paris, where they had to live in a miserable hovel. His mother managed their meager budget, even to selling her magnificent hair to a wigmaker when necessary to make ends meet. She was determined that he was to have the advantages that the city could offer.

Pablo's professional playing had begun many years before that. Known affectionately throughout Barcelona as "El Nen" (The Little One) he earned his living from the age of twelve by playing in cafes, slyly introducing better music into the expectedly trivial programs. When he made his official debut at fourteen he played the usual showy claptrap which was the typical cello fare of the nineteenth century. The year before he had discovered, with a sense of blinding revelation, the unaccompanied cello works of Bach in a dusty corner of a Barcelona music shop. He worked at them for twelve years before daring to play them in public.

In learning these works and the other fine cello music by Beethoven, Brahms, and others which he resurrected, Casals revolutionized the entire art of cello playing, which was then so limited in repertoire and so rigid in technique. At thirteen, experimenting on his own, he made cello technique more natural, changed the arm position, extended the reach of the fingers—in short, he became the father of modern cello technique and repertoire. The music of Bach has remained to this day a kind of religion for him. He said recently that for over eighty years he has started each day in the same way—by playing Bach. Though in his nineties he is still active, playing, teaching, composing and conducting. Wherever he chooses to live (in recent years it has been Puerto Rico) always becomes a shrine for lovers of music and for lovers of peace.

It was fortunate that even as a child Gregor Piatigorsky (1903–   ), the great Russian cellist, was tall. By the age of nine he was able to help his destitute family by talking himself into a job as cellist in a movie orchestra. (The manager hid him below the stage level so that no one would see a child playing late every night.) Early years of struggle with school by day, playing at night, and practicing in between paid off. By fifteen he was the first cellist in the Imperial Opera Orchestra in Moscow.

Gregor had left home long before that, spending many a night sleeping in a classroom or night club, eating cat food, playing with gloves on to keep his fingers warm. A series of hair-raising adventures ensued when he smuggled himself across the Polish border at the time of the Russian Revolution. It was in Poland that he first made his mark as a soloist, going on to become the most esteemed cellist, after Casals, in the world. He was also, like Albeniz, one of the great prankster-prodigies in music. When he was eighteen, Gregor attached a cord to the cello of one of the older, dignified players in the Warsaw Orchestra, having previously arranged for a friend backstage to hoist the instrument gently into the air just as the bow was about to touch it during the performance. Gregor never regretted the week's salary this little joke cost him.

If cello prodigies are comparatively rare, the picture of a young person becoming a prodigy on the double bass, which stands taller than a full-grown man, is incongruous, even ludicrous. Yet Serge Koussevitzky (1874–1951), who in later life became one of the world's greatest conductors, earned his earliest fame as a double-bass prodigy.

Serge left his tiny Russian village home when he was sixteen, with three groschen in his pocket, and determined to study music seriously in Moscow. Until then he had learned a little violin from his father, picked up a bit more from strolling musicians whom he followed for days at a time, and had done a bit of composing and arranging for a provincial theater company.

At a music school in Moscow he found that there were only three openings for which scholarships and living expenses were available; they were the horn, the trombone and the double bass. Serge chose the latter—the most clumsy and despised of all the instruments. So determined was he to make something of himself and his chosen instrument that he covered the five-year course of study in five months. Within a year, while still in school, he was admitted to the Imperial Theater orchestra, and shortly after that he ventured on stage as a double-bass soloist.

His appearances aroused intense curiosity. What would he play and how would he play it? He added to the almost nonexistent repertoire by making ingenious arrangements of cello music, and he elevated the instrument to solo status by his magnificent tone and striking mastery of the enormous difficulties the double bass presented. Much of modern double-bass technique owes its inception to the driving need to succeed, coupled with his remarkable energy and persistence, of Serge Koussevitzky.

Among guitarists, today's finest classical player and the world's outstanding flamenco player both started out as prodigies.

When Andrés Segovia (1893–   ) was born the guitar was a curiosity on the concert stage, like the double bass. It had been one of the most beloved and esteemed instruments during the early 1800's. But, by the turn of the century, however, it was considered to be completely vulgar, beneath the notice of any serious musician, fit to be played only in the most disreputable taverns. Andrés' father wanted him to be a lawyer, but he himself had other ideas. There was no one to teach him (even if his father had consented) the instrument he loved. So he taught himself, secretly, practicing in a neighbor's garden. Teacher and pupil were one, he later explained, and there was never a serious quarrel between them!

Thus, entirely on his own, he gradually perfected his technique to a point where he was complete master of the instrument—but with no modern music to play on it. He solved that problem by arranging for the guitar music written for half a dozen other instruments. His debut at the age of fifteen was a revelation to both the audience and to his father, and marked the beginning of a career that saw him single-handedly restore the classical guitar to a place in the concert hall. He resurrected the old guitar music and many of the finest contemporary composers have written new works (over five hundred of them) for that instrument after hearing Segovia display its capabilities.

One interviewer reported that, at seventy-eight, Segovia "still talks about the guitar with the rapture of a newly-smitten teen-ager." From being only a folk instrument he made it musically acceptable, and through his teaching has passed his inspiration on to younger artists. One of them is the Englishman Julian Bream (1933–   ) who has also revived the lute, a favored instrument of Renaissance times. "The future of the guitar is assured," Segovia said recently. "I have broken the vicious circle. . . . Guitarists of worth did not appear because great composers did not write for the guitar, and the latter did not write for the guitar because it lacked virtuosos of talent." As late as 1971 a prominent critic marveled at the "rapt, almost hypnotic spell he [Segovia] casts over his audience."

With Carlos Montoya (1903–   ) we come to our first prodigy who does not read a note of music. He plays flamenco guitar, and is the first such guitarist ever to give solo recitals. Flamenco music is difficult to define. It originated in the Andalusian province of Spain, which was the crossroads for the meeting of Moorish music brought in by the Arabs, native Andalusian folk song, and the music of the gypsies, that wandering people believed to have come originally from India. Whatever its origins, flamenco music is a blend of oriental wavering pitches and unusual intervals, complex rhythmic patterns and ornamental vocal flourishes. It is a theater art, usually a mixture of singing, dancing, guitar-playing, hand-clapping and castanet-playing, with the audience reacting audibly by shouting its approval or encouragement to outstanding performers.

Most of all, flamenco is deeply emotional music, often expressing a tragic sense of life, something like the American Negro's blues, and occasionally reflecting joyous abandon and gayety. It is based on certain short melodic and rhythmic figures and is largely improvised by the individual artist.

Carlos Montoya is a gypsy. From childhood he has been steeped in flamenco experiences in his native Madrid. At the age of eight, he studied for two years with a local barber who played flamenco guitar as a hobby. Otherwise he is entirely self-taught. The guitar played a secondary role in flamenco music, mainly accompanying the singers and dancers, and only occasionally being played solo for a few seconds. Carlos served an apprenticeship during his teen years, playing at the age of fourteen with some of the finest flamenco troupes. His extraordinary skill soon brought him fame. The greatest flamenco dancers of modern times, Vicente Escudero and La Argentina, chose young Carlos to play for their world-wide tours.

When Montoya made his extraordinary breakthrough he was in his forties and living permanently in the United States. He decided to try, for the first time, to hold an audience for an entire evening with flamenco music on the guitar alone, without benefit of dancers or singers. By then he had found ways of suggesting these missing elements on the guitar, so that the listener, closing his eyes, could hear the passionate, fervent melody of the singer, the throbbing guitar chords behind, the clicking of castanets, the clapping of hands. The only thing he couldn't reproduce was the ecstatic reactions of the audience, but his own audience supplied that. His sense of improvisation was, and is, so luxurious that he has never played a particular work twice in the same way.

For many years Montoya has commanded a following which can only be described by the intensity of its devotion. It buys out his concerts as soon as tickets go on sale. In 1971, when the artist was sixty-eight, a New York reviewer wrote of his dazzling playing: "Mr. Montoya is the master virtuoso and interpretive artist, achieving just the right balances of light and shade, statement and insinuation, gravity and gaiety." The critic found his playing to be full of the "eagerness of youth." Montoya's domain has remained uniquely his—there is no other flamenco guitarist to match him either in artistry or in capturing the public's admiration.

There was another prodigy we know by name from thousands of years ago who also couldn't read music" (there being no musical notation available then). He was the David of the Bible.

It is not a certainty, but biblical evidence suggests that David was in his early teens when King Saul's emissaries, scouting the entire kingdom for an outstanding musician to relieve the king's melancholy, discovered him. David and his "harp" (actually, it was a related instrument, the lyre) became a cherished feature of King Saul's court, where the boy's great powers of improvisation in both music and poetry (see the Psalms) were much appreciated. In later life David proved to be a great organizer as well, putting musical instruction and performance on a systematic basis which enabled the musical traditions of his people to survive and flourish through the centuries thereafter.

There have been several musicians who, if they are recalled at all, are remembered only as prodigies, because they died before they were twenty-one. Juan Arriaga (1806–1826) for example, was a violinist and composer. Some of his delightful overtures, symphonies, and concertos, written before he was eighteen, are still performed and recorded today. George Aspull (1813–1832), just two years younger than Franz Liszt, was compared seriously to Liszt by the London critics. He died at nineteen on the threshold of a brilliant career. Of Karl Filtsch (1830–1845), whom Chopin greatly admired, Liszt once said, "When this little one goes on the road, I shall shut up shop." Liszt need not have worried. Karl, unfortunately, was dead at fifteen.

There are some prodigies who, in later life, abandoned music for other fields. André Philidor (1726–1796), who came from a famous line of French musicians, was responsible for important innovations in opera. He started playing and composing at a very early age. At the Chapel Royal at Versailles card-playing was not allowed, but a long table inlaid with chessboards was provided. André's mind was as brilliant in chess calculation as in puzzling out problems of musical composition. All his life he was torn between his two loves—music and chess. At nineteen, he left France and music to seek, and find, fame and fortune in chess. His book *The Analysis of Chess* was revolutionary in its time, being the first book to explain the reasons behind particular chess moves. He was the ranking chess player of Europe for fully forty years, and a famous chess opening is named for him. After about ten years devoted almost exclusively to chess, however, Philidor returned to France to continue his considerable career in the world of music.

William Herschel (1738–1822) when only fourteen years old was an oboist in the court band at Hanover. When the band moved to England he took up the organ and soon became a respected professional performer and teacher. He also branched out into conducting and composing. While becoming one of the best-known organists in England he also dabbled in astronomy with the help of his devoted sister. Not until he was forty years old did he finally give up his music for the greater demands of his scientific genius. He eventually invented large-scale telescopes, discovered the planet Uranus, catalogued over two thousand hitherto-unknown nebulae, and discovered several double stars. Universally recognized as one of the great pioneers in his field, as one biographer said: "He opened the path to all the principal branches of modern stellar astronomy."

When Maurice Dengremont (1866–1893) made his violin debut in New York at the age of fifteen, he had already been subsidized by the king of his native land, Brazil, to study in Europe, and had enjoyed a hundred or more successful appearances in Europe and South America as a prodigy. He ended up, however, as a celebrity not in music but in billiards, becoming the world champion of that game.

In our own time, it is not generally realized that Victor Borge (1909–   ), best known as a comedian who deftly weaves musical humor at the piano into his night-club act, was a child prodigy. He made a successful piano debut at thirteen, and continued for twelve years to do concerts (he did some composing as well). His flair for comedy gradually took on a professional tinge. As he acquired varied experience as actor, composer, pianist, writer, and radio and film director, music became more and more an adjunct to the comedy routines for which he is best known. Coming full circle, however, in 1971 he returned to serious music by conducting concerts at the Romantic Music Festival at Butler University in Indianapolis, Indiana. According to the critics, he acquitted himself very well in that unaccustomed role.

Rarest of all have been prodigies among wind, brass or percussion players. The reasons are not difficult to find. Until recently, there was too small a repertoire of solo music of the virtuoso level to sustain a

full concert. Even if there had been sufficient music, the sight of someone blowing an oboe, for example, has very little visual appeal. There
is no room for the grand gesture, the compelling rapport with the audience, that a great violinist, pianist or singer has. Also, some of the
brass and woodwind instruments were perfected only as late as the nineteenth century. So it has remained for the twentieth century to produce prodigies on wind and percussion instruments, and, even so, most
of them have been in the jazz rather than the classical field. But that is
another chapter.

There have been some musical prodigies who stayed in music, but
changed their instrument or specialty. Harold Bauer (1873–1951),
for example, was a struggling violin prodigy who also played the piano
a little. In desperation, when he was eighteen, he took a temporary job
as piano accompanist to a singer. He went on to become famous as
one of the world's greatest pianists.

Daniel Barenboim (1942–   ), at nineteen, with a fine reputation
as a prodigy pianist, decided to turn to his second love, conducting; he
now divides his time almost equally between the two. One incentive
for his conducting career is the opportunity of conducting with his
wife, the excellent cellist Jacqueline DuPré (1945–   ), as soloist.
She too was a prodigy. The sight of her very emotional involvement
with the cello, while following the beat of her husband's baton, has
made theirs an irresistible musical romance—the twentieth-century
equivalent of the story of Robert and Clara Schumann.

Classical piano was the springboard for several prodigies who later
switched to jazz. Hazel Scott (1920–   ), was born in Trinidad,
daughter of a well-known scholar and a cultured musical mother. She
had classical training and began playing in public at five, making her
formal debut at twelve in Carnegie Hall. Her formal music study ended when her father died. She then played for a time (saxophone as
well as piano) with an all-girl band, "The American Creolians," which
her mother had organized.

By sixteen Hazel had her own regular radio series, and began what
was to become her specialty—swinging the classics. As one reviewer
said of her playing of Liszt's Second Hungarian Rhapsody in a recital
when she was twenty: "It was impudent music criticism . . . witty,
daring, modern, but never irreverent. I think Liszt would have been
delighted." When she made her first movie at the age of twenty-two
Hazel also sang, and from that time on she combined singing and

playing in a highly successful night-club act and on many recordings. Hazel Scott was one of the first black musicians to refuse to play for segregated audiences and drew national attention to the plight of black musicians. After several years of living abroad, she made a successful comeback in 1971.

Friedrich (Fred) Gulda (1930–   ) has an equally dramatic story of a turned-around musical career. He has been called "the best classical pianist now playing jazz and the best jazz pianist now playing classical music." And he takes each seriously. Starting out as a classical prodigy in his native Vienna, he first heard jazz recordings when he was sixteen and soon began playing with a small group. His life since then has been balanced between the two idioms. Jazz has given his classical playing "extraordinary rhythmic buoyancy," and classical training has given him the supple technique necessary to play (and compose) jazz with versatility. Sometimes he plays a combined classical-and-jazz tour; sometimes he finishes an evening at a concert hall by making a late appearance in a nightclub. He has tried to revive improvisation (so important an element of jazz) in serious music, and occasionally caps a classical concert with jazz encores. Not all his audiences have been ready for these innovations. In 1971 he affronted an Austrian audience in a castle courtyard performance by deciding on the spot (with no printed advance program) what he would play, including his own jazz compositions and improvisations, while wearing a business suit and turtleneck sweater instead of the usual formal concert garb. In recent years he has added jazz baritone saxophone playing to his accomplishments.

Herbie Hancock (1940–   ) made his piano debut at eleven with the Chicago Symphony Orchestra and studied music composition at college, but he is now known as a fine jazz pianist and composer. He has written the music for the sound tracks of many movies, some very popular hit songs such as *Watermelon Man,* and some very adventurous and ambitious jazz works.

One composer who started out in classical composition but later expanded his composing horizons was the Russian, Vladimir Dukelsky (1903–1969). He had already written successful ballets and other music when, at eighteen, he heard George Gershwin's song *Swanee* (written when that composer was nineteen). Vladimir immediately traveled to the United States to meet the composer. Entranced with the jazz idiom, he continued his classical writing but also branched into jazz. Under the name "Vernon Duke" which he reserved for his nonclassical works, he became known for such fine songs as *April in Paris* and *I Can't Get Started.*

In 1946 a tiny black girl of three played fourteen classical selections for a church audience in Chicago. Her name was Margaret Harris and she was a veteran of the concert circuit by the time she was six. Now she not only plays concerts but also conducts theatrical productions. Her most recent conducting assignment was the original Broadway production of the musical *Hair.*

Perhaps the most versatile of all is André Previn (1929–   ), whose family fled Germany at the time of World War II, when he was a mere youth. He had been studying piano in the Berlin and Paris conservatories before his family settled in Hollywood. Even before graduating from high school there, he was playing jazz in local night clubs on week ends, and doing arranging and scoring for the MGM movie studio. He wrote or arranged the scores for dozens of movies—several of which won him an "Oscar." Before he was out of his teens he had developed a highly individual jazz style which was captured on several recordings. All this did not prevent him from continuing to appear as a classical soloist, playing with leading symphony orchestras.

As if all this were not enough—arranger, composer, jazz pianist, classical pianist—André Previn is now embarked on still another career—that of conductor. After years of conducting for films and on television, he has now graduated to the symphonic podium, and is the permanent conductor of two important orchestras, the Houston Philharmonic in this country, and the London Philharmonic in England. In 1959 André Previn told an interviewer: "I don't think I'll ever go as far as I want to go." It would be difficult to imagine his saying that today!

Wolfgang Amadeus Mozart played in concerts at the early age of seven.

Thirteen-year-old Franz Liszt made his Vienna debut at the age of eleven.

*Clara Schumann (née Wieck) shown here
when she was thirteen.*

At the age of twelve, Felix Mendelssohn was an accomplished pianist and composer.

Anton Rubinstein, shown here at the age of twelve, made his debut when only nine years old.

Leo (15), Jan (13), and Mischel (12) Cherniavsky, billed as the Cherniavsky Trio, were going on world tours at the turn of the century.

Eleven-year-old Josef Hofmann was on an American concert tour when this picture was made.

At the age of eleven, Ruggiero Ricci had already taken his place "with the handful of great living violinists."

Ruth Slenczynska gave her first public performance at the age of four.

*Chubby ten-year-old Yehudi Menuhin began
taking violin lessons at the age of five.*

*Jascha Heifetz, shown here at the age of nine,
made his Berlin debut when only twelve years old.*

Philippa Schuyler, shown here at the age of nine, was playing piano on the NBC radio network coast to coast when she was four years old.

Thirteen-year-old Yong Uck Kim was to be called a genius by Leonard Bernstein.

Nine-year-old André Watts played a Haydn Concerto with the Philadelphia Orchestra.

Lorin Maazel conducted
a major symphony orchestra
when only ten years old.

Margaret Harris gave a piano recital,
playing selections from Bach, Brahms
and Mozart, when only four years old.

Twelve-year-old Lawrence Foster began studying the cello at the age of seven.

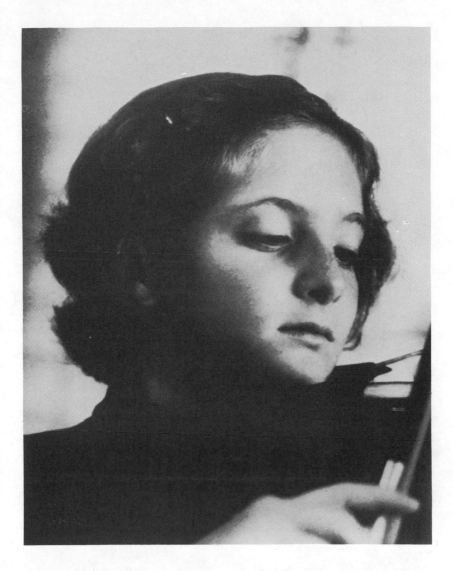

Violinist Lilit Gampel appeared with the New York Philharmonic at the age of twelve.

Michael Jackson, lower left, a member of the well-known family group, the Jackson 5, was nine years old when this picture was taken.

10

The New Generation in the Concert Hall

Young concert artists today are refreshingly individual in their approaches to their careers, and in the ways they meet today's challenges. To illustrate this point, consider the three young Americans—Zukofsky, Perlman and Buswell. No three violinists could be more unalike. Paul Zukofsky (1943–   ) looks like an antihero, emerging on stage with what was once described as a "rapid, open-toed, Chaplinesque shuffle." But for the knowing public and professional musicians he occupies a unique and highly respected niche as outstanding performer and advocate of contemporary violin music.

Brilliant intellectually as well as musically, he was tutored by his parents, receiving his high-school equivalency diploma at the age of thirteen. Paul made his professional debut at eight, and had given three major recitals in Carnegie Hall by the time he was seventeen. A prodigious winner of major competitions, he also composes and conducts, and has taught at several important music centers.

Paul Zukofsky's real distinction lies in his extension of the violin repertoire to include twentieth-century works generally neglected by other violinists. Many composers have written works for that instrument under the impetus of Zukofsky's promise to accord them a hearing in the concert hall or on a recording. He has given many composers short courses on bowing and fingering in order to help them to use the full resources of the instrument. As one critic put it in 1968: "At twenty-five he can play rings around many fiddlers twice his age, in a repertory that few of them would even dare touch." As Zukofsky himself put it, he is against the "masterwork mentality," which leads most violinists to play the same familiar old repertoire over and over. "I am simply trying," he has said, "to keep the violin alive."

Itzhak Perlman (1945–   ), Israeli-born violinist, came to the United States when he was thirteen to appear on the Ed Sullivan television show. He stayed on to study, and has lived in New York ever since. His New York debut, when he was seventeen, made the front pages of all the newspapers: overshadowing his playing, however, was the news that his valuable Guarnerius violin had been stolen while he was receiving congratulations backstage after the concert.

That he is a relaxed extrovert, with spontaneous humor; an avid basketball fan, self-assured and burly; as well as one of the finest violinists in the world, would not be surprising except for the fact that Perlman contracted polio when he was four years old, shortly before he started playing the violin. He walks with crutches and does all his playing sitting down. This has hindered neither his artistry nor his ebullient personality as his brilliant career and his personal life both go triumphantly forward.

An unlikelier name for a prodigy than James Oliver Buswell IV would be hard to find. He stems from an old Puritan family which includes ministers, college professors and anthropologists. Born in 1946, he was eight years old when the New York Philharmonic invited him to appear in its annual Children's Concert. When he won an important competition at the age of fifteen, a critic wrote: "Young Buswell has the maturity and assurance and the technique of a veteran. Some are comparing him to a youthful Menuhin, and to Buswell's favor." Later reviews were even more glowing, commenting on his "supernatural command . . . and gloriously luminous tone."

What is unique about young Buswell's career is the way he has combined it with formal education. He spent two years after high school practicing and performing intensively, and then entered Harvard University as a full-time student. "Leonard Bernstein persuaded me," he once said. "He told me I could play concerts all my life, but I would not always be able to get an education." At twenty, with a schedule of fifty concerts a year, he still managed to get on the Dean's List at Harvard, doing most of his studying on planes and trains between concert appearances.

Buswell is now well past that frantic period when he led a double life as student and as concert star, but he has no regrets. If anything, he believes, it made him a better performer and person. "I think the intellect plays a great part in today's music," he says.

Another obvious note about the prodigies who were born in the forties and who began their careers in the fifties and sixties, is the broad geographical diversity of their birthplaces. For example, a trip by the great pianist Rudolf Serkin to Korea resulted in bringing the first Korean violinist to the world's attention. Yong Uck Kim (1947–   ) had already, at eight-and-a-half years of age, carried off the top prize in a Korean national competition and had appeared with the Seoul Symphony. Mr. Serkin, dining with the family one evening, taped Yong Uck's playing and also his sister Dukju's. Not long afterward they learned that Curtis Institute, in Philadelphia, one of the great music conservatories, would give each of them a five-year scholarship. Serkin's faith was not misplaced; by the time he was sixteen Yong Uck had won an important American prize and was launched on a brilliant career. Conductor Eugene Ormandy has called him "one of the great talents of this generation." Leonard Bernstein introduced Yong Uck Kim as "a genius . . . and I do not use that word lightly."

There is also a whole new group of Japanese prodigy violinists, (all of them women!) who have become well-known names in Western concert halls. Their very names are musical, like Masuko Ushioda (1942–   ), who won top honors in Japan before being invited by the Soviet Government to study in Leningrad. Several competitive prizes later she returned to Japan for extended concert appearances. When she came to the United States in 1964 her playing was a revelation of the exceptional standards of musical performance in Japan. She has since been in great demand around the world. A Moscow critic said of her: "An artist of exceptional lyricism; hers is a deep and probing insight into the composers's ideas. . . . When she plays, audience excitement is at fever pitch."

The diminutive Teiko Maehashi (1943–   ) has had a career parallel to Miss Ushioda's, and has been equally successful. She, like Takako Nishizaki (1944–   ) completed her studies while on a scholarship at the Juilliard School of Music. *The New York Times,* commenting on Miss Nishizaki's playing when she had reached the ripe old age of twenty, cited her "virtuoso technique, virtually flawless intonation, silver tone . . . complete knowledge of musical styles, and . . . clear understanding of what is involved in playing expressively."

When he made his debut on the classical guitar at fourteen, the young American, Christopher Parkenning (1947–   ) was judged "altogether amazing." His playing reminded many listeners of Segovia, who indeed was one of his teachers. Segovia has said of him: "He belongs to that special group of my disciples of which I am so proud." Five hours' practice every day hasn't prevented Parkenning from pursuing many other interests while becoming his country's foremost classical guitarist; he has been Flycasting Champion of the Western United States, and fellow Californians are used to seeing this tall, handsome young man out riding his motorcycle, with a guitar strapped on the back.

Lawrence Foster (1954–   ), of Chicago, began studying the cello at seven, fascinated by its richness and sonority of tone. By fourteen he was among that very small number of performers dubbed "genius" by Leonard Bernstein. Still under twenty, he is already acquiring a reputation as a leading cellist with a brilliant future ahead of him.

Among today's young pianists, Tong-il Han (1941–   ) comes of a musical Korean family which fled from the Russian troops after World War II. In South Korea, a friend arranged for Tong-il to practice piano at the headquarters of the U.S. Fifth Air Force. Word of the phenomenal eleven-year-old pianist quickly spread around the base, and after hearing him play in an Air Force show the military personnel on the base contributed to a fund (over four thousand dollars was raised in all) to enable him to study in New York for two years. He then made his debut there. Not only was the debut notably impressive but Tong-il went on eventually to win the greatest American musical competition, the Leventritt Award, which assured him of an opportunity to appear with the leading orchestras and thus acquire an international reputation.

Inevitably, the careers of all the performers of this era were affected by World War II. Pianist André Watts (1946–   ), for example, owed his very life to it. Born in Nuremberg, Germany, of the union of a black career Army officer and a white Hungarian war refugee (both musical), André spend his earliest years in and around American Occupation Army camps in Germany. The family moved to Philadelphia when he was eight years old. With his mother as his first teacher, he soon showed unusual ability, winning an appearance with the Philadelphia Orchestra when he was nine.

André's story differs from that of many other prodigies in its dependence on a lucky break. That break came when Leonard Bernstein heard him perform on television at the age of sixteen. A few weeks later pianist Glenn Gould, who was scheduled to play with the New York Philharmonic, became ill two days before the concert. Bernstein recalled the extraordinary impression the young André had made on him, and asked André to substitute for Gould. As André later said: "Of course one must be ready when the big break comes. . . . Bernstein thought I was ready and that was enough." He must have been quite ready, for the orchestra as well as the audience gave him a standing ovation and catapulted him into instant fame.

On another occasion André observed: "Being discovered by someone like Bernstein means that you don't have to go through so much to get engagements, but you have to go through just as much to develop and build musically." Perhaps the most disciplined of all the young concert artists today, André has for years practiced six hours a day, six days a week, while establishing himself as a specialist in the music of the romantic period, particularly that of Liszt, his idol from childhood. In this too he had a lucky break: romanticism as a musical period is undergoing a great revival, thus putting André Watts in the vanguard of musical taste. "Mr. Watts is a throwback to an older generation of pianists . . . the Artist-as-Hero," said Harold Schonberg in the *New York Times.*

In his preoccupation with his career and college studies, André has had little or no contact with contemporary music or with his fellow musicians. He is essentially a loner. As a youngster, he encountered his share of racial prejudice. He feels that the experience of great joys and great sorrows is part of the essential background for expressing emotions convincingly in art. "If I have inner wounds, then maybe if I'm careful I can turn them to my advantage," he said. Happily, he has found that the world of music now tends to accept an individual on the basis of talent and personality. Getting to the pinnacle of his field is, he feels, the way he can contribute most.

In recent years Watts has expanded his repertoire to include other than romantic works, but the critics still have highest praise for his special area. Of a 1971 program, one critic said "He swarmed over the Rachmaninoff Third Piano Concerto like a madman with a purpose. Everything was fluent, magnificent, and at top tension. He took every freedom in the book . . . but he never outraged the spirit of the work." They speak of the "indefinable electric quality" of his playing. As for his own opinion, he has said recently "I'm never good enough, but I'm not standing still."

Lorin Hollander (1944–   ) started out as an "ordinary" prodigy, with the usual early triumphs that spoke of him at twelve as "a miniature red-haired virtuoso . . . a strikingly assured young pianist who

gives vast promise of a sunlit career." Intense and intellectually curious, he was a youngster of many interests and hobbies which never
obscured his overriding love of music. At seventeen, while he was on
tour, a neglected ceiling began to shed plaster over him during a concert. The next morning's review was headlined "PLASTERED PIANIST
PERFORMS PERFECTLY." This young pianist became the youngest performer ever sponsored for an international good-will tour by the U.S.
State Department.

Lorin has thought a great deal about music's place in the modern
world. He is aware of the rising median age of audiences, of the falling
attendance at concerts, of the apparent alienation of the young people,
his contemporaries, from the concert halls and from classical music in
general. He feels that the alienation is due not to the message—that is,
the music itself—but rather to the medium—the artificial solemnity,
inherited from European traditions, of the concert-hall setting.

His first attempt, in 1969, to get into closer rapport with his audience took the form of abandoning the full dress with white tie and tails
traditional to the concert stage. "Clothing is so pitifully unimportant in
today's situation," he explained. After that concert one review called
him a "rebel in velvet." What he wore was attractive, if unusual: a
blue velvet jacket, gray bell-bottom slacks, a white silk ascot, and long
hair. But he felt that was still not enough—that the young, hip generation was intimidated by such New York City locations as Carnegie
Hall and Lincoln Center, with their stuffy atmosphere. He took adver-
tisements in the leading youth newspapers, such as the *Village Voice,*
which read: "Lorin Hollander wants to share some beautiful sounds
with you this Sunday at Fillmore East." Fillmore East, downtown in
the East Village, was the very bastion of rock-and-roll and light
shows! The text continued: "If you'd like to get into classical music,
but Lincoln Center isn't quite your pot of tea, come hear Lorin Hollander closer to home."

Because of the peculiar acoustics of the very long and narrow hall,
Lorin introduced still another innovation—he used a new experimental electronic piano able to overcome some of the acoustical difficulties. On that sleety, snowy Sunday evening the young showed up in
droves, as did other professionals of the concert hall and music business, curious to hear the piano. Lorin "rapped" briefly at the micro-
phone with the audience before each selection, setting it in a frame-
work which would be meaningful to the listeners. The program was
identical with the one he had played uptown, except that it concluded

with his own composition, *Up Against the Wall,* which expressed his frustration with the chaotic state of humanity. The evening was a daring experiment, but the artist felt it had succeeded; a new audience had found a bond with old music.

But Lorin felt that the true music lover must be caught even younger for it to really take. So, in 1971, he began taking his music to the streets, playing without fee in vest-pocket parks and in playgrounds. Using his new electronic piano to compete with street noises, he was bringing classical music to audiences young enough to crawl under the piano to get closer to the sound. "I can't play if you yell," he was heard to say. If other concert artists follow his example they could well revolutionize the musical taste of the generation to come.

In the matter of dress, many other performers have already followed his lead. Pianist Peter Serkin has been known to play in a purple hip-length shirt. Jeremy Menuhin, pianist son of Yehudi Menuhin, has admitted resentment at having to don "that absurd waiter's suit." Violinist Jaime Laredo abandoned the traditional garb after a college concert at which he noticed many of the audience in bare feet. And Itzhak Perlman has appeared in a wide-lapeled blue business suit with red-striped shirt. He summed up what seems to be the common denominator of this clothes revolt: "I want people to listen to me, not look at me."

This, then, is the younger generation of concert prodigies. Judging by their integrity, their superlative musicianship, their individuality, the future seems to rest in good hands.

11
Two Prodigies of Early Jazz

The lives of two men, whose childhoods and early musical achievements were in some ways parallel, give us great insights into the early days of jazz. One was black, one was white. They were born within a period of ten years, around the turn of the century.

First there was Louis Armstrong (1900–1971). He was still going strong shortly before his death, enjoying a comeback in *Hello, Dolly!* after he had been thought to be finished artistically for some years.

Louis was born in New Orleans on the Fourth of July in 1900, exactly the right time and place for a youngster with his exceptional musical and personal qualities to make good. His was, however, a hard-won success that called for incredible stamina as well as the drive to succeed, quite aside from musical talent.

Jazz itself was born in New Orleans at just about this time. It could only have originated in that city with its peculiar mix of peoples and their music. The Cajuns, white descendants of Canadian refugees, had drifted down the Mississippi to New Orleans, where they made their dialectic French the dominant language and brought French folk songs and, later, opera to New Orleans. Add a generous portion of ex-slaves and freed men from Cuba and other Spanish-speaking areas, who brought their sinuous, syncopated dance rhythms; add some Haitians who carried with them the voodoo drumming that stemmed even more directly from Africa. Stir pretty thoroughly for several generations, and then settle them on the east, or "downtown," side of Canal Street.

The whites lived fairly amicably with all the shades of mulatto Creoles. They all were fond of good food and crazy about music. No occasion from cradle to grave—whether baptism, birthday, wedding, party, picnic, club affair, restaurant gathering, civic ceremony or funeral procession—was complete without a string band or brass band. Band instruments were plentiful. The pawnshops were particularly full of instruments left behind by the Confederate bands which had broken up around New Orleans after the Civil War. Almost everyone studied with a music teacher. At first music was a side line; the musicians had trades ranging from cigarmaker to tinsmith to barber, and played mostly for pleasure rather than for the "ice-cream money" music-making provided. Professional musicians, as such, were looked down upon socially. These semi-amateurs had to be versatile, playing Old World dances like quadrilles and schottisches, Cuban habaneras and tangos, military marches and minstrel-show cakewalk rhythms. Many of them became accomplished "legit" musicians, playing from written music and mastering European instruments like the flute, trumpet, trombone, clarinet, and guitar.

By the 1880's the old order of things had begun to break up. The slums on the uptown side of Canal Street were by now teeming with black ex-slaves who had drifted in from the countryside, seeking big-town opportunities. Theirs was a different sort of music—more frenetically African-based in its rhythms and call-and-response work songs; more spiritual- and blues-oriented in melody, rough and searing vocally. Here was no tradition of polite opera, sedate dancing, or European purity of tone.

Not only was the love of music perhaps even deeper on the western side of Canal Street but music itself was seen as a passport out of the world of deadening manual labor in town or on the docks. It seemed as if every little black boy managed to improvise or acquire an instrument of sorts. "Baby" Dodds' first drum was a tin can he played on with chair rounds for sticks. Cigar-box banjos and fiddles, toy violins and fifes, old pieces of water pipe punched with holes were typical first instruments in the poverty-ridden "uptown" sector. By playing in small combos on street corners and in local saloons some of the more talented musicians gathered enough pennies to buy real second-hand instruments for the few dollars they cost at the time. Few ever amassed enough to pay for lessons, however.

By the turn of the century there were as many black bands playing in the new hot style, compounded of syncopated rhythm and ebullient vitality, as there were older-style Creole bands. By now, too, poor whites were competing with the Creoles for jobs. Music had assumed a new importance as a way to make a living. The Creoles had "put down" the rough, tough characters from the wrong side of Canal Street; they scorned playing by ear rather than by notes, but the hate, fear and jealousy that existed on both sides had to erode—for each group needed the other.

The musicians listened outside each other's dance halls to the different musical styles, and before long the Creoles discovered that the real vitality and more money was to be found in notorious Storyville, the sporting-house and honky-tonk area of New Orleans. As one Creole musician put it: "These hot people—they play like they killing themselves." For their part, the black musicians polished their technique and learned to read music from the downtowners. Urbane sophistication fused with slave-bred sorrow; classical tone and technique merged with "dirty" tone and deep musical instincts; written musical know-how melded with on-the-spot improvisation—and out of it all came jazz.

Where did "Little Louis" (as the undersized Armstrong kid was known throughout his teens) fit into this picture? Born in the poorest, most crowded and toughest "Back of Town" area, he went to school through the fifth grade. If, during lunch recess, the signal on the bass drum and the short trumpet fanfare announcing the approach of one of the popular brass bands of the day was heard, Louis, along with his friends, headed out of school in wild excitement, "second-lining" the band. They played kazoos, harmonicas, home-made instruments, whistled or sang—anything to be ecstatically close to their heroes, following the band ten or twenty blocks before trudging reluctantly back to school.

To these kids the players in such bands as Bunk Johnson's or Tio Perez's were idolized as if they were the present-day Beatles and Joe Namath rolled into one. There was no other recreation—no sports, no radio or television; music-making was the great outlet for competition, emotion, amusement and high spirits. And musical competition there was! If a man died who had belonged (as was very likely) to several social clubs or funeral organizations, there might be as many as three or four bands playing in the long and solemn cortege wending its way to the cemetery—each band followed by its faithful string of second-liners. The youngsters hoped for the great honor of holding the instrument case or perhaps even the instrument of their particular hero during the band's frequent stops for liquid refreshment. All solemnity ended after the moaning and chanting of the funeral service at the graveyard; the music on the way back to town was chosen and played with the dead man's life-style in mind—and it was usually "hot" all the way.

Competition was especially keen when two social functions were to be held on the same night. All that day the band from each dance hall would advertise its talents by giving free samples of its playing while traveling around on a horse-drawn wagon. Signs on the sides of the wagon told when and where the event would take place. When, as often happened, the paths of the wagons crossed, the street crowd would encourage the bands to engage in "cutting contests" in which they tried, playing their hearts out, to "cut each other down" musically. In order to prolong a good contest it was not unusual for the crowd to chain the wheels of the wagons together, happily sacrificing traffic and working time, in the same spirit in which the goalposts are demolished in a hysterical stadium after a last-second football victory.

In between selling newspapers, delivering beer, collecting cans and bottles and shooting craps, Little Louis second-lined his favorite cornet-players, Joe Oliver and Bunk Johnson, and trombonist Kid Ory whenever he could. Every cent Louis earned went "home," which was sometimes with his mother, most often with his grandmother, and later, at times, with his father. Sometimes by singing as a quartet, with Louis accompanying on a cigarbox guitar strung with discarded copper wire, he and his friends played for tips in Storyville.

Things seemed destined to happen to Louis on holidays. His birthday fell on July Fourth, and the turning point in his life came on New Year's Eve when he was thirteen. On that occasion he and a friend were picked up by the police for (what to them was just a bit of fun) "discharging firearms without a license within the New Orleans city limits," and sent to a kind of reform school known officially as the "Waifs' Home," and unofficially as "back of Mr. Jones."

Once he had become used to the change (it was actually a better environment than the one he came from) Louis thrived on the military atmosphere of the Home. Instead of police whistles, there were bugle calls. Mr. Jones loved boys and knew how to handle them. They were all taught the practical arts, such as scrubbing floors, washing, ironing, cooking, making beds, repairing clothing, and so on. They also engaged in sports, and a number of successful baseball players and swimmers were among the Home's graduates.

Best of all, despite a slim budget, there were lots of musical instruments, and a band trained by Mr. Jones personally. After a few false starts Louis finally attained his heart's desire. He was given a cornet, taught to read a few notes, and worked his way not only into the band (eventually becoming its leader) but also into the bugler spot. Never was a horn polished more lovingly, guarded more carefully, or practiced more assiduously.

The "bad boys' band" often left the grounds to play at private picnics, at summer resorts, at the fair grounds, and in all-day parades. On
one occasion the boys walked, playing all the time, more than twenty-
five miles in one day. And once, to Louis' great satisfaction, they pa-
raded in his old neighborhood, where all his friends turned out to hear
and see him. The boys' caps were passed among the crowd that day
and netted enough coins to buy new uniforms and instruments for the
entire band. By the time he was fourteen years old Louis had left the
Home, carrying with him the nickname "Satchelmouth." Even then he
had a wide, irrepressible grin, and the shortened form "Satchmo"
stuck with him the rest of his life.

Louis' earnings were more important than ever, because he was now
helping to support a cousin and her baby. It was a grim struggle for
survival, but Louis' natural insouciance and wonderful physique saw
him through a variety of imaginative schemes for making money. He
would follow the garbage wagons to the city dump and rescue
"spoiled" produce which his grandmother would manage somehow to
prepare so that it was sufficiently edible to be sold to local cheap cafes;
he helped load banana boats; and while doing that, if he noticed any
spilled coal, coke or charcoal on the levees in the evening he would
collect it, load it onto a pushcart and sell it door to door the next
morning at five cents a bucket. He also collected rags and bones for a
junkman, and worked on wrecking jobs.

It was a lucky day when Louis began running errands for Stella
Oliver. Her husband Joe paid him with occasional lessons on one of
his old worn cornets. After a while Louis began to play, at first only
for tips, on street corners in the "Battlefield" area (aptly named in
light of the nightly fights that took place there). He averaged perhaps
a dollar a night for his "act" that combined playing, singing and genial
clowning.

Louis bought his first cornet on the installment plan—it was in the
pawnshop more often than not—and formed his first band when he
was fifteen. The job in a local sporting house which they were able to
land didn't pay very well, so he hauled coal in the daytime. His daily
schedule went something like this:

7 A.M. to 5 P.M.—haul coal (five tons) for 75¢ a day.
Sleep a couple of hours.
Play cornet until four o'clock in the morning for $1.25 plus tips.
Sleep a couple of hours.
Then up again at seven o'clock and start all over again.
Saturday nights were special—instead of quitting at four o'clock in

the morning he played until eleven o'clock Sunday morning, but the tips made it all seem worthwhile.

When the police closed the honky-tonk the band broke up, but Louis was beginning to be known. He played for dances, picnics, funerals, and an occasional parade with the great Joe "King" Oliver himself. Even the music-reading Creole bands called on him to help spark their parades. He didn't abandon the coal-cart, however, until King Oliver went to Chicago and Louis was asked to fill Oliver's spot with Kid Ory's Brown Skinned Babies, the best band in New Orleans. At the same time Louis played in the famous Tuxedo Brass Band. Soon he was being offered more jobs than he could handle.

Louis was now eighteen and married. His wife Daisy was three years older than he. She was illiterate, jealous, and given to settling arguments with a razor. It was just as well that fate, in the form of a fine musician named "Fate" Marable, stepped in at this time. The opportunity Marable offered him took Louis away from New Orleans (and from Daisy, whom he later divorced) and completed his heretofore sketchy musical education.

When any musician got the enviable job of playing in Fate's riverboat band it was said that he was "going to the Conservatory." Fate had heard Louis in a "band war" and must have been greatly impressed with his tone, phrasing and general style, for his was the most musically polished and prestigious band on the river. It was very embarrassing for Louis to sit in rehearsals in which everyone else could read perfectly any music put in front of them. One of the other players took it upon himself, however, to teach Louis for half an hour daily for several months until he was sight-reading with the best of them.

At first Louis played only the night cruises. The twelve-piece band would assemble on the wharf at eight o'clock in the evening, playing for half an hour or so to drum up business. Then the big stern-wheel boat would cast off, returning by eleven o'clock. The band played steadily during this time, stopping only for two very brief intermissions. It was a kind of floating dance hall, with gambling and refreshments, and the band playing through many a brawl. Louis thrived on this regime physically as well as musically. Soon the river air and regular hours developed his appetite, and no one ever called him "Little Louis" again.

Soon after he was twenty, Louis left New Orleans for a seven-month, two thousand mile trip upriver. This time there were daytime excursions out of a different town each day; at night the musicians would make the rounds of the local cabarets, awing the local musicians whenever they took over the bandstand. In many small towns they were often the first colored band ever the townspeople had seen. They were always able to overcome initial prejudice with their playing, carrying the "good-time" New Orleans jazz sound north with them.

Chicago, rather than New Orleans, was the new land of opportunity for jazz musicians, and when King Oliver sent for Louis in 1922 to join his band Louis readily accepted. This marked the beginning of Louis' rise to eminence in jazz, for he soon began recording, playing in New York, winning an enormous European reputation with his records, eventually duplicating that success in the States, opening the door to night clubs and movies for black jazz musicians, and representing the United States in cultural missions everywhere.

In a popularity contest for great Americans held at the Brussels World's Fair in 1958, the only American, living or dead, who rated higher than Louis Armstrong was Albert Einstein. Abraham Lincoln ran third. Armstrong, more than any other single figure, made jazz the United States' most important cultural export. It was in Europe that his recordings were first appreciated; his trumpet playing and "scat singing" (with nonsense syllables) transcended all language barriers and created a generation of European jazz lovers long before similar recognition forced the Jim Crow barriers at home. Louis' complete virtuosity as well as his showmanship, rich tone, fantastic, driving rhythm, and keen sense of phrasing, along with his sensitivity and great originality of musical ideas have influenced not only every trumpet player but also the musical inflections and styling of other brass players and even pianists. Louis literally extended the range of notes deemed possible on the trumpet, and invented techniques that have since become standard on all brass instruments. And not least, his completely individual and unorthodox vocal style revolutionized jazz singing.

Before Louis Armstrong came along, jazz had emphasized collective improvisation, a kind of composing by committee in which the players read each other's musical mind and were able to perform as a group without musical chaos. Louis changed all that—his ideas were so original and broad in scope that he initiated a "star system" in jazz: the individual musician of great talent could now soar on his own, not restricted to the more mundane inspiration of a group trying to soar together. There have been reactions to that idea at various times, of course, but we have had scores of great jazz soloists, both instrumental and vocal, as a result of that liberation of the individual. Louis earned his place as the greatest jazz musician of all time by a combination of extraordinary talent, powerful, impassioned skill in improvising, and a warm personality.

Among the twelve children of an impoverished refugee from Russia anti-Semitism, he was number eight. He became a key figure in American jazz, the carrier of its message from black to white audiences. And he became a millionaire while doing it. In a paragraph, that's the story of Benny David Goodman (1909–   ), the prodigy from Chicago.

Benny experienced the same grinding poverty and occasional hunger that marked Louis Armstrong's childhood, but there the resemblance between the lives of the two ends. Benny's parents had brought with them a love of classical music which prompted them to take their brood to every free park band concert available; they realized that since advanced education was out of reach, music might give their children the approval, recognition and security which was part of the golden promise of the United States.

Thus the ambitious father wangled three of his boys into community bands at a local synagogue and, later, at Chicago's Hull House settlement. The assignment of instruments was purely pragmatic, based on the size of the child and the needs of the band. As Benny later said: "If I had been twenty pounds heavier or two inches taller, I would probably be blowing a horn now instead of a clarinet." Besides the twice weekly rehearsals at the synagogue, Benny, who was ten years old, also walked several miles to the bandleader's house every week for private lessons.

Chicago was the underworld capital in those post World War I days. Benny once said that it was probably his clarinet that kept him from going the gangster route traveled by so many of the kids in his neighborhood. The underworld, like the tough honky-tonk operators of New Orleans, owned the night clubs, the showcases for musical talent. Chicago had for several years been the Mecca for jazz musicians —Louis Armstrong was not the first to be attracted by the opportunities for a steady job and higher pay. And white bands, notably the New Orleans Rhythm Kings, were interpreting black jazz (and diluting its "hotness" in the process) for white audiences.

Benny and his fellow members of the Hull House band "dug" the new jazz, although it had no relation to the military and concert music they played in parades on holidays. There were quite a few of these kid bands which held their own variety of "cutting contest," by simply trying to outdo each other in volume, spectacular uniforms or fighting ability. Benny described a church picnic where, after playing their program and gorging on the food, they spent the rest of the day "jamming" (group improvising) in the surrounding woods.

One of the well-known clarinetists of the day was Ted Lewis. When Benny, at the age of twelve, entered a jazz Amateur Night contest, he was wearing a Buster Brown collar and bow tie, along with his usual short pants. His perfect imitation of a Ted Lewis record solo, anything but childish, won him both first prize and his first professional job. Weighing seventy-five pounds at the time "with a clarinet in my hand," he made five dollars each time he appeared at a weekly jazz night held in a local theater. For fear of prosecution under the child labor laws the manager had him play from the pit at night, and on stage only for daytime matinees.

Before long, the three Goodman brothers began scouring the neighborhood for other kids who played. They formed a band of sorts, practicing stock arrangements in each other's homes and experimenting freely with the written notes. Occasionally they played for high-school dances on Saturday afternoons. It was at Austin and Harrison High Schools that Benny first met some of the intense young jazz-minded boys: Dave Tough, Bud Freeman and Frank Teschemacher, among others.

Benny was asked by a booking agent to play for some house parties and proms at Northwestern University. Thus, at thirteen years of age he became the youngest member of the musicians' union. Still wearing short pants by day, he played college dates at night, wearing long pants to conceal how much younger he was than the collegians he played for. He soon earned enough money to buy his own clarinet and first tuxedo, which had to be made to order because of his small size. Other jobs followed: at an amusement park, and on a day excursion boat. By the time he was fourteen, the upper age limit for compulsory education, money was too badly needed at home for him to pass up a steady job at a dance hall for forty-eight dollars a week. In his spare time he made the musical rounds, listening to good bands, including King Oliver's, in which Louis Armstrong was playing. Musicians took to calling him "the kid in short pants who plays clarinet with So-and-So." The "So-and-So's" kept changing as he found better bands that wanted him. Socially it was pretty rough on a kid who didn't shave yet, being thrown with adult musicians toughened by years of travel.

For a boy who had never been a hundred miles from Chicago it was quite a break to be called out to California when he was sixteen to join Ben Pollack's big band that played real jazz and gave soloists like Benny very good backing. When the band came to Chicago, a Victor recording agent heard the band and set up a recording date. But most of the time they played one-nighters (in one memorable week playing in six different states in six nights). Before he was eighteen years old Benny had made his first record under his own name—a piece called "Clarinetitis," which led to further recordings under the name of Benny Goodman's Boys.

By the time he was nineteen Benny was playing at the Little Club in New York, and word got around that it was the only "hot" white band in town. It was spoken of in the same breath with the great Duke Ellington band. Still, there were plenty of slack periods between jobs, and once he was reduced to appropriating bottles from his hotel hallway for resale to raise enough cash for food. Then the jobs began to build; recordings for Victor and many small-label companies multiplied, and Benny Goodman was on his way to enormous commercial success.

But there is more to his story than that. Benny was, and is, a very complex man as well as a superb musician. He listened to and learned well his father's admonitions to strive for security and success. His early training was classical but his earliest talent and earnings came from jazz. That somewhere along the line he had suppressed a desire to play classical music is obvious. Once he was established he became one of the few jazz musicians to also make it big in the concert hall, playing and recording Mozart and Beethoven, and having great modern composers like Bartok compose special works for him.

Benny Goodman was unique in other ways, too. He felt, in the nineteen-thirties, that the white American public was not ready to accept completely improvised jazz (there was only limited opportunity for personal appearances by the great black jazz bands of the day), but he sensed that jazz's vitality, infectious rhythms and emotional impact were the wave of the future. He hired outstanding black arrangers such as Fletcher Henderson and brought together the finest jazz musicians, thereby displaying very early in life his great organizational ability. He exposed his growing audiences to preconceived, written-down jazz, and succeeded in giving to jazz middle-class respectability and acceptance. In the process, of course, true improvisation all but disappeared, so that purists insisted on changing the name from jazz to "swing."

Benny's greatest contribution, however, was a personal one. Never did he forget the Negro roots of jazz and the fine black musicians. There were few precedents for the early recordings he made with black musicians such as Billie Holiday and Coleman Hawkins in 1933. His small combos, which included such black stars as Teddy Wilson and Lionel Hampton, were the first integrated groups of their kind. Having broken the color barrier, he paved the way for wider personal appearances by the great Negro bands of the day such as Chick Webb's, Erskine Hawkins' and Cab Calloway's. In the long run, that foresightedness may prove to have been the greatest single contribution to the history of jazz made by Benny Goodman, graduate of the Chicago ghetto.

Many critics and jazz buffs have accused Benny Goodman (and Louis Armstrong, too, for that matter) of "selling out." That's a glib conclusion which overlooks many of the basic facts of musical life. In every art a particular style must be pushed to its limits, known and understood by enough people, before a new style can be appreciated as a contrast or corrective. A reaction can only be felt, and be artistically valid, as a "reaction to something." Only by exposure to hot music, translated for ears with different backgrounds into "swing," could the rebellion of "bop" be understood. Bop in turn, with all its musical and social implications, had to be heard, and loved or hated enough, to lay the groundwork for "cool" jazz.

Louis Armstrong and Benny Goodman were innovators *in,* as well as caretakers *of,* their musical traditions. For that role they fortunately had the stability to withstand the usual hazards of the musician's life. Unlike so many other great young jazz talents, from Bix Beiderbecke to Charlie Parker, their early gifts were not destroyed by drugs or drink.

12
Nonclassical Prodigies—Jazz, Blues, Folk, Rock

In 1958 Paul Anka (1941–   ) wrote and sang a song called *Diana* which made him a millionaire at seventeen. Does he qualify as a musical prodigy? A business prodigy he certainly was, making a new million every year in a row for several years. In all, he sold thirty million records in five years, meanwhile establishing two music publishing companies, "Spanka" and "Flanka," to promote his three-hundred-odd songs. He still has a huge loyal following, besides writing songs for other singers such as Frank Sinatra and Tom Jones. He obviously had an uncanny awareness of the trends of the new teen-age music market of the fifties, a taste for promotion, plus a degree of personal flamboy-ance. Musically, however, he was (and is) undistinguished in quality as composer or performer, and therefore not a prodigy by our defini-tion. His kind of exceptional success without exceptional talent is only possible in an age of sophisticated marketing techniques, and with the wide use of microphones, echo chambers, and other electronic equip-ment to disguise mediocrity.

Returning to the area of sheer musical talent—generally, everything about the nonconcert-prodigy scene is vastly different from the con-cert world. Even for the most truly talented, the millions of dollars don't accumulate very easily. For the young "pop" music composer there is no royal patron, no opera manager clamoring to rush his latest production onto the boards. For the jazz or "pop" performer there is no wealthy music lover ready to subsidize his study on a fine instru-ment; no widely respected music critic whose pronouncement that the performer is an exceptional talent will be a guaranty of overnight suc-cess; no well-established contest to enable him to pit himself against

147

his contemporaries with, should he win, resultant fame and fortune or, at the very least, a cash award and the certainty of important concert engagements.

As has already been touched upon in discussing Louis Armstrong and Benny Goodman, the road for a blues singer, a jazz pianist, a pop arranger or would-be composer has always been a devious one. It might start (as with Bessie Smith, the great blues singer) in endless one-night stands at carnivals, barrooms, "rent" parties, brothels and the like; gradually the talented young performer could play or sing with better groups in better cocktail lounges, night clubs and theaters; movie possibilities might open up. Even recordings, when made on obscure labels, were a slow road to recognition unless an unusual lucky break gave them national exposure.

The road was most devious and slow for black performers, condemned by unrelenting segregation to perform only for blacks most of the time. They often sat by and watched their material (written by and/or first performed by them) appropriated by white performers who had access to bigger audiences, both live and through recordings.

Universal recognition of prodigies in the jazz, rock or blues world therefore often came quite late in their lives because of all the obstacles they had to overcome. It also becomes more difficult to decide just who among them *were* prodigies. The first professional appearance of a talented performer playing with a traveling group playing in obscure little towns is hardly equivalent to the professional debut of a classical performer before a large audience and the critics. Here, attention will be called to those few nonclassical performers and composers whose outstanding talents did somehow manifest themselves early enough and with sufficient recognition to make a clear impact on others in their field.

The black guitarist Charles Christian (1919–1942) is a good case in point. In the brief twenty-three years of his life, he revolutionized jazz guitar-playing. There is not a jazz or blues guitarist, from Wes Montgomery to B. B. King to Eric Clapton, who is unwilling to admit the enormous debt his playing owes to Charlie Christian. Starting with a cigar-box guitar he made in a manual training class at school when he was twelve years old, he was still playing a five-dollar wood guitar at "jam" (group improvising) sessions when he was eighteen. But *how* he played it was another matter. Brought up in Oklahoma City, he came from a thoroughly musical family; his father played the trumpet, his mother the piano in silent movie theatres. Later the males in the family—father on trumpet or mandolin, one brother on violin, another on string bass, and Charlie on guitar—formed a strolling band. They played requests, but sometimes concocted their own rich brew of opera, blues, ragtime, ballads and light classics, enriching all with spicy harmonies and improvisations; then they passed the hat at the end of the performance.

Many fine jazz groups played Oklahoma City on their cross-country tours, but in these jazz bands the guitar was traditionally part of the rhythm section, playing nothing but chords on or off the beat. Charlie didn't even bother to listen to the guitarists; he had ears only for the horns—the great trumpeters, the great saxophone players like Lester Young. He dreamed of making the guitar a melodic instrument. When he was eighteen the electric guitar had just recently been developed. It had a wider range of tone quality, greater volume of sound, and the ability to sustain tones than did the traditional instrument. It wasn't long before musicians were carrying the word back to New York of a remarkable young electric guitarist out in Oklahoma City who could play single-note melodies that twined imaginatively around the trumpet and saxophone melody lines, and managed to play rhythmic chords at the same time!

New Yorker John Hammond, a Columbia Records executive, has done more than anyone else to discover and create opportunities for the development of jazz talent. Discerning, energetic, generous of time and money, he soon went to hear Charlie Christian for himself. Immediately he became aware that this boy held a new world of guitar-playing at his fingertips. Hammond arranged for Charlie to meet Benny Goodman, who was then playing in Los Angeles. Later referring to it as one of the most exciting days of his life, Hammond had Charlie play in a local restaurant where Goodman would hear him. During the performance, instead of playing his allotted single chorus, Charlie played twenty, holding the roomful of listeners spellbound for over forty minutes!

Charlie soon became part of the integrated Benny Goodman Sextet, which was highly successful both in personal appearances and on recordings. When the sextet played in New York, Charlie would lug his guitar and amplifiers from the midtown night club up to Minton's, the Harlem club where every important jazz musician in town gathered after hours to experiment with new sounds. Charlie was a vital part of these intensive sessions out of which bop and, later, cool jazz were born. The two or three years that remained to him before illness forced him off the bandstand provided enough recordings with his name on them to become a textbook for guitarists.

Thomas ("Fats") Waller (1904–1943) earned his nickname as a child and used it to advantage all his life (a short man, he weighed 280 pounds at the time of his death).

In the words of John S. Wilson, the noted jazz critic, Fat's "desire to find acceptance as a serious musician was buried under a heavy coating of pervasive geniality." He was more than genial—he had an endearing ability to make people laugh, to relish and create comic effects, which gave his devoted public a sense that Waller was primarily a clown who exploited his musical talent to that end. Only those intimate friends who heard him play hymns, spirituals and Bach by the hour in his hotel room on a rented organ while on tour really understood his serious aspirations. Another critic once concluded that to Fats the organ was the instrument of his heart, the piano that of his stomach.

That the piano eventually provided him with a good income was not due to his business acumen. That he did not have. For example, during the course of his life he wrote over three hundred songs. Some of the best of these, such as *Ain't Misbehavin'* and *Honeysuckle Rose,* he sold outright in a bundle with a dozen others for a few hundred dollars; the money they subsequently earned went into the pockets of other people. No doubt he composed with reckless fecundity, good material and bad, but there can be no question of his enormous influence on later pianists. His famous "stride" left-hand style, full of power, was balanced by a remarkable delicacy in the right hand which resulted in airy, graceful, lilting music, quite incongruous visually with the short, pudgy, eye-rolling, gesticulating figure at the piano.

Fats' upbringing, as the twelfth child in a religious, musical middle-class New York home, gave little inkling of what his future was to be. While his father was speaking on street corners as a volunteer preacher and his mother sang, he began at the age of five to accompany them on a harmonium (a small portable organ). His inability to resist "ragging" the hymns on the organ caused his father to denounce ragtime (a predecessor of jazz) as "music from the devil's workshop." Fats studied classical piano for several years, for a time with the great pianist Leopold Godowsky, but the lure of the pipe organ in the Lincoln Theater, which showed silent movies, was too much for him. Already well-known for his piano antics at his high school, he began substituting for the theater organist when he was fourteen years old. By the time he was fifteen he was appointed regular organist, with all his schoolmates shouting and stamping, encouraging him to rag his accompaniments.

The death of his mother when he was sixteen was a great blow to Fats. He left home shortly afterward and began his multifaceted career in jazz. Although he recorded a number of classical organ solos, he became famous for his consummate ability to turn that instrument, so unusual for jazz, into a vehicle for every kind of musical expression. He was, in fact, the first and greatest jazz organist. Later he began to sing, with piano or organ, scattering comic remarks infectiously throughout each song, to the delight of his thousands of fans. When he died at thirty-nine, he was at the height of his powers. He was evidently getting tired of the trivial material on which he wasted so much of his massive talent, and was about to try a more disciplined approach to composition, but that chance never came.

Among prodigy vocalists none has had a happier career than the "First Lady of Song," Ella Fitzgerald (1918–   ). Her career began at Amateur Night at the Apollo Theater in New York's Harlem, which was for many years the prime showcase of black talent. Ella's appearance there when she was sixteen was inauspicious—she was timid and frightened and sounded that way. Nevertheless Chick Webb, one of the many bandleaders who invariably scouted those amateur shows, detected a promise, a quality in her voice and personality, and he hired her to sing with his band. For the first six months Chick simply coached her; after that she was on her own, bringing fame to his band for the next four years that Chick led it before he died. She continued with the band as leader and singer after his death.

From the age of seventeen, when she scored her first success, *A Tisket, A Tasket,* it was obvious that Ella had rare musical qualities—the incredible ability to express every emotion with subtle vocal shadings, the almost tangible communication of mood. She also excelled in "scat" singing in which, using nonsense syllables, she used her voice like a fast trumpet or saxophone solo. Early on, her sense of mimicry enabled her to poke fun at the changing musical fads as they occurred. Even today she is still able to sing in any style, whether jazz, popular, blues, rock, bossa nova, or calypso. Her career has been a steady crescendo of success, her appeal reaches every kind of musical taste, in every part of the globe. On "Ella's Night," in 1968, fifteen hundred fans gathered to pay tribute to her as she was presented with New York City's first Cultural Award, an honor awarded for "exceptional achievement in the performing or creative arts." She deserved it.

How differently did life treat Billie Holiday (1915-1959)! It is no wonder that this queen of jazz singers had a deeply ingrained sense of the blues, with the harshness and moaning, the pervasive despair and defiant outcry against fate—her life provided her with plenty of firsthand material. Brought up in Baltimore by relatives, running errands for a brothel madam so that she could hear the Louis Armstrong and Bessie Smith records being played there, she was raped at ten— and sentenced to a correctional institution by a judge who didn't believe her when she told her age.

Afterward, reunited with her mother in New York, Billie, by then a tough young loner, scrounged around for any kind of job that would provide food and shelter, running the gamut from domestic to waitress to prostitute. One night, when she was fifteen, she begged a Harlem barroom owner to try her out as a dancer. Instead, he asked her to sing. When she finished the song *(Body and Soul),* no one applauded for a moment; the stunned, tearful audience could respond only with silence, before showering her with coins that amounted to the sum of thirty-eight dollars . . . and turned her into an instant singer.

Billie's book, *Lady Sings the Blues,* is a revealing commentary on the seamy side of Harlem life at the time, the corruption and gambling, the drug traffic that pervaded it and left its mark on her. She once said, "I don't think I'm singing; I feel like I am playing a horn. What comes out is what I feel. I hate straight singing. I have to change a tune to my own way of doing it. . . . There are a few songs I feel so much I can't stand to sing them."

The white downtown musicians heard about Billie and made the trek to Harlem to listen and be conquered. John Hammond helped her, as did Benny Goodman and others. But she was caught in the mesh of humiliating segregation incidents, exploitation by unscrupulous managers, and a heroin habit which put her in and out of hospitals and cost her the precious cabaret license without which she could not perform in New York. The considerable amount of money she earned through her recordings and personal appearances evaporated under the pressure of cures, relapses, arrests and acquittals, intermingled with occasional singing dates. Her life seemed to be in an irreparable shambles.

She tried and failed, with sporadic recordings, to make some kind of comeback. Her death at forty-four marked the end of a hopelessly tragic life and the waste of a great talent. In 1972 Diana Ross tried, not quite successfully but still very poignantly, to portray Billie in the filmed version of her life, which was called "Lady Sings the Blues."

When Aretha Franklin (1942–   ) was fifteen years old, she sang *Precious Lord* on her first recording, called "The Gospel Soul of Aretha Franklin." In 1972, coming full circle, she sang it again for a new album of gospel music and music sung in gospel style. What had happened in between those years?

Aretha was brought up in the gospel tradition: her father, the Reverend C. L. Franklin, is one of the most dynamic of all evangelical preachers, and it was while traveling with him on tour that Aretha found her voice as a solo singer. A thrilling voice it was from the beginning.

John Hammond, that ubiquitous explorer in the world of black music, heard her when she was eighteen and felt at once that her fervent singing style could be applied to secular "pop" music too. Her recordings under his direction, modeled partly on certain white singers' styles, somehow never caught on, although for several years she made the night-club circuit with some success.

When she switched to another recording company, with which Jerry Wexler was associated, he took a different approach. "I just took her to church, sat her down at the keyboard and let her be herself," he said. While it surely was not quite that simple, this much is certain: Aretha found for herself a way to fuse the contagious rhythmic drive of gospel, its projection of conviction and honest, direct emotion, with jazz and blues material.

They called her "Lady Soul," because, as one fan explained, she was the incarnation of all that is meant by that. "Her voice and style have the totality of the experience of the black people in this country." What was most remarkable was her appeal to white people as well as blacks, for it was they who helped make her the best-selling female vocalist year after year. Aretha is a brilliant jazz pianist as well, completely self-taught, with an uncanny ear and a harmonic and rhythmic flair that permeates her playing as well as her singing.

What does an artist who is at the top of her profession, equally recognized in blues, pop and jazz, do for an encore? Perhaps only the daring step Aretha has taken was possible—to go back to her roots, to see if her huge white following was ready to accept the pure black gospel on which she grew up. Hence her 1972 album, "Amazing Grace," recorded live in a church with a thirty-five voice choir, which John Hammond suspects will provide, as he says, "the final breakthrough of black gospel music to mass appreciation. . . . I wonder if popular music will ever be the same again."

When she appeared at the Apollo Theater in Harlem in 1971 the marquee read "ARETHA'S HOME." Recalling her childhood gospel idols, Clara Ward and Mahalia Jackson, and summarizing her later successes, her father has said, "Everything Aretha does is gospel. She has never left the church." According to Jerry Wexler, Aretha's interests in music span the world, so it is quite possible she will be singing African or Asian music some day.

There is an interesting group of young composer-poets who write their own lyrics. In each of these cases, music and words are equally important—in a sense the songs are sung poetry. Jim Webb (1946–   ), for example, began composing songs at the age of fourteen. He has produced a string of very dramatic songs from the age of eighteen on. These include *By the Time I Get to Phoenix, Up, Up and Away,* and *Wichita Lineman.* By 1970 he had a firm reputation as composer, lyricist, pianist, arranger, record producer and music publisher; on the other hand, his attempt to perform his own songs met with somewhat less success.

Equally versatile is Steve Winwood (1948–   ), an English multi-talented star who began his musical life as a choirboy. From the age of eleven on he played with skiffle bands (similar to American jug bands). At the age of fifteen, when Spencer Davis spotted him, he had taught himself to play several instruments. He later joined the Davis group on rhythm, guitar, harmonica and vocals. By the time he was sixteen he was the featured singer on a recording which became the greatest English hit of 1964. The quality of his voice was amazing—gravelly, rough, powerful, driving; it reflected his complete absorption in American blues. He was the epitome of what is called "white soul."

Steve left the Davis group after a very short time, at the height of his popularity, and retired to a quiet country place with a group of carefully picked musicians, determined to concentrate on composing. The music he subsequently wrote for this new group—*Traffic,* and later *Blind Faith*—is among the best ever to come out of the cross-breeding of rock, jazz, rhythm and blues.

Meanwhile, in the United States a teen-age girl was writing and singing unusual songs of very high caliber in both music and words. Laura Nyro (1948?–   ) sings with the same unexpectedly rich, "black" quality as does Steve Winwood, but her melodic inspiration is entirely her own. Before she was twenty she had helped make the reputation of several other singers by writing such songs for them as *Eli's Coming, When I Die* and *Save the People*. Her musical moods swing wildly between the sweet and the sensational. It remains to be seen whether as a vocalist she will live up to the expectations of her avid following, and whether her later compositions will fulfill the early promise.

Among the nonclassical prodigies are several who have one trait in common—all are sightless. Some of them are pianists, some singers, some guitarists; some are English and some American. In each case the listener has a sense not so much of deprivation or handicap as what seems to be a heightened awareness of sound compensating for the absence of sight. As the first teacher of Alec Templeton (1910–1963) expressed it: "Tone is the fibre of his life."

The Welsh youngster, Templeton, when three years old was able to recognize his friends by the varying sound of their bicycles. When only four years old, he could reproduce any melody he heard, standing in front of the piano, his hands higher than his shoulders, using only the four fingers of each hand because he had not as yet discovered the usefulness of the thumb. For many years he learned his music entirely from recordings. By listening and reproducing it over and over again, he was able to memorize the most complex piano work within a week or ten days. Only after he entered the Royal Conservatory of Music did he begin to learn by reading "Braille," that ingenious raised system whereby music as well as words can be "read" by touch.

Composing and improvising were the passions of Alec's life; he didn't aspire to become "merely" a concert pianist, although he did in fact became a very respectable one. He found the interpretation of other men's music too confining for his musical exuberance and his sense of humor. He could capture with uncanny accuracy the personality of an individual in a musical improvisation. From a few notes suggested by a member of the audience, he could improvise in the style of any well-known composer, and he could combine (in a totally different style from Hazel Scott's) the classics with jazz, which he did in such compositions as *Mozart Matriculates,* and *Mr. Bach Goes to Town*. Templeton could spoof not only the clichés of composition of different periods and composers, but also certain absurdities of performance, as in his take-offs of Wagnerian sopranos. His was an infectious charm and humor, which, added to exceptional musicianship and pianistic ability, made him a great entertainer.

Another young blind English lad, George Shearing (1919–   ) who came from a poor mining family, learned to read books and music in Braille at the special school for the blind which he attended. In his early teens he heard American jazz recordings for the first time and was attracted to the idiom. Leaving school at the age of sixteen, he began to play piano professionally; first with small groups in local pubs, later joining an all-blind band. It was during a jam session one night that American jazz critic Leonard Feather discovered him and arranged for several recording dates.

Shearing's recording debut at the age of nineteen quickly made him England's leading jazz pianist, with regular appearances on records and radio. After a slow start in the United States, the George Shearing Quintet became one of the most successful groups of the fifties. In the late sixties he regrouped it and won acceptance all over again. As a critic said of him in 1968, "Shearing's sound is as soft and sinuous as ever." He is an all-around musician. For several years, he resumed the study of classical piano in order to enrich his playing. He has also composed some fine jazz "classics," the best-known being *Lullaby of Birdland*.

A far greater figure in jazz than George Shearing, and one of Shearing's idols, perhaps the idol of all jazz pianists, was Art Tatum (1910–1956), who was himself almost completely blind. From the very beginning he made a remarkable adjustment to his handicap. Indeed his entire life showed a self-sufficiency, an ability to become, in a balanced, capable way, a happy, fulfilled person. This, in itself, was as admirable as his fantastic musical achievements. That they were fantastic was obvious to the many great classical as well as jazz painists who stood in awe of Art's playing. Pianists Artur Rubinstein and Vladimir Horowitz, fabulous in their own classical sphere, never missed an opportunity to hear him.

Art's technique was fully formed by the time he was twenty, for he had begun playing by ear at the age of three and quickly showed both prodigious memory and aural acuity. One hearing fixed a piece in his mind so firmly that he could play it. Later, after one "reading" of a piece in Braille, he never had to read it again—it was memorized. His mother taught him classical piano for four years; after that he began experimenting with his own imaginative and unorthodox piano sounds. He would invent harrowing harmonic problems for himself, then set about solving them with the great daring and spontaneity that later made his performances so unpredictable. Hours in every day were devoted to developing the nimbleness of his fingers and increasing their span by his own devices, so that his playing was later characterized as "lightning execution."

This black, almost-blind boy growing up in the musical bywaters of Toledo, Ohio, managed to acquire by himself not only a brilliant technique, with the touch, speed and accuracy usually reserved for concert pianists, but also the rhythmic and harmonic imagination that made him the greatest jazz pianist ever. One critic mentioned his "gossamer touch—the keys became feathers." Another summed up his improvisational genius by saying: "He expressed in one measure more ideas, more subtleties of phrasing and dynamic and harmony, than could his predecessors in four."

Art Tatum had no real followers, he established no "Tatum school" of playing, because he was only to be envied rather than imitated, even by the most gifted jazz pianists. They packed the rooms wherever he appeared and followed him to the "after-hours" places later out of sheer homage. He was the Liszt of the jazz piano, and, like Liszt, established new goals for performers yet to come.

In describing the rise of Ray Charles (1932?–   ) to wealth and fame on a bedrock of great talent, a critic said of him in 1970, "Ray Charles *is* the American Dream." But on closer examination the dream, for much of his life, was more of a nightmare. Born in Georgia, he became blind at six and was an orphan by the time he was fifteen years old. By then he could play the piano, alto saxophone and various other musical instruments, and had taught himself how to arrange and compose. Determined neither to beg nor to make brooms for a living, he played intermittently with bands in Georgia and Florida, with many periods of semistarvation between jobs. Paid off once with a tin of jam, he later recalled being so tormented by hunger that he "jabbed the can opener into the top too quickly, and everything inside fell on the floor." It was at the age of sixteen that he became a heroin addict, with all the heartbreak that entails. His intermittent brushes with the law over narcotics kept him out of night clubs, as they had Billie Holiday.

But Ray's talent could not be held down. His first recordings, when he was nineteen, scored an immediate success, and from then on, no matter what field he turned to—gospel, rhythm and blues, jazz, popular tunes—his hoarse, sometimes harsh, sometimes warm, always intense voice had a hypnotic force that was sometimes actually embarrassing in the depth of feeling and anguish it conveyed to listeners. Black writer James Baldwin has called him a "great tragic artist." Certainly the tragedies of his life have lent poignancy to his singing of the blues; there is gospel fervor in it, vitality and pathos. One critic spoke of its "pain-drenched timbre." His singing is not "beautiful," lapsing as it often does into moans, falsetto, growling roughness, any means that help project the emotionalism that makes Ray Charles the "living embodiment of soul."

Ray was a forerunner of Aretha Franklin in applying the gospel beat to many kinds of secular music that appeal to white as well as black audiences. One field that he has made his alone is that of country and western music, in which he was, incidentally, the first black performer to become a national star. Having grown up in the Deep South, he sensed the connection of country music with the blues. Country music, he once said, is about the "little folks who are having a tough time of it just staying alive—exactly like the blues." The real hillbilly tunes, he felt, are about the basic struggle for existence, except for being about poor whites instead of poor blacks.

A keen businessman as well as outstanding performer, Ray's was the first black jazz group to appear successfully on sponsored television. A steady stream of blues, gospel-like jazz, and popular commercial song hits have made him a millionarie several times over. His influence on such black singers as Aretha Franklin and Otis Redding is considerable, and for at least ten years almost every well-known white singer of popular songs has been in his debt to a lesser or greater degree.

The achievement which meant most to him personally was undoubtedly his successful campaign in 1965 to cure himself of his narcotics addiction of nineteen years' standing. *Billboard,* the entertainment world weekly, put out a special issue partly in recognition of that accomplishment. And in 1966, his 20th year in show business, the U.S. House of Representatives passed a special resolution honoring him, which read in part: "The pain of his early life and the hardships he has overcome are part of the Ray Charles sound."

In order to give an award to another blind musician a critics' group once had to invent the new category of "MISCELLANEOUS INSTRU-

MENTS" for Roland ("Rahsaan") Kirk (1936–   ). Unable from infancy to see anything and barely able to distinguish light from darkness, he played the clarinet and saxophone in grade school, and by the age of fifteen was playing with well-known bands and with his own group throughout Ohio.

When he was sixteen years old, Kirk, browsing through the wind instruments in a music store, came upon a discarded heap which included some strange and unusual instruments. One, the "manzello," was something like an alto saxophone; another, the "stritch," was a kind of cross between a soprano and alto saxophone. Kirk bought them and learned to play them. He was fascinated by the idea of playing more than one instrument at once. Experimenting with them, he finally succeeded in playing manzello, stritch and alto saxophone all at the same time, by using incredible breathing devices and even trickier fingering techniques.

It looked like a gimmick, but the resulting sound is a very musical self-harmony. As jazz critic John S. Wilson said, "He plays them simultaneously not simply as a novelty but to produce valid musical results." During the course of a performance Kirk also switches at times to playing flute in limpid, beautiful tones. Sometimes he hums along with it to produce a second melodic line. Or, again, he will add a nose flute to create flute duets. Whatever the combination, he has achieved a highly individual, virtuoso, forceful jazz style.

Having won acceptance first in Europe, and now increasingly in the United States, Roland Kirk feels he is exploring rather than revolutionizing with his multi-instrument experiments. Since 1971 his unique style, his highly original compositions, and his showmanship have won him a large following on college campuses.

In the early 1950's a young Puerto Rican teen-ager carrying a guitar in a brown paper bag approached one Greenwich Village coffeehouse owner after another. He pleaded for a chance to play and sing a few folk songs for coins during the intermission between the scheduled acts. Many of the owners gave in to the youngster, perhaps because he was blind. His name was José Feliciano (1945–   ). It was not easy, being blind and living in Spanish Harlem. Getting lost while getting about in the big city, with the alternative of lonely isolation, plus grinding poverty, made for a hard childhood. At first José fooled around on guitars borrowed from friends. When he was nine years old, a family friend spent ten dollars to buy him one of his own. He had a little classical guitar training, otherwise he is entirely self-taught, not only on guitar, but also on bass, banjo, organ, piano, harpsichord, bongos, mandolin and harmonica.

José left high school at the age of seventeen to take his first professional job. Only a year later a critic recommended him to those who "want to witness the birth of a star." He called José a "ten-fingered wizard who romps, runs, rolls, picks, and reverberates his six strings in an incomparable fashion." Beginning to get more important engagements, he also started making recordings for one of the larger companies. His first successful albums were done in Spanish for Latin and American Spanish-speaking audiences. Originally, his voice was a rather thin and quavery high tenor, completely engulfed by his guitar-playing. Later, a tour of South America seemed to accomplish a double purpose: while discovering his ancestral roots his voice became stronger and richer, yet never lost its haunting, melancholy overtones.

By the time José returned to the United States his style was mature if unpredictable. The beat was that of blues or jazz; the voice, vibrant and expressive, reminded many of Ray Charles with a Latin tinge; the guitar sounded, someone said, "like Segovia if he had taken up pop music," and the rhythmic drive and oral percussive sounds added to the general excitement of his performances. Some of his songs show an offbeat sense of humor which spills over into his verbal expression at times, as when he says, "The only people I'm prejudiced against are blind people; they just can't see things my way."

In 1968 he sang the *Star-Spangled Banner* before a broadcast and televised World Series baseball game and became a controversial figure overnight. His blues-rock version of the anthem caused a national furore, making the front pages of newspapers and provoking heated commentary on radio and television. His justification was very simple: "That's how I feel the song."

Stevie Judkins (1950–   ), a blind little black boy ten years old, had been dismissed from his church choir the year before for singing rock and roll music. Now, child of a broken home, raised in a teeming industrial slum, he was playing harmonica and singing on a street corner in Detroit. A member of a successful singing group heard him and took him to audition for Berry Gordy, the head of Motown Records. Stevie sang for almost an hour, nonstop, for the fascinated Gordy, who said later, "He came up here and we never let him go." They renamed him "Little Stevie Wonder." It was an appropriate name on all counts. He was barely four feet tall and twelve years old when his first single record, a driving song called *Fingertips,* sold over a million copies, making him one of the first artists in the great Motown success story, and catapulting the Motown label for the first time before the white record-buying public as well as the black.

Often one talent obscures another. If he had never sung a note, Stevie Wonder would still have to be considered an exceptional prodigy. Starting with a miniature four-hole harmonica that came on a key chain, he quickly developed an expressive, almost vocal quality on that underestimated instrument. Eventually he became one of the very few great virtuosos of the chromatic harmonica, a very difficult instrument indeed.

Somehow Stevie was able to sing continuously throughout his adolescence. His formal education was in the hands of a tutor who traveled around the world with him. Meanwhile he learned to accompany himself on piano, drums, and organ as well as the harmonica. He also wrote many of his own songs. By the time he was twenty years old (and over six feet tall—"Little" Stevie Wonder no more), he had added haunting ballads to his repertoire of soul and novelty songs. His own rendition of *Blowin' in the Wind* became as famous as Bob Dylan's. As one critic said, "He was able to overcome almost any material by the sheer strength of his talent."

The most obvious of his many talents are his voice and the force of his personality. The impression he creates is one of such vast exuberance and energy, such vibrancy and urgency, that no one in hearing range can help but succumb. "The closer you sat to him, the more roped in you were by his magic," wrote the critic Alfred Aronowitz, calling him "one of the most compelling performers I have ever seen." After watching him perform in 1970, Mr. Aronowitz concluded, "Stevie isn't a freak show. He's an honest prodigy of flawless taste and superb talent."

Of all the blind performers, Stevie Wonder is perhaps most the sensitive and responsive to the needs and aspirations of the blind everywhere, and he has done much to help them. He once expressed his own attitude this way: "I'm glad I'm blind. I can see more of life that way."

These (along with Louis Armstrong and Benny Goodman) are some of the nonclassical prodigies. Most of them succeeded despite incredible personal and social handicaps. In terms of the sheer number of listeners whose lives their talent have enriched, they surely belong in the same book with Mendelssohn, Menuhin and Montoya.

13

The Role of Heredity

In 1950, Isaac Fishberg celebrated his one hundredth birthday, in New York City, forty-three of his 150 living family members were professional musicians; many more were talented musical amateurs. For five generations they have been playing with major orchestras, acting as concertmasters, conducting, giving solo recitals. Two hundred years before, in 1750, when Johann Sebastian Bach of the fifth generation of musicians in his family died, there were still two talented generations of Bachs that followed him. Without ever reaching the towering genius of Johann Sebastian, the two generations still included excellent composers and performing musicians.

Between the Bachs and Fishbergs, there have been many other examples of family continuity in musical life, instances in which music has seemed to run in families. In France there were six generations of Couperins, three of Philidors; in England four of Purcells. Among Czech musical families the Bendas, as well as the Nerudas, persisted through three generations. Wilma Neruda (1839–1911), a magnificent violin prodigy, was the only woman ever to become the most famous member of a musical family. The Nerudas—brother Franz, sisters Amalie and Wilma—were one of the earliest traveling family acts, after the Mozarts. Another family act was the Swedish Björlings. The father and three of his sons formed a very successful vocal quartet which performed in Europe and the United States. The youngest member, "Jussi" (1911–1960), was six when he first traveled with them. He went on to become one of the finest of lyric tenors, esteemed especially for his skill in the Italian repertoire, at the Metropolitan Opera, La Scala, and other great opera houses of the world.

There have been other musical dynasties, such as the Scarlattis in Italy, the Strausses of Viennese waltz fame, and the Webers, among

163

others. But of special interest to us are those more recent families whose offspring are well-known on today's musical scene. Wilhelm Busch was an unsuccessful nineteenth-century German musician who had to give up music for carpentry and violin-making. But he realized his dreams through his nine musical sons, two of whom achieved world-wide fame. Adolf became one of the finest violinists of the early twentieth century, and his brother Fritz, one year younger, became one of the most brilliant of operatic conductors.

The Russian-Jewish Serkin family, the father a former singer, emigrated to Bohemia (Czechoslovakia) and came upon hard times. But when parents and eight children are living in a single room talent is pretty difficult to conceal. It was soon obvious that Rudolf Serkin (1903–   ) was a piano prodigy. When he was seventeen years old his path crossed that of Adolf Busch and the two soon became fast musical and personal friends. Adolf's daughter Irene was four at the time. By the time she married Rudolf Serkin in 1936 he was thirty-three, she was twenty.

It is interesting to speculate on what heredity will decree for the offspring of two such distinguished musical lines as the Serkins and the Busches. Enough time has passed to enable us to know that not all of their six children are outstandingly musical. At least one, however, Peter Serkin (1947–   ), has followed in his father's footsteps as a piano prodigy; indeed, he surprised critics at his earliest concerts with his uncanny resemblance to Rudolf at the same gangling, awkward age. At first, inevitably, headlines read "YOUNGER SERKIN, VIRTUOSO SON," and "YOUNG SERKIN TAKES AFTER HIS FATHER." In the last few years, however, Peter Serkin has come into his own, taking after his father in a profound, serious approach to music. His is an unprepossessing stage presence little concealed by his "far-out" clothes, but he has an intense, searching, individual approach to the instrument, and a commitment to what he considers best in the modern, experimental idioms of such composers as John Cage and Oliver Messiaen. With his enviable versatility, his recordings of Mozart and Bach are as much sought after as his Bartok or Schoenberg.

Jan Kubelik (1880–1940), son of a musician, was a Czech violin prodigy at the turn of the century who amassed a fortune by becoming the idol of Europe and the United States, where he was called "The New Paganini." He once said "I believe in heredity, of course, and believe that whatever skill I possess as a violinist came from my father, and will in turn be communicated to my children." At least one of his children, Rafael Kubelik (1914–   ), has carried out his father's prediction. From an early start as a pianist, Rafael became a conductor at the early age of twenty-two. In 1972, as a climax to his very successful career, he was appointed permanent conductor of the Metropolitan Opera House. His nonmusical claim to fame was his organization of a musicians' boycott of Czechoslovakia at the time of the Russian occupation.

The new influx of talent from the Orient includes the Korean Chung family with its seven musical children. Each has achieved separate honors. Kyung-Wha, the oldest boy, is a violinist who won the Leventritt Award at the age of eighteen; his brother, Myung-Whun, a pianist, was an outstanding soloist with the Little Orchestra Society at the age of sixteen, having made his debut in Korea when all of seven years old.

What, if anything, does this prevalence of musical ability in families tell us about heredity? There have been many theories, which might perhaps better be called myths, about the inheriting of musical ability. As far back as 1874 musical precocity was defined as "inherited ripeness," based on an inborn capacity unrelated to training or intelligence. Just as specific blood types or certain diseases seem to predominate in certain ethnic or racial groups, so, it was argued, does musical ability. This theory accounted very conveniently for the preponderance of Italians among the outstanding singers, many Jews among the great violinists, and so on.

It was believed until fairly recently that musical talent is transmitted most often by the father rather than by the mother, and that it is weakened in the transmission, so that children are rarely as gifted as are their parents. Mozart has usually been cited as a supreme example of genius that evinced itself too early to be accounted for in any way other than by heredity. Convenient, too, was the theory of "early ripe, early rot," which held that any extreme aberration such as genius or overwhelming talent dooms its possessor to a life of eventual failure, if not to early death. Part of this theory recognized a one-sided imbalance in the life of a person of unusual endowment, an imbalance which would warp his personality, even to the point of insanity, and would, in any case, make him incapable of functioning as a healthy, whole personality. His life would be one long sacrifice to his unusual talent.

There was a certain amount of evidence to support these views which, in the absence of any scientific proof to the contrary, were widely held by knowledgeable people in both music and science. The fact that not all the Bachs were musically talented seemed to indicate that, given the same environment, not all had inherited the "divine spark." The idea that heredity sometimes comes up with a "mutation," or unpredictable variation from the normal, may account for certain defects which appear at birth. Some have argued that a mutation may have the opposite effect, i.e., produce someone exceptionally endowed in one respect, yet otherwise normal. Certainly when Claudio Arrau (1903–   ), the Chilean piano prodigy, revealed that at the age of seven his greatest thrill was not the frenzied response of audiences to his playing, but the miniature motorcar given him by the Princess of Saxony, he demonstrated that a superb achievement in one direction does not imply equally advanced behavior in another. He was still a child in every way other than his musicianship. Also, there have been such prodigies as Handel and Toscanini, who came from totally unmusical families. And Giovanni Martinelli, the famous tenor, was the only musical one in a family of fourteen children. "Mutation" has been a convenient umbrella under which to account for unexpected outcroppings of musical ability.

In recent years, however, with the tremendous acceleration of scientific knowledge in general, and genetics in particular, some beginnings have been made in applying scientific method to the problem of the origin of unusual talent in all fields. Often these gains have been a part of larger studies of superiority in intelligence. The first serious attempts to link musical ability to heredity can be traced to Carl Seashore, a pioneer who, beginning in 1919, created ingenious tests of certain specific constitutional abilities which he felt were basic to musical achievement. These included tests for perception of pitch, loudness, rhythm, time, timbre and tonal memory. After following up a large number of subjects over a period of years he concluded that innate ability to perceive these separate factors changed very little—that whatever the individual was able to do by the age of ten remained the same at the age of twenty or older. Therefore, he argued, these capacities and limits of the sensory organs must be hereditary in the same sense as the level of visual ability is fixed at birth.

Though the Seashore Tests, with modifications, are still widely used, a number of psychologists and other investigators have devised their own versions of such tests, each striving for greater validity. Hardly an issue of the *Journal of Research in Music Education* appears without some ingenious refinement designed to shed further light on the elusive problem. No matter what approach is used, all the tests have led to certain common conclusions. One is that the sensory capacities are independent of each other, and that, therefore, someone with a high score on tonal memory may also have a very low score on pitch and timbre perception. When school music teachers use these tests in recommending children for instrument study, they take this knowledge into account. No child with a poor sense of pitch would be recommended for the violin, for instance, nor one with a poor sense of rhythm for the drums. The teacher also knows that on *any* instrument the chances for success will increase if the child has a fairly good score on *every* element, since a good score on one element doesn't compensate for a poor score on another.

Although few of them have ever been tested in this way, there is no question that every prodigy or outstanding adult musician would score very high on every item of these tests. Does that, in turn, mean that a child who scores very high on every item has the potential to become an outstanding musician? It would be wonderful if things worked out that way, but they don't. It seems that although all these and other aptitudes are essential for superior musical technique, they do not in themselves guarantee unusual talent. There also seems to be another factor, which so far has not proven to be measurable, needed for truly outstanding performance in music. The unknown factor has been called by many names—musical intelligence, musicality, "extra-talent gene," and so on. Especially in the case of composers there are factors such as creative imagination, taste, and inventiveness, which require entirely different kinds of tests from the purely musical and isolated ones described above.

There has been a growing awareness in recent years of the importance of these factors in *all* areas of life. Organizations such as the Creative Education Foundation, as well as individual investigators in the behavioral and social sciences, are striving constantly to find ways of measuring these traits, and of separating their hereditary and environmental strands. Their success so far has been rather limited. When such methods are found, and to them are added accurate tests of purely musical inherited abilities, there will be real progress towards understanding and perhaps even predicting outstanding musical achievement.

There have been various studies to determine the genetic roots of musical talent, including studies of the musical abilities of twins, of the child singers in the Sistine Chapel, and so on. One geneticist, Amram

Scheinfeld, used data from questionnaires filled out by a large number of the leading virtuoso instrumentalists and opera singers of the time, on which he based certain hypotheses. Among these was the hypothesis that musical talent could be in accord with genetic principles, inasmuch as his study showed that where both parents had musical talent, 70 per cent of that individual's brothers and sisters also would have talent; with one talented parent the percentage dropped to 60 per cent; with neither parent talented it became 15 per cent. He also made a particular study of absolute pitch (a kind of "mental tuning-fork" which enables its possessor to identify any musical tone and to reproduce it accurately upon demand). He traced this ability as it had occurred in the musical family of the singer Kirsten Flagstad, where it seemed to have followed Mendelian principles of inheritance.

As a result of these investigations, Scheinfeld's hypothesis was that musical talent is probably inherited through the combination of a number of genes acting together (at least two of them being dominant), and that without the required combination there can be no musical talent. This theory solved the problem of sudden talent, since it is possible for several generations to go by before the right combinations of genes comes along to produce talent.

Obviously, new developments in genetics should and undoubtedly will lead to reappraisal of the genetic role in musical talent. For the most part, that role is still a fascinating speculation, an unsolved mystery.

14

The Role of Environment

In the Russian home where Isaac Fishberg was brought up, the musical instruments played by the father, and eventually by eleven of the thirteen children, were so numerous that some of them were hung from hooks in the parlor ceiling. "From another house," Fishberg once said, "we might all have turned into glaziers or pawnbrokers. It's no use trying to prove anything about heredity in a family that literally cut its teeth on violins."

What these musical teething-rings may better prove is something perhaps about environment; given the basic biological equipment for musical talent, it would have been improbable that any member of the Fishberg family would *not* have been a musician. Similarly, in the Bach family, early exposure to an environment of enthusiastic and gifted musicians, plus the strong family tradition of music-making, must have been a powerful stimulus to each young Bach. In our own century, pianist Daniel Barenboim tells of being brought up, an only child, in a room-and-a-half in which both parents gave piano lessons all day. "Until I went out into the street I did not meet anybody who could not play the piano," he has said. His parents were his only teachers. Surely his home environment could almost in itself account for his remarkable progress as a child musician.

It takes, of course, an exceptional parent like Mozart's father to shape his child's environment and learning as successfully as he did (measuring the success in purely musical terms). Many parent-teachers, as with the fathers of Carl Maria von Weber and Ruth Slenczynska, fail doubly, producing only fleetingly successful prodigies who are haunted in later life by the shortcomings of their upbringing. The opposite has also happened—obstinate parents, as in the cases of Robert Schumann and Hector Berlioz, have sidetracked an obvious musical

169

talent in a misguided attempt to do what they thought was best for their offspring, thus sacrificing that early training without which musical ability cannot be fully realized.

It takes gifted parents to raise a gifted child, particularly a musically gifted child. Merely recognizing the potentially great talent is difficult in itself. For one thing, there may be general genes for creativity that make for talents along more than one path. Some musicians, for example Charles Gounod and George Gershwin, have had great painting ability too. It takes keen observation and acute sensitivity to direct the energies of a multi-talented child into the one direction that has the greatest potential for his artistic expression. It takes even greater parental vision to allow two or more talents to develop freely without an effort at control.

The dilemma is this: If a real musical talent exists and is to be fully realized, it must not only be discovered but also fostered from an early age. The Seashore and other similar tests are without value for very young children; instead, the age-old indicators of musical talent are still operative. Violinist Josef Szigeti (1892–   ) chimed in with a harmonizing line to a sung melody when he was only three years old. At about the same age pianist Artur Rubinstein, instead of talking, sang for the sheer pleasure of making up melodies. Some prodigies have reacted violently to unpleasant or out-of-tune sounds from infancy on; some could sing on pitch before they could talk. Some began early to pick out tunes on any handy instrument; others responded rhythmically as infants. All of them paid keen attention to the world of sound, man-made or natural. Whether these manifestations of musical awareness and ability blossom into real talent is subject both to the constitutional factors that were probably inherited and to the environment that nurtures it.

Intensive training of musical abilities must start early. Only in that way will motor responses become automatic and dependable, with the concentration and discipline that will be needed thereafter built into the child's work habits. There is too much ground to be covered to allow for postponement. Single-minded enthusiasm and energy must be used before the onset of puberty and its emotional complications. Music critic and composer Virgil Thomson has pointed out that professional training in music is more rigid than that of any other profession because it must begin in childhood. Speaking of a musician, he said: "He must work very hard indeed to learn his music matters and to train his hand, all in addition to his schoolwork and his play-life." Rather than being overworked, Mr. Thomson felt, a musician was more "elaborately educated" than others, living, as it were, an extra life. This may all sound like making a childhood of painful drudgery. For the shamelessly exploited prodigy it has been just that; for most prodigies, however, the absence of toys and the ordinary distractions of childhood were voluntary. They simply found more fun in doing what interested them most. Music was the source of their play as well as their work.

It is hard to overestimate the importance of the teacher in all this. Even more difficult is determining what makes one teacher particularly well-suited to develop the talent of a prodigy. Some have seemed to have a magic formula. Violinist Leopold Auer (1845–1930), himself a prodigy, accounted for more successful prodigies than any other teacher in musical history. He was immortalized in George Gershwin's song *Mischa, Jascha, Toscha, Sascha* in which the songwriter pointed out that to be a successful violinist one should have a Russian name and have arrived at Carnegie Hall via the Auer studio.

From wherever in the world they might be concertizing, his students followed Auer to various summer retreats to refresh their technique and to find new inspiration. Many of them have commented that he never imposed his own personality upon the pupil. He taught them a superb technique, gave them interpretive ideas, guided them along general lines, but let the personality of each student develop without losing its original qualities.

Among his outstanding prodigy-students (in chronological order) were: Jan Kubelik (1880–1940), Bronislaw Huberman (1882–1947), Efrem Zimbalist (1889–   ), Mischa Elman (1891–1967) and Jascha Heifetz (1901–   ). As each one rose to the height of his fame, there always seemed to be a younger competitor waiting in the wings to snatch the crown. Heifetz was only twelve when, on hearing his Berlin debut, violinist Fritz Kreisler said to his fellow violinist Efrem Zimbalist, "You and I might as well take our fiddles and break them across our knees." There is also the often-told story of Heifetz's New York debut at the age of sixteen. The audience was full of professionals eager to hear the much-heralded boy wonder of Europe. Among them were Mischa Elman, for almost twenty years the king of violinists, and his friend, pianist Leopold Godowsky. As the concert progressed, Elman kept mopping his forehead. Finally he whispered, "Rather warm in here, isn't it?" Replied the imperturbable Godowsky, "Not for pianists."

Among living violin teachers (Louis Persinger having died in

1966), Ivan Galamian is best known for his work with very young talents. Among his students have been such successful prodigies as Jaime Laredo (1941–), Charles Castleman (1941?–), Michael Rabin (1936–1972), Pinchas Zukerman (1948–), and many others.

Some of the finest teachers have been prodigies who, for one reason or another, turned early in their careers to teaching instead of performing. One of these was Georges Enesco (1881–1955), who said of his most famous pupil: "I learned more from Yehudi [Menuhin] than he learned from me." Leon Fleisher (1928–), piano prodigy and teacher, expressed his teaching philosophy thus: "I'm not here to turn out little Fleishers." Few performing prodigies have made great teachers. Byron Janis (1928–), a fine pianist, once said that it took him "three years to acquire a fabulous Horowitzian technique from Vladimir Horowitz, but much longer to shake it. The important thing is to say something artistically that is you. . . . There are many ways of performing a given work, but an artist must be convinced that *his* way is right."

Another great artist who has taught so authoritatively as to overpower most of his young pupils is Jascha Heifetz. Of all his students only the fine prodigy-violinist Erick Friedman (1940?–) has had a successful career as a soloist. In later life, prodigy-violinist Josef Szigeti (1892–) complained of the shallow training he had received at the Budapest Conservatory, where the teachers bowed to parental pressure and concentrated on showy trash requiring dazzling virtuosity instead of stressing great music which would lead slowly but more surely to greater musicianship.

Of all the things a teacher can do to ruin a prodigy—both in his career and in his personal life—the most certain is to rush the student into public appearances before he is ready. Often this is the result of parental or managerial insistence, but the good teacher strives to prevent this disastrous course. Probably more of the failures (far outnumbering the successes) among talented prodigy-musicians have resulted from premature exposure than from any other single cause.

From the desire to cash in on the prodigy while he is at his peak of earning ability stems the pernicious practice of falsifying the youngster's age. Witty pianist Moritz Rosenthal was so scornful of this custom that once, on meeting a child prodigy for the second time, he asked, "Tell me, how old are you *still?*"

Patrice Munsel (1925–), a seventeen-year-old coloratura soprano from Spokane, Washington, in 1943 became the youngest singer ever to win the Metropolitan Opera Auditions of the Air. Instead of a seasoning process to round out her negligible operatic experience, she was permitted to take leading roles that season. The public was delighted with her youthful freshness and charming voice. Not so the critics. Virgil Thomson reported that she was "far from being prepared for her present glory." Others spoke of her vocal immaturity, her "mingled brilliance and ineptitude." One critic wrote, "Perhaps the management felt that her youth condoned her vocal sins." Another called one particular role a "schoolgirl effort." After leaving the stage Patrice Munsel eventually became a mature artist, but she did it the hard way by going down in order to come up again. It was only after several years of study and appearances in musical comedy that she took her rightful place at last.

This brings us to the whole question of public performance and the prodigy. Music, like the drama, is a public art. Norbert Wiener, a scientific prodigy, pleaded in his *Autobiography of an Ex-Prodigy* that prodigies "not be thrown to the lions of popular entertainment." He was thinking, however, of mathematical geniuses, who were then being publicly tested on radio as "Whiz Kids." Such performances did nothing toward fulfillment of their gifts. In musical performances, on the other hand, there is a need for successful performing experiences in order to build confidence and to become familiar with the stage before self-consciousness and stage fright set in. Few prodigies ever go through the agonies on stage that older debut performers often experience.

The story of Josef Hofmann (1876–1957), one of the greatest of piano prodigies, demonstrates dramatically both the benefits and the pitfalls of early public performance. A sensational American debut when he was eleven years old led to a ten-week tour during which he was to play fifty-two concerts. His drawn, nervous appearance led the Society for the Prevention of Cruelty to Children to interrupt the tour. An anonymous benefactor guaranteed an income to his family for several years, the sole proviso being that Josef was to be kept off the stage and permitted to spend those years in study. Anton Rubinstein then took on Josef as his only private pupil. When Josef reappeared after six years of complete seclusion it was to make a notable success. Eventually he became director of the Curtis Institute of Music in Philadelphia. His fiftieth jubilee was celebrated in 1937 with all the honors due to one of the greatest pianists in the world.

Hofmann himself, however, bitterly regretted the six-year interruption of his career. He felt that playing in public was natural to him, a normal experience, and that on his return he was forced to struggle to regain ground that he had won effortlessly in his boyhood. He believed that the critics listened to him supercritically and that they asked more of him than they would have if he had been allowed to appear continually. In his extreme sensitivity to the critics' skepticism he reacted by playing coldly, almost indifferently, as if to show that he didn't care what they thought. Having made his boyhood reputation by a pulsating vitality and colorful technique, psychologically he was now driven to the opposite extreme.

The best teachers are those so sensitive to their students' needs that they can unerringly make the right decision about when the careers should start, as well as recommending the degree of intensity of self-application. The wise teacher will prevail on manager and parents to limit recitals severely at first, increasing them gradually, while allowing for normal physical and emotional growth along the way.

Not only does the prodigy need opportunities to perfect his art through performance, but he must also have the opportunity to develop models whom he can emulate, and to hear the great performers both on his own and on other instruments. This is why, incidentally, all prodigies gravitate quite early to the great urban centers of musical culture. Many prodigies have referred to particular musical heroes whose playing (or even conversation) was a key factor in their career. For pianist Leonard Pennario (1924–   ) this happened when he was eight years old, on his hearing Rachmaninoff play. Pianist Clifford Curzon (1902–   ) described the sense of revelation he felt as a young boy upon hearing Artur Schnabel. Violinist Fritz Kreisler felt the same way about Anton Rubinstein, even though Anton was a pianist.

One of the reasons for the significant upsurge in prodigies in America between 1900 and 1950 is undoubtedly the ingathering of talent through the visits and immigration of Europe's finest artists. Whether they came to escape persecution, to seek adventure, or to make money, they gave the American prodigy access to the best practices and teachers of the older European musical tradition. For there is such a thing as a good "climate," an especially good environment for prodigies; time and place have a great deal to do with their successful development. Italy, for example, with its several centuries of popular enthusiasm for opera, would be the natural breeding ground for singers. In Italy there were always dozens of small opera companies where a young singer could serve his apprenticeship before a receptive public.

Early nineteenth-century Europe—with its proliferation of concert halls, its newly blossoming bourgeoisie eager for culture hitherto the exclusive property of the nobility, plus the new romantic attitude toward children—was a good time for prodigies. Today, in the United States, the emphasis on youth as an ideal has permeated the world of music. Rock groups start out in their early teens. Family groups, some with very young children, have flourished; these have included the BeeGees, the Cowsills, the Carpenters, and the Jackson Five, among others. Because of the peculiarities of music as a business it is difficult to sort out the degree of genuine talent in these youngsters. How does one tell how much of their performance is pure mimicry? Or if their "original" material was actually written by them? How much does their success owe to superb control-room engineering? Or to adroit press agentry? Or to unusual marketing expertise? In any case, the American climate today is right for young talent, whether on the concert stage or off.

On the other hand an unfavorable environment can discourage the prodigy and actually suppress his talent altogether. Yehudi Menuhin's father put it this way: "I am sure that there are many other young men, now nobodies, who might have become as great artists as my son if their talents had been immediately recognized by their parents and they had been given equal opportunities for training and development." This raises the tantalizing possibility that there may be hidden youthful talent around us which has never been permitted to grow and fulfill itself.

Nowhere has this possibility, labeled the "veto" power of the environment by Amram Scheinfeld, been more evident than in considering girl prodigies. Until well into the nineteenth century, a girl's place was so clearly in the home that music for her was merely a way of ornamenting the home more gracefully. This she could do best by playing the accepted instruments for girls, meaning those that could be played in a demure, seated position—the harp and the keyboard instruments (not including the organ). As for girl singers, for years their appearing professionally on the stage automatically put them beyond the pale of respectability, reducing them socially to the same level as actresses, i.e., barely a notch above prostitutes. In 1874 an observer wrote: "Any effort on the part of a girl to learn the violin, flute or even the organ was frowned on as unsuited to her sex . . . crushed out of them. Almost any boy with a strong passion for an instrument could find means to slip out and practice every day, but the girls, being watched closer, had to stay in and do as they were bid."

It is remarkable that *any* prodigies before 1850 were female, what with the lack of opportunity, the family responsibilities, the social pressure to "play at" rather than to "play" a musical instrument. Yet the two greatest male composer-prodigies both had enormously talented sisters—girls who were prevented from becoming professional musicians by their strong-minded parents. One was Mozart's sister Marianne (1751–1829), or "Nannerl," as she was called. Their brother-and-sister act, the talk of the royal court circuit, was stopped by Leopold Mozart, the father, in time for her to learn the womanly arts of the household. In the much more enlightened Mendelssohn family, Felix's sister Fanny (1805–1847) was given the same excellent music instruction as he was. Felix claimed in later years that her piano-playing was far superior to his. Throughout his life he sought and took his sister's advice about his compositions, for she had herself written works which he admired. Several short pieces called "Songs Without Words" were actually written by her, as Felix was the first to admit with delight, although modern editors have tended to attribute them entirely to him. Even though she was not permitted to become a concert artist, the family could hardly interfere with the privacy of her study. Fanny wrote a number of songs, piano pieces and chamber music, some of which were published during her lifetime, some after her death. A line from one of her songs is engraved on her tombstone: "Thoughts and songs go straight to the kingdom of Heaven."

In our own century, prodigy-pianist Ampara Iturbi (1899–1970) played "second fiddle" to her brother, José Iturbi. Yehudi Menuhin's sisters Hephzibah and Yalta, both very talented pianists, were not encouraged to devote themselves to concert careers. That they did so later was their own adult decision.

Mention has already been made of several girl instrumental prodigies—Gertrude Mara (who was forced to give up the violin for voice training), Clara Schumann, and Teresa Carreño. Through the course of the nineteenth century there were many others, mostly pianists such as Anne Belleville-Oury (1808–1880), Arabella Goddard (1836–1922) and Sophie Menter (1846–1918). Camilla Urso (1842–1902) was an outstanding violin prodigy, as were the Milanollo sisters, Maria (1832–1848) and Teresa (1827?–1904), who toured together. Occasionally, also, a girl composer in a family of professional musicians managed to obtain recognition on her own. Such was the case with the short-lived Lucile Grétry (1770–1790), and with Elizabeth de La Guerre (1659–1720), who from childhood on was a brilliant star on the harpsichord, in both improvisation and composition, at the court of Louis XIV.

There might be some inclination, in light of the overwhelming number of male prodigies, to believe that talent is sex-linked or biochemical. So far, however, there has been no scientific evidence to support the idea. When the environment, as in opera, has been such that the demand for female talent has equaled that for males, somehow the talent was there in surpassing abundance. When the Victorian idea of women's role began to wane, more and more girls developed into musical prodigies. And yet, although in the last fifty years women have been well on their way toward equal opportunity with men, there have still been far more male prodigies than female.

One of the exceptions is Erica Morini (1908–   ), not merely a fine violinist who started out as a prodigy, but one whom *New York Times* critic Harold Schonberg has called "the greatest violinist of the century." Her experiences are instructive. The Vienna Academy would not admit her because girls were permitted only in the piano classes. Within a few short years, however, her phenomenal playing won her the Austrian State Prize, but she could not collect the much-needed cash award, because the wording of the award specified: ". . . to the man who . . ." Her assessment of the failure of women prodigies, made over thirty years ago, will not endear her to feminists. She said at that time: "Most of my sex lack the concentration, the will power and the willingness to sacrifice everything else to art which are absolutely necessary if one is to become a fine artist. Music is probably the most demanding of the arts. . . . I'm sure there are just as many women born with great talents for music . . . as there are men. But most of them haven't the single-minded drive and determination to bring them to fulfillment."

Whatever it did take, Erica Morini had in abundance. She recognized that marriage and children present greater problems to women in art than to men. As for herself, she was fortunate enough to marry a man who agreed not to let their marriage interfere in any way with her musical career. About having children, she said, "I don't think it's possible for a woman to be a good mother and a good artist, too." At least, she felt, it was impossible for her; she therefore decided to have no children. In recent years Ms. Morini has combined her concert schedule with teaching. "I won't bother with mediocrities," she said. Despite her high resolve, no student of hers has achieved prominence on the violin as yet.

Until quite recently, the dominance of men in the practical world of concertizing certainly limited talented women's opportunities to perform, whether as prodigies or adult performers. Men have always held the purse strings in concert management. On the community level, women, who make the choices among various artist for social functions, have tended to favor men performers.

As more women win the highest international awards, however, this picture is changing. Perhaps Erica Morini has underestimated the determination of many talented young women who may still make their mark as musical prodigies.

How, then, can we summarize the relative importance of heredity and environment in the development of a musical prodigy? Pianist Jan Smeterlin once said, "Heredity without training would not go far, but training without heredity would not go anywhere." Put differently, no environment, no matter how conducive to development, can *create* talent. But given the inborn talent, environment can make it or break it —stifle it or cause it to flower to full potential. But of course "music genes" don't exist in a vacuum. The individual's character traits, whether inborn or acquired, constantly interact both with the inborn talent and with the environment, molding the environment and being molded by it. This complex interaction accounts for the uniqueness of every prodigy. There is no magic formula for achieving success; that is why each prodigy's life is different and unpredictable.

15

The Prodigy Personality

A music critic once said that every prodigy should bear a tag marked "DESTINATION UNKNOWN." Yet a consideration of the basic character of a prodigy as a person rather than as a musician should help us to discern the landmarks of that mysterious voyage.

Musical memory has more to do with memory than with music. And every prodigy needs it in abundance, although only the rare, spectacular feats are noticed. Think of Mozart and Liszt, both capable of playing a complicated piece of music after a single hearing; or Josef Hofmann, at the age of ten, rehearsing a concerto with an orchestra for the first time, leaning over from the piano to tug excitedly at the conductor's jacket because he heard the cellos playing a particular passage inaccurately (something the conductor had not noticed at all). Then there was pianist Walter Gieseking, who once memorized a composer's new manuscript during an intermission at a concert and then played it from memory as an encore at the end.

Another aspect of musical memory is visual rather than aural. Harold Schonberg once noted in an article the number of musical artists who have been able to learn new music entirely by eye. After studying a work on a ship, train or plane, they have been able to play it perfectly at the end of the journey. This could be called "photographic memory," but what does one call Camille Saint-Saëns' uncanny ability to read a complex orchestral score of fifteen or more simultaneous lines of music, reducing them at sight at the piano so easily that it sounds like a fluent piano piece? These are intellectual as well as musical feats, calling for a peculiarly gifted musical intelligence which is capable of improvement with training.

The other traits to be considered apply to any prodigy, not just to musical ones. What is evident very early is a certainty of purpose, a

179

clear vision of a high goal. When he was seven years old, American composer Samuel Barber (1910–   ), in a playfully creative mood, wrote an "opera" with the family cook. At eight he wrote a letter (note the precocious use of language) to his mother which said: "I was not meant to be an athlete; I was meant to be a composer and will be. I'm sure . . . so don't ask me to forget this." Artur Rubinstein was no more than four or five years old when he distributed cards which were engraved *"Arturic* [his nickname] *the Great Piano Virtuoso."*

Accompanying this clearly defined purpose must be persistence of motivation, single-minded determination, and the sustained effort necessary to achieve the goal. Mozart once wrote to his father: "You know that I am, so to speak, swallowed up in music, that I am busy with it all day long, speculating, studying, considering." Sir George Grove, commenting on this letter, wrote, "His inner world was beyond the reach of any disturbance." The quest for perfection, whether in composition or performance, never ends. As Deems Taylor said of Jascha Heifetz: "He has only one rival, one violinist whom he is trying to beat—Jascha Heifetz." There have been prodigies who hated the discipline of practicing but submitted to its necessity with good grace. Artur Rubinstein told an interviewer once: "When I was young I used to go into the practice room and lock the door behind me. I'd put a beautiful novel in with my sheet music, a box of cherries on the right-hand side of the piano and a box of chocolates on the left. I'd play runs with my left hand and eat cherries with my right, and all the time be reading my book." A far cry from the pianist André Watts with his six-hour, six-day practicing week, yet each achieved his objective in his own way.

Being a prodigy demands hard work and great stamina. Fortunately, as psychologist Lewis Terman found in testing 1,500 children with high intelligence and conducting follow-up tests thirty years later, gifted children tend to be physically stronger and longer-lived than "normal" children. This is largely true of prodigies as well. We have referred to a certain number of prodigies who died early, but they were comparatively few and lived at a time of lower life expectancy. Today many prodigies, such as Pablo Casals, Andrés Segovia, Artur Rubinstein, not only live into their nineties, but are still active musically in their old age. In 1971 a review of a concert given by Artur Rubinstein, then in his eighties, was headlined "THE PERENNIAL PRODIGY." As Rudolf Serkin had noted just a few years earlier: "His music is becoming more reflective, but at the same time it is becoming younger. It's almost as if he's playing everything for the first time."

The physical hardships of constant touring, which is exciting and adventurous at first, do take their toll. Beethoven's piano pupil Carl Czerny (1791–1857), in addition to a shyness that made him reluctant to perform in public, dreaded the strain of travel and gave up a promising prodigy career at the age of fifteen. This was fortunate for the future of piano playing, because from that time on he devoted himself to teaching, for which he had an unusual gift. His pupils, including Franz Liszt, became the leading pianists of the mid-nineteenth century. Saint-Saëns, an amazing prodigy in composition, organ and piano, also found the fatigue of travel too high a price to pay for early success.

In our own times travel is more luxurious but no less strenuous, what with jet lag and tight schedules of world-wide appearances creating hazards Czerny and Saint Saëns never dreamed of. There were few fatal accidents in the carriages of a hundred years ago, but in recent years Ginette Neveu (1919–1949), a wonderful French violin prodigy, met her death at thirty in an airplane disaster, and two talented young rock prodigies, Buddy Holly and Richie Valens, died in an automobile accident.

At a performance, an audience expects the artist to be poised, confident, ready to play or sing his best. When Artur Rubinstein made his first American tour at the age of seventeen, he learned to his sorrow that he couldn't quite get by on his magnificent stage presence. "I played with more fire than accuracy. In those days I dropped maybe 30 per cent of the notes" (a pardonable exaggeration). "My difficulty was that I had so much vitality and dash that I could get away with murder in Europe. But in America they felt that because they paid their money they were entitled to hear all the notes." Accidental errors do creep in, however, in the most polished performances. The audience was quick to appreciate her aplomb when Guiomar Novaës (1895–   ), the Brazilian piano prodigy, once punished a note that came out wrong by thumbing her nose at it.

There are performers who can play on the feelings of an audience as skillfully as they play their instruments. One of the listeners, in Thomas Mann's short story "The Infant Prodigy," thinks: "Ah, the knowing little creature understood how to make the people clap!" Today that elusive quality, needed by successful prodigies (and politicians, for that matter) is called "charisma."

Throughout the history of music prodigies there have been musicians with magnificent technical attainments who lacked the healthy exhibitionism needed to communicate with an audience. Daniel Auber (1782–1871) began composing when he was eleven years old, eventually becoming the leading composer of French light opera. Not only did he refuse to conduct his own works but he couldn't even bear to be present when any of them were performed. Henri Alkan (1813–1888), a fantastic piano virtuoso at the age of seventeen, suffered from such paralyzing self-consciousness that he went into virtually monastic seclusion rather than continue to appear in public. Chopin, too, shrank from playing before large crowds, and consented to appear only in intimate salons before small groups of his admirers.

The very thought of a concert was enough to make pianist Adolf Henselt (1814–1889) physically ill. His morbid fear of the public made him remain offstage until the last possible moment. Then he would rush on stage and dash to the piano bench, running off again when he was finished. While performing he seemed to forget that the audience was there at all, for he repeated pieces he liked and he would hum along with the music, no longer so much frightened as oblivious of the audience.

Somewhat different is the case of Leopold Godowsky, the idol of Josef Hofmann and Sergei Rachmaninoff and considered a virtual wizard of the keyboard in both playing and composing. He was a "pianist's pianist," who played at his incredible best not in public but in his New York home for his awestruck friends and admirers, among whom were always to be found any pianists of note who happened to be in the city at the time.

The complexities, the distractions, and the natural hazards of life for a prodigy demand great strength of character. The needed self-confidence, if fed by too much praise given too soon, turns easily into smugness and conceit, dangerous both to the personal and professional future of the prodigy. Pianist André Watts tells how he guards against complacency: "As I take my bow, one side of me is saying, 'You're a good pianist, you've done your homework,' and the other side is saying, 'This could really be bad. Don't be too sure of yourself.' Always the two voices, one active, one observing."

The artist's intensity of feeling, sometimes called "temperament," also must have an outlet. If expressed in the prodigy's life off-stage rather than on, it can become destructive eccentricity. Loneliness too can be a real problem. The prodigy spends most of his time either completely alone while practicing or before an audience of interested strangers when performing. There is little opportunity for the ordinary give-and-take of human relationships. André Watts, once more, expressed the isolation and also the advantages this way: "If you want to be the boy next door I guess you just can't be an artist. But there are compensations. There's a chance to travel to interesting and exciting places and to meet some of the great and inspiring personalities of our times." He went on to describe the stimulation and excitement of concerts, the warmth and enthusiasm of some audiences, and the great inner satisfaction that comes with the awareness of having played well. "I guess the rest of living will just have to come later on for me," he said.

A prodigy must have a willingness to face difficulties, the courage to overcome obstacles, and a joy in solving problems. He needs the resilience to relish success, but must not be overwhelmed by failure. Most difficult of all to survive are the crises of adolescence, when the sense of self is fragile, and when there are periods of doubt, of clashes with teachers, with parents, and with surroundings. It is the dangerous time when physical and emotional growth must somehow catch up with the precocious musical growth if the prodigy is to emerge as a balanced person and, eventually, a mature artist.

Part of that balanced growth, at least in the twentieth century, requires that a successful prodigy be someone with breadth; total preoccupation with music alone has too often resulted in a narrow, inbred approach to music which limits the expressive horizons of the performer. This, in turn, keeps him from that total understanding and communication which characterizes the very greatest artists. Speaking of child wonders, Leopold Godowsky once said of their adolescence: "The wonder usually disappears and the child remains."

Some versatile prodigies have managed to combine other interests and attainments with their unusual musical talent. Violinist Charles Castleman (1941?–   ) made his successful debut recital at the age of ten. His extraordinary intelligence, coupled with an excellent general education, allowed him to appear at the same time with great success as a "Quiz Kid" on radio, in competition with some of the best young minds of the day. Pianist Walter Gieseking was an ardent entomologist. He once stopped playing in the middle of an outdoor concert when a rare moth flew by, and did not resume his playing until he had caught it.

Most astonishing of all was the case of many-talented violinist Fritz

Kreisler (1875–1962). Not only did he become an accomplished pianist and painter, but he was also a linguist and book collector, a student of medicine and an army officer. He once spoke of a favorite daydream: "In those youthful days I had some very weird thoughts about my future career. I envisaged myself operating on a patient in the morning, playing chess in the afternoon, giving a concert in the evening, and winning a battle at midnight."

There are implications in all this of the need for co-operation and understanding on the part of the prodigy's parents, siblings, playmates and teachers. First of all there is the obvious need to begin music study early and with excellent teachers. He will also need a good general education. Above all, he needs wise but limited direction by both parents and teachers—"limited" to give him extra room for growth. There must be the necessary scope to allow him to achieve for himself the right balance between self-discipline and self-expression. All these ingredients are necessary in order to bring his potential into full fruition.

This, then, is the personality of musical prodigies. They may not always be likeable, but hardly ever will they be uninteresting.

16
The Crystal Ball

Violinist Isaac Stern (1920–　) once said: "Every young musician comes up against this wall, at one time or another, of needing influence, money, attention, a chance to get on in the concert world. . . . And because there is no set channel in society through which he can go to reach his goal, he has to depend on the generosity of private people and on chance circumstance."

While that statement is not universally true, it does indicate the crucial role that economics plays in the life of a prodigy. One has to understand that role in order to assess a prodigy's chances of success as an adult and also in order to speculate on the future of prodigies in general.

Among those rare prodigies, like the Mendelssohns, who came of wealthy or aristocratic families, the long, slow training process was no burden. When it was time for a concert debut, it was not unusual for the family to hire the services of an orchestra and a conductor for the event. But the preponderance of prodigies have come from middle-class or poor families—Handel's father was a barber, Dvorak's a butcher, for example. And Josef Szigeti remembers his family cutting pencils into four pieces in order to make them last longer. Both poverty and political oppression are powerful motives for producing a prodigy when musical talent shows itself early. It often presents itself as an escape route to an undreamed-of freedom and affluence. Many families have undergone incredible hardship to achieve that dream. Sometimes it is the mother, sometimes the father who, leaving the rest of the family at home, undertakes long, arduous journeys with the hopeful prodigy, seeking an audition with a famous teacher, or admission to an august conservatory.

185

It was a particularly daring enterprise for a Jewish family in Czarist Russia, where the status of Jewish musicians was humiliatingly low and they were very poorly paid. Those periodic massacres called "pogroms" served as ever-present reminders to the Jews that they were not even second-class but fifth-class citizens. Beyond that, Jews were not allowed to leave their communities without special permission, which was seldom, if ever, granted.

Mischa Elman's father permitted a local Russian countess to sponsor the phenomenally gifted Mischa for his first formal instruction, until he realized that Jews would be barred from attending the boy's debut recital. The father then sold his house, left his wife and children to the care of friends, and set out with the five-year-old Mischa for Odessa, where the boy was promptly admitted to the Odessa Academy. The family was soon reunited, but the tiny stipend barely kept them alive until the father, a Hebrew teacher, found a number of pupils. Only after several years of bitter economic hardship was the father able to get permission to stay in St. Petersburg for two months in order to settle Mischa in the hands of the great teacher Leopold Auer. All these early hardships and deprivations did not, of course, prevent Mischa Elman from soon becoming at once the despair and envy of every young violinist in Europe.

Leopold Auer wrote, in his autobiography, of the misery and cold endured by Mrs. Zimbalist (also Jewish) in trying to locate a family in which to lodge her young son Efrem, who was to study with Auer. Hounded by the police for remaining illegally in St. Petersburg, she finally turned to the teacher for help. Only through his intervention with the police was she able to remain long enough to complete her mission. Auer exclaims: "How her heart must have grieved when she was obliged to leave this inhospitable city, to entrust her child to the keeping of strangers, and to face the depressing prospect of not being able to visit him when her mother love prompted!"

Sometimes, as with the American prodigy Leon Fleisher, it is not sacrifice, but rather a well-planned parental ruse that provides the turning point in the boy's career. Knowing the great Artur Schnabel's well-documented distrust of prodigies, the Fleishers awaited with impatience his next appearance in San Francisco, where they lived. As friends of Alfred Hertz, conductor of the San Francisco Symphony, they were able to prevail on the Hertzes to invite the Schnabels for an evening of dinner and bridge. Planted unobtrusively at the Hertzes' piano in an adjoining room, the nine-year-old Leon began to play.

Bridge was soon forgotten, as the highly impressed Schnabel also forgot his long-standing antipathy and agreed to take Leon as a pupil.

Such parental maneuverings (so well-described in Slenczynska's book *Forbidden Childhood*) might be called the do-it-yourself approach to musical patronage. Then, again, sometimes the government of a country becomes aware that outstanding talent can be a national asset, and provides some much-needed help. It was in 1910 that his mother left their tiny earthquake-ridden Chilean town with seven-year-old Claudio Arrau (1903–   ) for the capital Santiago. Once there, she arranged for him to play at musicales held in the home of every member of the Chilean legislature; she won her point, and the government soon appropriated a sum sufficient for the entire Arrau family to go to Germany for several years so that Claudio could obtain the best training. It never regretted the decision, for Claudio Arrau became Chile's most famous cultural export.

Even so poor a country as Bolivia gave a tiny subsidy to the Laredo family to enable them to bring talented young Jaime Laredo (1941–   ) to the United States for study. When he became, at eighteen, the youngest violinist ever to win the international Queen Elizabeth Competition in Brussels, he returned triumphantly to Bolivia. His grateful country promptly issued an airmail stamp with his picture on it and the three notes that spell his name, La-Re-Do. They also appointed him to a high diplomatic post in the United States.

Occasionally a group of interested persons collaborate in helping a promising prodigy to pursue further study. Such a committee of citizens paid for a year and a half of study for Ferruccio Busoni (1866–1924), a remarkable pianist who, when he conducted his own *Stabat Mater* at the age of thirteen, had already played over one hundred concerts and composed more than one hundred and fifty pieces. By the age of fourteen he was admitted to the Philharmonic Academy of Bologna, the youngest musician since Mozart to be so recognized.

Pianos themselves have played an interesting role in prodding the careers of impoverished prodigies. Back in the late 1700's, the composer-pianist Muzio Clementi opened a piano showroom in London. Who could better sell pianos by demonstrating his improvisational skill on them than his promising twelve-year-old pupil, John Field (1782–1837), who had made his debut two years before? This was a formal apprenticeship, personal support in exchange for music lessons, an arrangement that some observers felt short-changed young Field, who was noticeably ill-fed and ill-clothed for his efforts. Also, piano manufacturers, for their own commercial reasons, have underwritten and managed many a prodigy's debut or first tour as a valuable endorsement of their product. Josef Hofmann, Teresa Carreño and Artur Rubinstein have been just a few of the many prodigy pianists who have taken advantage of these opportunities.

On a more dignified, professional level, there are numerous national and international competitions judged by outstanding musicians. Many of these carry a cash award and, even more important, a guaranteed appearance with a major symphony orchestra or at an important opera house. This carries the double advantage of both defraying the often-prohibitive cost of a privately launched debut and also assuring critical coverage. There are contests for composers, too, as well as foundation grants to enable them to be composers-in-residence at various colleges and universities. And of course there are foundations as well as orchestras and individual artists who commission works directly from a particular composer.

Governmental sponsorship for gifted young musicians and composers varies among countries from an ample flow to a mere trickle. In the Soviet Union, various tests of children are carried out systematically at the earliest age possible to ferret out musical talent. The ones chosen are sent to special schools, then pitted against each other periodically in regional competitions that send the best on to the music conservatories. When a truly exceptional talent is uncovered, he is trained with lavish care for the international competitions. Josef Szigeti once observed: "Other governments gave their candidates good wishes; the Russian team was granted support as generous as though the Olympic Games were in question. Moscow provided its children with superb instruments to play upon; it sent them to Brussels, together with trainers and accompanists, long before the competition opened." The Soviet system doesn't concentrate on prodigies, because early debuts are not in the best interest of the state, but it has produced some great mature musicians such as violinist David Oistrakh (1908–   ) cellist Mstislav Rostropovich (1927–   ), and pianists Sviatoslav Richter (1914–   ) and Vladimir Ashkenazy (1937–), who in 1968 settled permanently in the West. The great defect of this system, from the Western point of view, is that there is no room for individual initiative by parent or prodigy. The state effectively controls the development of musical talent by having the only and final say on who will have the opportunity for superior musical training.

Israel adopts a halfway position. It hold periodic competitions for musically talented children regardless of how or where they began their training, awarding over a hundred scholarships to those deemed worthy of encouragement. A second competition is held several years later. This time all the contestants who are judged to show the most promise and who need financial help are subsidized by the government to study intensively either in Israel or in fine conservatories or with good private teachers of other countries. Out of this enlightened policy have sprung, in a few short years, such prodigies as Daniel Barenboim (1942–   ), Pinchas Zukerman (1948–   ), and Itzhak Perlman (1945–   ).

In the United States government subsidy of music and the other arts is in its infancy, actually minuscule by world standards. For example, the allotment of a single German city like Hamburg to its major musical organizations is larger than the total awarded to all the arts for the entire United States by the National Foundation for the Arts. Of course, an enormous amount of money is raised privately through the generosity of the public and is channeled, directly and indirectly, through foundations and musical institutions, to performers and composers.

In the international competition sweepstakes, it was not at all unusual, twenty-five years ago, for the Soviet entrants to win five out of six awards, but that is far from being the case today. For whatever combination of reasons—the presence of outstanding teachers and conservatories, an unaccountable increase in the number of "prodigy personalities," and perhaps an unusual run of luck, the United States, with its unpredictable, free-wheeling musical atmosphere, has in recent years outdone all other countries in the number of award winners on all instruments.

The problem of providing a prodigy with a good general education along with his musical training is a serious one and not easily solved. So far, American schools are still groping with the problem of how to cope with the gifted in any field. Enrichment of the curriculum has been tried with only moderate success. For truly unusual talents, segregation of the talented in schools of their own has been tried, as in New York City's special high schools for the performing arts and for science. (The earliest proponent of this idea was Plato, the Greek philosopher, who suggested the separation of superior students in order to train them to become community leaders.) There are, of course, harrowing tales of geniuses who were judged to be washouts by teachers in traditional schools. The recently published *Einstein Papers* tells about the teacher who insisted nothing good could possibly be expected of young Albert Einstein! Surely we cannot look only to the schools to uncover exceptional musical talent, although this has happened occasionally. For example, it was the discovery by an alert kindergarten teacher that Byron Janis (1928–   ) could play tunes by ear on a toy xylophone that started him on a very successful career as a piano prodigy.

Private tutoring works to increase the normal isolation of a prodigy's life, when what he needs is not only the company of other young people, but also the stimulation of young people with similar unusual abilities and interests. The answer may lie in a controlled environment especially planned for the musically gifted. Interlochen, an unusual summer music camp in Michigan which has always emphasized intensive expert instruction, severe competition, musical excellence, and concentrated performing opportunities, decided several years ago to enlarge its scope. By creating the Interlochen Arts Academy, a year-round boarding secondary school with a double curriculum of music and general education, it has helped to fill a real need, and has turned out extremely well-trained musicians with solid academic backgrounds.

But high-school age is too late for a controlled environment to help the prodigy in his early, formative years. Yehudi Menuhin, remembering the rich, quasi-school environment his parents had provided for him and his sisters, decided on an experiment. In 1963 he set up a boarding school for twenty-seven musically gifted children between the ages of eight and fifteen (the school was later expanded to hold twenty more). The student's day is long, what with both private and group music lessons in addition to everything else, but it provides for recreation, and includes chores which help to make the group a kind of extended family. Both faculty and students perform frequently, and the atmosphere is congenial, though serious. The children seem to thrive on it, physically, intellectually, and musically. It is too early, however, to tell whether a higher incidence of prodigies will develop—so far they have not.

Another experiment in environment control, bolder and more far-flung, was begun in 1945 in Japan by Shinichi Suzuki, a violin teacher. The children chosen were not preselected for unusual talent, since the aim was to produce skilled performers who would love music rather than being professionals. In all, 150,000 Japanese children have been trained by Suzuki's "Talent Education" method. Suzuki felt that the way children learn to speak their native language has important implications for teaching methods, and that if he could develop a "mother-tongue" approach in teaching an instrument, other experimenters would be able to apply the idea in the teaching of different subjects as well.

Starting with children at the age of three or four, he requires one parent of each to take lessons at the same time. Furthermore, he insists that the recordings he has prepared of the pieces the children and parents will be studying shall be played constantly at home. At first there are preliminary games involving rhythmic play and "pre-violins." A real instrument is given to the child only when he asks for it. Just as the child knows how to speak before he can read or write, so he knows each piece thoroughly by ear from recordings before he tackles it. The actual reading of music is postponed until he has played by imitation the first three volumes of the ten-volume carefully graded set of Suzuki instruction books. The resulting eagerness to play as well as possible the music already so familiar and beloved, the excitement of playing it with a parent, the opportunity to play with hundreds of other children at the periodic Suzuki "festivals," the warm praise and encouragement every step of the way—all combine to make for very rapid progress.

Starting in 1962, American violin teachers began going to Japan to study this method under Suzuki. Many came away convinced that, with modifications, it was applicable to American children. Among them was Louise Behrend, a New York teacher who uses many elements of the Suzuki "Talent Education" method. She finds parents reluctant to continue the lessons with their children as long as the Japanese parents do, chiefly because the youngsters soon begin to outpace them. Instead, the adults supervise the practice period very positively and actively. Miss Behrend also begins the reading of music somewhat earlier, as do most American teachers. But she is convinced the underlying principles of the Suzuki method are sound, and will enable any normal child to become a competent musician and a life-long lover of music.

What is of interest here, however, is whether, as a bonus, any unusual talent will be uncovered in the course of equalizing the environment of so many children chosen at random. Several Suzuki graduates, the best-known being Miss Toshiya Eto, have already become successful concert artists. Several others are concertmasters of important orchestras, a highly demanding professional attainment.

Lilit Gampel (1960?–   ), an American prodigy and a product of the Suzuki method, was ten years old when she won the Los Angeles Young Musicians Foundation competition, a competition usually restricted to musicians eighteen or over. She had already played several concertos, with a technical sweep, poise and expressive intensity that strongly impressed public and critics, performing with the Los Angeles Philharmonic and the Vienna Symphony among other major orchestras. In June of 1972 she appeared with the New York Philharmonic. "PLAYS LIKE A MATURE ARTIST," read one headline. In describing her as a violinist of unusual gifts, the accompanying article continued: "She drew a large, firm and beautiful tone from her instrument . . . produced with an incisiveness and sensitivity that cannot be taught."

An interviewer found her enchanting, with a childlike, open, volatile personality. "I play the violin because it's fun," she said. Math, too, was fun, and reminded her of the violin, because, she felt, with hard work any problem, mathematical or musical, could be solved. The interview made her restless, because she doesn't like answering questions, and she said, "I talk with my violin. All violinists do." She reported that she was never nervous, for that would take the pleasure out of playing, but she appreciated the recognition of applause. "That means they like it," Lilit said. "That's what violin playing is for."

There have been great changes in parent-child relationships in the last fifty years. Exploitation of children, for whatever reason, is frowned upon not only by child labor laws but socially as well, since it is considered too high a price to pay regardless of the result. Even the word "exploitation" has wider connotations now. It suggests an unbalanced education, or deprivation of the opportunity to grow up normally.

In their concern about the effect on the child's personality and his happiness, many parents today tend to look upon their offspring's extraordinary talent as a curse, rather than as a God-given gift. They realize how much more education than formerly is needed to cope with the complexities of modern life, and they hesitate to burden the child with the extra and arduous training that would be involved in bringing his special talent to early fruition.

The economic drives, too, are different now. In the early 1900's, the parents of a large family often would have all the older children go to work early in order to send one or two of the younger ones to college, the theory being that the educated children would eventually raise the standard of living for them all.

The economic, or financial, motivation is strongest among the disadvantaged and minority families. For them, the goal of fame and riches, whether achieved through music, the other arts, or sports, is strong and vivid. These accomplishments depend on the person himself, and offer the talented one and his family a breakthrough from the cycle of poverty. Violinist Isaac Stern, commenting on the small number of violinists and prize fighters in our affluent society, once said, "You have to beat yourself up so badly if you want to be good that only poor people are willing to take the pain."

As for the youngster himself the higher standard of living and the greater opportunities for fun may well smother the overwhelming determination to succeed which is essential to a prodigy's development. Violinist Mischa Mischakoff (one of the younger members of the Fishberg dynasty) once expressed his doubt that very many first-rate musicians would turn up in our times: "Kids are too much in love with the ball and the bat." And Harold Schonberg, in a 1968 article entitled "Too Itchy, Too Hungry," deplored the tendency of musical artists already on their way to look for short cuts to success—short cuts which, he said, in the end prove very costly to their talent.

Developments in recent years have made it much harder to become a successful prodigy than ever before. There is the relentless competition with the recordings of the established artists in the field, the higher expectations of audiences made sophisticated by exposure to the best performers through the mass media, and the almost incredible explosion in technical skills which has raised performing standards to new heights.

We can only conclude that there probably will always be some musical prodigies. Many of them will come from the ranks of the underprivileged as always, and more and more of them probably will be girls. All will have to be exceptional to choose at an early age so distant and difficult a goal. For there seems to be only one thing more difficult than raising a prodigy, and that is *being* one.

Supplement: Other Musical Prodigies

This is a listing of musical prodigies who were not written about in the main text, although a few were briefly mentioned. It is not all-inclusive, but helps to give a more balanced picture of the number and scope of prodigies in music history. If it appears that all major musical figures were prodigies, it should be remembered that Richard Wagner and Hector Berlioz, Bob Dylan and Van Cliburn, are just a few examples of relatively late starters.

Some of the prodigies are listed merely by name, date and nationality, while others are discussed in one or two paragraphs. This does not reflect their relative importance, but instead indicates that there was something unusual or noteworthy about their lives as prodigies.

We have divided the music field into classical and nonclassical. Under these heads the categories are arranged in alphabetical order. The arrangement of names is chronological within each category of musical endeavor. The classical prodigies are listed first, in this order:

cello	horn
composition	multiple prodigies
conductors	organ
double bass	piano
family groups	violin
guitar	vocal
harp	

The nonclassical prodigies follow, in this order:

composition	percussion
family groups	vocal
guitar	woodwind and brass
keyboard	

CLASSICAL PRODIGIES

CELLO

Forqueray, Antoine (1671–1745), French. Viola da gamba (related to the cello).

Gérardy, Jean (1877–1929), Belgian.

Cassadó, Gaspar (1897–1968), Spanish.

Feuermann, Emanuel (1902–1942), Polish.

Garbusova, Raya (1908–   ), Russian.

Parisot, Aldo (1920–   ), American (born in Brazil).

Nelsova, Zara (1920?–   ), Canadian.

Starker, Janos (1924–   ), Hungarian.

Rostropovich, Mstislav (1927–   ), Russian. A third-generation cellist, he made his formal debut at the age of fifteen in a Soviet Composers Concert, appearing in the triple role of composer, cellist and pianist. He made his final decision in favor of the cello at the age of seventeen. Perhaps the greatest of modern cellists, he has communicated the urgency and vibrancy of his playing to his most famous pupil, the brilliant young Jacqueline DuPré. Many contemporary composers have written new cello works especially for him. It has been said of him that he is "no dazzler, no hypnotist, no demon of the bow" but rather a "sober, serious, intense and devoted" musician.

Several times Rostropovich has accomplished the extraordinary feat of playing over forty major works from memory (virtually the entire standard cello repertoire), within the space of three weeks. He has come into open conflict more than once with the Soviet authorities over his passionate defense of the principle of freedom from censorship for artists in various fields.

Moore, Kermit (1929–   ), American.

La Marchina, Robert (1928–   ), American. Arturo Toscanini, himself an ex-cellist, placed Robert in the NBC Symphony cello section when he was only sixteen years old. After a brief career as a cello soloist, La Marchina (like Toscanini) turned conductor, and was appointed in 1963 Assistant Conductor of the same orchestra (renamed the Symphony of the Air).

Domb, Daniel (1944–), Israeli.

Wilson, Eric (1949–), Canadian, made his debut at the age of sixteen with the Winnipeg Symphony Orchestra. He is a very promising young cellist, having received numerous international awards. He has given concerts extensively in Canada and the United States.

COMPOSITION

Monteverdi, Claudio (1567–1643), Italian.

Purcell, Henry (1659–1695), English. He came of a family of accomplished musicians. Henry became a chorister in the Royal Chapel (the youngest ever to be admitted) and at the age of eleven was chosen to compose a special anthem for King Charles II's birthday (it was published later). Evidence is not altogether reliable about this period, but he seems to have contributed a number of songs and religious anthems to various collections while still in his teens. By the time he was twenty, an accomplished organist, he had become permanent organist at Westminster Abbey. His most famous work, written later, was the opera *Dido and Aeneas.* A prolific composer of operas, choral works, songs and music for plays, he died at the early age of thirty-six, England's first great native composer.

Telemann, Georg (1681–1767), German.

Rossini, Gioachino (1792–1868), Italian. With an abundance of musicality which extended in many directions he studied cembalo (a keyboard instrument) early and was taught horn by his father. He learned to sing and to compose well enough to be admitted to the Philharmonic Academy of Bologna at fourteen—thus duplicating Mozart's feat of some years earlier. He also continued singing soprano operatic roles until the age of fourteen. By then he was friendly with a singing family who commissioned him to write songs and scenes from time to time. Out of this grew his first opera, which was not produced until he was twenty.

By that time, however, several operas, commissioned by opera houses and written with ardent haste spurred by economic necessity had already flowed from his pen. At least one, *La Cambiale di Matri-*

monio, was a significant foreshadowing of Rossini's mature operatic genius. It had his characteristic melodic and rhythmic verve, and his delightful insights into the inconsistencies of human character, along with his ability to illustrate them musically. Rossini's immortal comic opera, *The Barber of Seville,* was written in about twenty days when he was twenty-four years old. Its premiere, for a number of reasons, was a disaster!

Donizetti, Gaetano (1797–1848), Italian.

Strauss, Johann (the Younger) (1825–1899), Austrian. His father was already the internationally acclaimed waltz composer and conductor, largely responsible for the waltz craze that swept Europe in the 1830's, when the younger Johann wrote his own first waltz at six. The father was sternly against his son's making a career of music, so young Johann studied violin and composition secretly.

In a dramatic confrontation when he was nineteen, the son appeared with his newly-formed orchestra in a restaurant-garden where his father played regularly. Amid the partisan furore of his father's supporters, the son played a mixed program of his father's and his own works. He was soon acclaimed as his father's equal. Before long the truth became obvious—it was Johann Strauss the Younger who was the true "Waltz King," and it is his waltzes which are the classic masterpieces of the genre. They include *The Blue Danube, Tales From the Vienna Woods, Wine, Women and Song,* and many others.

Foster, Stephen (1826–1864), American. The first published song of this self-trained composer was in the classical vein, but soon thereafter he began writing minstrel-type songs inspired in part by the singing of black workers he heard on the levees near his home. *O Susanna,* which he wrote at the age of nineteen, went into twenty-two editions within three years. It was followed by such songs as *Camptown Races, My Old Kentucky Home, Beautiful Dreamer, I Dream of Jeanie.* Most of the words were written by Foster himself. He died at the age of thirty-eight, miserable, alcoholic, penniless, never dreaming of the immortality his songs would bring him.

Bizet, Georges (1838–1875), French, could have been a concert pianist. His very musical family had intended from the beginning that Georges be a musician, and he was a brilliant pianist by the time he was fourteen. Bizet's remarkable skill at sight-reading flabbergasted Liszt and Berlioz.

He wrote a number of works for voice, piano, and other instruments when still in his teens (having begun in his twelfth year), but the one that has earned a permanent place in music history is his First Symphony, written when he was seventeen. It is altogether delightful, with vitality, freshness and delicate charm. Showing Bizet's uncanny instinct for the potentialities of each instrument and a mature grasp of symphonic form, it is one of the most brilliant works ever written by one so young. It was discovered only as recently as 1933.

Cowen, Frederic (1852–1935), English (born in Jamaica).

Strauss, Richard (1864–1949), German.

Prokofiev, Sergei (1891–1953), Russian.

Lecuona, Ernesto (1896–1963), Cuban. He was a piano prodigy at the age of five, and had begun composing piano pieces at eleven. His very first work, a lively march, is still played by Cuban bands. At seventeen he made his New York piano debut and his first recordings of his own compositions. His best-known work, *Malagueña,* has been recorded in more than seven hundred different versions.

Korngold, Erich (1897–1957), Austrian. He set all of Austria on its musical ear with a series of large works in modern style which he wrote beginning at the age of ten. A pantomime of his was produced when he was thirteen, and two operas when he was seventeen. Critics and public acclaimed them. American critics were not quite so kind; Olin Downes, for example, called his music "remarkable for its technical precocity and its lack of originality." Infant prodigies, about whom he felt very strongly, Downes compared to mushrooms "best allowed to mature in the dark." In later life Korngold concentrated on writing film music in Hollywood.

Gershwin, George (1898–1937), American. He quit school at the age of fifteen to become a song plugger for a music publishing company. This entailed eight to ten hours of playing songs for interested performers to hear. Soon professional musicians were coming simply to hear the remarkable young man play. He studied classical composition technique sporadically, but was almost entirely self-taught in jazz piano playing.

After several earlier songs, the first of his great songs, *Swanee,* was written when he was nineteen and became an immediate success. Among the other songs he wrote, with words by his brother Ira: *I Got*

Rhythm, The Man I Love, S'Wonderful, Liza, and *Fascinatin' Rhythm.* With the folk-opera *Porgy and Bess* Gershwin realized his dream of combining the folk-blues-jazz idiom with symphonic instrumentation. It became a masterpiece of American opera and one of its leading musical exports, just as his *Rhapsody in Blue* became a landmark in the synthesis of the jazz and classical impulses in the concert hall.

Rodgers, Richard (1902–   ), American. He started writing musical comedies on a semiprofessional basis when he was fifteen. But it was his teaming up with lyricist Lorenz Hart when Rodgers was seventeen that began his brilliant career in the musical theater. The fruits of that collaboration included such shows as *The Girl Friend, Babes in Arms,* and *Pal Joey,* among others. After Hart's death, Rodgers' next collaboration (with Oscar Hammerstein II) proved even more fruitful, resulting in *Oklahoma, South Pacific, The King and I, Carousel,* and other musicals.

Shostakovitch, Dmitri (1906–   ), Russian. He began composing in his teens, mostly chamber music. The first of his works to become accepted permanently into the orchestral repertoire was his First Symphony, written when he was nineteen. It has a freshness and maturity which many of his later works have not equaled.

CONDUCTORS

Alfidi, Joseph (1949?–   ), American.

Brott, Boris (1946?–   ), Canadian.

Serebrier, José (1938–   ), Uruguayan.

DOUBLE BASS

Dragonetti, Domenico (1763–1846), Italian, was called the "Paganini of the Contrabass." Practically self-taught, he held a responsible first-chair position in an important opera house at the age of fourteen, and by nineteen he had already written concertos for the double bass which were unplayable by anyone but himself. Dragonetti expanded both the technique and the repertoire of his unwieldy instrument, managing to achieve astonishing feats of virtuosity on it unparalleled until the career a hundred years later of Serge Koussevitzky. It was doubtless Dragonetti's playing that inspired Beethoven to include virtuoso passages for the double bass in his Ninth Symphony, passages no one would otherwise have thought possible at the time.

FAMILY GROUPS

Holmes, Alfred (1837–1876) and **Henry** (1839–1905) English. These two violinists traveled together as a brother prodigy act from their early teens on.

Cherniavsky family (Russian). Three of the several musical Cherniavsky brothers formed a highly successful trio of prodigies. **Leo** (1890–   ) was the violinist, **Jan** (1892–   ) the pianist, and **Mischel** (1893–   ) the cellist. All three were at first taught by their father, who was a conductor. That three such uniquely talented youngsters, each a virtuoso in his own right, could perform together for over twenty years without noticeable clash of temperament is in itself noteworthy. Leo, the oldest, gave concerts alone until he was nine years old and Jan seven, at which time they began to tour as a duo. By the time Mischel was seven the trio took to the touring circuit together.

It was unusual at the turn of the century for artists to go as far afield as Australia, China, India, Africa and Oceania, but the three Cherniavsky brothers did just that, and were often the first well-known soloists to bring European music to those parts of the world. Called the "musical globe-trotters," they covered as much as 75,000 miles in those pre-airplane times. Their first American tour, in 1916–17, was a triumph. By 1937 the group had disbanded and they were giving concerts separately.

Romero family consists of four guitarists, father **Celedonio** (1918–   ) Spanish, and three sons, **Celin, Pepe** and **Angel.** All made their debuts long before they were twenty (Celin and Pepe when they were only ten years old). They perform together, playing works for various combinations of two, three or four guitars (and also lutes) in both classical and flamenco styles. They have also commissioned works for four guitars and orchestra. Having appeared with all the major orchestras of the world, they are considered superb performers, both individually and collectively, particularly in the classical guitar repertoire of all periods.

GUITAR

Bream, Julian (1933–   ), English. He made an astonishing debut at the age of twelve, and has since been considered one of Segovia's logical successors. He has done much to extend the guitar repertoire by resurrecting and arranging for modern guitar (and lute, which he also plays superbly) pieces from the sixteenth, seventeenth and eighteenth centuries. He is a great favorite with young people, of whom he has said: "The young love the clarity, order and logic of my music. They are people who are looking not only forward but back."

Barbosa-Lima, Antonio-Carlos (1944–   ), Brazilian.

HARP

Bochsa, Robert (1789–1856), French, demonstrated unusual early versatility, playing and composing for several instruments long before becoming Napoleon's official harpist at the age of nineteen. A year before that he had played a concerto on each of four different instruments at a concert—piano, harp, violin and flute. In all he wrote over a hundred and fifty works for harp, also a harp method which is still in use. An eccentric adventurer (with forgery and bigamy on his record), he is best remembered for having revolutionized the technique of the harp, and for elevating it from a purely accompanying role to that of a solo instrument.

Grandjany, Marcel (1891–   ), French. He still teaches harp, although he is in his eighties. There are no ten-year-old harp prodigies, since the instrument is too large to be handled by a young child. But Grandjany had the advantage of a thorough musical background from infancy on. He was an accomplished pianist, organist and composer by the time he made his harp debut at the age of seventeen. He greatly enriched the harp repertoire with his numerous original compositions and his skillful adaptations and revivals of neglected harp works. The dean of harpists, he founded the American Harp Society and has played a decisive role in furthering harp study and in winning acceptance of the instrument as a solo concert medium.

Zabaleta, Nicanor (1907–   ), Spanish.

Senior, John (1958–   ), American.

HORN

Brain, Dennis (1921–1957), English. He was a third-generation French horn player who made his debut at the age of seventeen, and was thereafter the best-known player on this instrument until his untimely death at thirty-six in an automobile accident. He performed and recorded with outstanding chamber and symphonic organizations, and many composers wrote new works especially for him. His remarkable tone and exceptional mastery of the difficult instrument made him one of the great instrumentalists of this century.

MULTIPLE PRODIGIES

Mattheson, Johann (1681–1764), German. Composition, singing

Scarlatti, Domenico (1685–1787), Italian. Composition, organ

Martinez, Marianne de (1744–1812), Austrian. Composition, clavecin

Clementi, Muzio (1752–1812), Italian. Organ, composition

Wesley, Charles (1757–1834), English. Harpsichord, organ

Wesley, Samuel (1766–1837), English (brother of above). Organ, composition

Crotch, William (1775–1847), English. Organist, pianist, later composer and teacher. At three he so astounded Johann Christian Bach who heard him play *God Save the King* that he was commanded by the King to play at Buckingham Palace. He was already, at that age, being exhibited from town to town in public houses, improvising and playing his own compositions on a small portable organ made by his father. He had an extremely good ear and was generally very precocious musically. His numerous compositions, however, were inferior, so that he never remotely earned the title of "the second Mozart," that many had predicted he would. Crotch became head of England's leading musical institution, the Royal Academy of Music, and did much to further English musical life.

Cooke, Thomas (1782–1848), Irish. A prodigy violinist and conductor, he later sang and composed extensively. At a recital he once performed in succession on all the following instruments—violin, flute, oboe, clarinet, bassoon, horn, cello, double bass, and piano.

Meyerbeer, Giacomo (1791–1864), German, began his musical life as a pianist, with a debut at the age of nine. By then he was a superb performer, but already had begun to turn his thoughts to composing. His brilliant but undisciplined musical mind led him in turn to compose operas (produced from the time he was eighteen) in the styles of each country he lived in. His earliest were Germanic, then Italian à la Rossini, later French influenced. His greatest success was *Robert the*

Devil, which swept Europe. Meyerbeer's influence is obvious in the early operas of Richard Wagner.

Potter, Cipriani (1792–1871), English. Piano, composition

Chopin, Frédéric (1810–1849), Polish. By the age of twenty he was well on his way toward becoming both one of the great pianists and one of the greatest composers for the piano in all of music's history. He was precocious in many ways—writing verse at six, drawing and acting with considerable ability as a child. His youthful works for the piano were written and published from the age of seven on, with his first major works dating from the age of fifteen. Also at seven he made his first public appearance as a pianist, soon becoming the darling of the aristocratic salons of Warsaw.

The elegance and refinement of Chopin's playing and composing styles (he has been called "the poet of the piano") were practically self-taught. An early interest in the native Polish dance forms permeated many of his compositions. Chopin revolutionized piano technique with the striking originality of his approach to both keyboard and pedals; equally striking was the piquancy of his harmony and melody. He was the quintessence of romanticism in his work and his life, and exerted a profound influence on pianists and composers who followed him.

Hiller, Ferdinand (1811–1885), German. Piano, composition

Heller, Stephen (1814–1888), Hungarian. Piano, composition

Bennett, William Sterndale (1816–1875), English. Piano, composition

Reeves, Sims (1818–1900), English. Organ, singing

Smetana, Bedrich (1824–1884), Czech. He seems to have been a born musician, able to play the violin by the age of five, and the piano in a public debut when he was six. At the age of eight he had already begun to compose, and later he sang in a church choir. With very little systematic instruction, he became a brilliant if superficial pianist. To his diary, however, he confided: "I wish to become a Mozart in composition and a Liszt in technique." It was only after years of economic struggle as a performer and teacher that his gift for composition finally flowered. Through his operas and orchestral works, so permeated with Czech feeling, nature reflections and history he eventually became one of the revered national heroes of his country.

Brahms, Johannes (1833–1897), German. Johannes almost went to the United States on a tour as a piano prodigy when he was fourteen. But family circumstances forced him to contribute financially by playing in sailors' taverns in his native Hamburg, instead. He wrote considerable popular music under an assumed name, while also writing serious music that no one would listen to. It was not until he was twenty that a tour accompanying a violinist brought him to Weimar and Franz Liszt. Liszt was much impressed with the early piano compositions of Brahms and was instrumental in helping him toward his eventual success as a composer (along with the invaluable help of Robert Schumann, another fellow composer of generous spirit). Brahms became one of the greatest nineteenth-century composers of symphonies, chamber music and songs.

Rheinberger, Josef (1839–1901), Liechtensteiner. He was the only famous musician that his tiny country has ever produced. Exceptionally gifted as a child on both piano and organ, he became organist of his parish church at the age of seven. His first composition, a mass, was produced in public when he was eight. He went on to become professor of piano and organ, conductor, organist-extraordinary and prolific composer. Many of his organ compositions are standard in today's organ repertoire. His works are not at all like Bach's, but rather are imbued with the romantic spirit of Beethoven and Schumann.

Bronsart, Ingeborg von (1840–1913), Swedish (born in Russia). Piano, composition.

Sherwood, Arabella Parepa (1861?– ?) English. Her posters called her "the wonderful musical infant, seven years of age, the smallest and youngest pianist, vocalist and actress in the world." She performed twice a day, a combination of piano recital, ballad concert and readings ("serio-comic"), illustrated musically. All was done in costumes to match the characters.

Bauer, Harold (1873–1951), English. One of the great pianists of the early twentieth century, he began his musical life as a violin prodigy at the age of nine. It was not until he was nineteen that, disgusted with the patronage practices of his native England, he settled in Paris. There, Paderewski encourage him to change to the piano (which he already played well). A musician of the highest integrity, he did much to further chamber music in the United States (where he eventually lived) as a highly successful performer and teacher. Many of his recordings of certain works are still considered definitive.

Dohnanyi, Ernst von (1877–1960), Hungarian. A pianist, conductor, teacher and composer, he had composed several works (including a symphony which was awarded the King's prize) by the time he was twenty. He had also by then been recognized as a pianist of the highest rank. A consummate musician, he was one of the few composers able to express wit and humor successfully in music.

Ganz, Rudolph (1877–1972), Swiss. Cello, piano (later conductor).

Kriens, Christian (1881–1934), Dutch. A quadruple-threat prodigy, he made his debut with orchestra when he was fourteen in four capacities—he played Beethoven's Violin Concerto, also a Beethoven Piano Concerto, and he conducted a symphony he had written himself. He first made his mark in the United States in 1906, when he conducted an opera in New Orleans. He thereafter enjoyed some repute as a composer and conductor. But his career came to a bitter end. Despondent over his discharge as musical director of a radio station, he committed suicide at the age of fifty-three.

Nat, Yves (1890–1956), French. Composition, piano.

Stassevitch, Paul (1894–1968), Russian. Violin, piano.

Gould, Morton (1913–   ), American. The piece he composed at six, called "Just Six," was played on radio a year after he wrote it. He was giving piano recitals, and displaying a talent for improvising, by the time he was thirteen. At the age of sixteen he gave a concert of his own compositions; some of which, a critic reported, showed "the flash of unmistakable originality." At fifteen some of his piano works were first published. Economic necessity now led Morton to play in movie theaters and with dance bands, so that he was exposed to jazz. His compositions at first remained purely classical. Later he combined jazz idioms with his classical works in writing numerous film scores, ballets and operas. His music, commercially successful, linked Broadway and symphonic idioms and is distinctly American in sound.

Foss, Lukas (1922–   ), American (born in Germany). This conductor, composer and pianist began composing from the time he was seven years old, using the classical masters as his model, but eventually developing a style all his own. As early as at the age of seventeen some of his piano pieces had been published, and he was commissioned to write the score for a production of *The Tempest* even before graduating with honors from the Curtis Institute.

Foss was already a brilliant pianist when he emigrated to the United States in his early teens. He began conducting professionally as guest conductor of the Pittsburgh Symphony when he was seventeen. He has continued twin careers as conductor and composer ever since.

Schuller, Gunther (1925–   ), American. He was a prodigy on the French horn, but he is best known today as a composer and as the inventor of the term "third-stream music," by which he meant the merging of classical music and jazz to form a new musical idiom. Starting as a boy soprano in a church choir school, he took up flute at first, but by the age of fourteen began studying the horn. He made such phenomenal progress that he was playing professionally with the New York Philharmonic (under Arturo Toscanini, that most exacting of conductors) by the time he was sixteen. By the time he was nineteen he had played his own Concerto for French Horn with leading orchestras, but after a few years gave up playing to concentrate on composing, teaching, conducting and writing.

Lewis, Henry (1932–   ), American. Double bass, conductor.

Ran, Shulamit (1948–   ), Israeli. This pianist-composer gave her debut recital at the age of twelve in Israel and her first orchestral work was performed by several orchestras when she was fourteen. She has since completed her musical education in New York, and has appeared extensively in American and European tours. She played her own *Capriccio* for Piano and Orchestra in a nationally televised concert with the New York Philharmonic under Leonard Bernstein. One critic said: "There has never been a front-rank woman composer, but Miss Ran might be the one to break the barrier."

ORGAN

Strungk, Nicolaus (1640–1700), German.

Couperin, François ("le Grand") (1668–1733), French. The fact of his having been an organ prodigy is often obscured by his fame as a prolific composer of magnificent works for the keyboard instruments as well as church and chamber music. He also wrote extensively on music theory and on performance practices.

Daquin, Louis (1694–1772), French. He also played clavecin. His immortality was achieved later through his works for harpsichord.

Tausig, Karl (1841–1871), Polish. At the age of fourteen he quickly became Liszt's favorite pupil. He was a phenomenal technician, considered Liszt's equal in many ways, from the time of his debut at seventeen. He was outwardly calm, even wooden-faced, but could galvanize an audience by his superb command and stupefying effects. Even in his short life (he died at thirty) he was an influential teacher, and produced a considerable body of compositions and arrangements.

Napoleão, Arthur (1843–1925), Brazilian.

Menter, Sophie (1846–1918), German.

Holmès, Augusta (1847–1903), French. Later a composer.

Krebs, Marie (1850–1900?), German.

Hyllested, August (1856–1946), Danish.

Janotha, Natalie (1856–1932), Polish.

Rivé-King, Julie (1857–1937), American.

Friedheim, Arthur (1859–1932), American (born in Russia).

Rosenthal, Moritz (1862–1946), Polish. From his earliest public appearances he showed an astonishing technique that put him in a class with Anton Rubinstein. So stunning was his debut at the age of fourteen in Vienna that he was immediately appointed Court Pianist by the King of Roumania. After sensational appearances in Paris and St. Petersburg, Moritz retired at sixteen for six years to acquire a thorough general education. After that he resumed a brilliant career in Europe and the United States as one of the great pianists of the world.

Soldat, Marie (1863–1955), Austrian.

Zeisler (Bloomfield), Fanny (1863–1927), American (born in Austria).

Albert, Eugen d' (1864–1932), German (born in England). At fourteen he was an excellent pianist; at fifteen and sixteen his concerts included piano and orchestral works written by him. Liszt called him "our young lion" and described him as a "dazzling talent." Later in life he turned entirely to composing. Eventually he became Court Conductor at Weimar, the post Liszt had once held. The second of d'Albert's six wives was Teresa Carreño, who had herself been a piano prodigy.

Beach, Amy ("Mrs. H. H. A.") (1867–1944), American.

Lhevinne, Josef (1874–1941), Russian, made a brilliant piano debut at the age of fourteen, but continued to study at the Moscow Conservatory until he was seventeen. He then toured Europe and taught at the Moscow Conservatory. His appearance in the United States in 1907 caused a furore; he thereafter returned every season.

Lhevinne's wife, **Rosina** (1880–   ), who had been one of his students, carried on the Rubinstein-Lhevinne teaching techniques as late as 1972, when she was the revered senior member of the piano faculty of the Juilliard School, still actively teaching although in her nineties.

Hegner, Otto (1876–1907), Swiss.

Hambourg, Mark (1879–1960), English (born in Russia).

Friedman, Ignaz (1882–1948), Polish.

Schnabel, Artur (1882–1954), American (born in Austria). If Vladimir Horowitz was the high priest of piano technique, Schnabel was the high priest of intellectual musicianship. From his earliest days as a performer, making his debut in Austria at the age of eleven while studying with Leschetitzky, and his Berlin debut at sixteen, he had a seriousness of purpose, a strength of character and intellect, which lent unusual depth to his interpretations (and to his own numerous compositions, which he himself never played). His talent was not showy, so that its true dimensions were only gradually appreciated by the general public. His son, **Karl Ulrich Schnabel** (1909–   ), a fine pianist and musician in his own right, was also a prodigy. Both, as teachers, exerted a profound influence on two generations of pianists.

Backhaus, Wilhelm (1884–1969), German.

Leginska (Liggins), Ethel (1886–1970), English.

Merö, Yolanda (1887–1963), Hungarian.

Saperton, David (1889–1970), American.

Hess, Myra (1890–1965), English.

Horszowski, Mieczyslaw (1892–   ), Polish.

Hilsberg, Ignaz (1894–1961), Polish.

Novaës, Guiomar (1895–   ), Brazilian. She was the one out of nineteen children in her family who showed marked musical talent very early in life. When the Brazilian government subsidized her trip to Paris at the age of fourteen to audition for the Conservatory there she had already performed extensively in South America. At her audition (Claude Debussy was one of the judges) she won over more than three hundred and fifty contestants. Almost unbelievably, the judges asked her to *repeat* the same selections they had heard so many times, for their own pleasure! She has since become one of the world's great pianists, particularly recognized for her interpretations of the romantic repertoire.

Cohen, Harriet (1895–1967), English.

Arriola, Pepito (1897–   ), Spanish. He is one of the spectacular failures among child prodigies as adults. In 1908, when he was eleven, English newspapers called him "the reincarnation of Mozart." He was the highest-paid performer in Europe, captivating interviewers with his grownup expressions as much as the public and critics with his playing. "Chopin has not spoiled my taste for toy soldiers, and Schumann does not interfere with me when I want to row, bicycle, or play ball. There is nothing like broadmindedness for the artist," he said. American critics proved far less susceptible to his talents than the Germans and English who put him on a pedestal.

By the time he was eighteen he was simply a pianist whom Spain was proud to claim. By the age of forty-eight he had disappeared so completely from the news that he was reported to be dead. Instead, very much alive, he wrote a letter in 1945 to a music magazine to bring his biography up to date. He and his family had lived in Germany, had been displaced during the Second World War, and had had their share of adventures. He had continued performing, but it can be gathered, reading between the lines of this poignant letter, that since his teens Pepito Arriola has been a very minor figure indeed in the concert world.

Levitzki, Mischa (1898–1941), American (born in Russia).

Rubinstein, Beryl (1898–1952), American.

Casadesus, Robert (1899–1972), French.

Horowitz, Vladimir (1904–   ), American (born in Russia) Horowitz is to the piano what Jascha Heifetz is to the violin—the pace setter for younger performers. He studied under Anton Rubinstein, and at first aspired to composing.

The Russian Revolution, which deprived his family of its possessions and home, forced Horowitz on to the concert stage in his teens. At the twenty-fifth anniversary of his American debut, critic Howard Taubman wrote: "He has transformed himself from a fire-eating virtuoso into a self-critical, searching artist." After a mysterious retirement of twelve years, Horowitz returned, in 1965, a legend renewed, as exciting and forceful, but more reflective and introspective an artist than ever. In the words of a newspaper: "Horowitz again unleashes his magic."

Kentner, Louis (1905–   ), Hungarian.

Echaniz, Jose (1905–1969), Cuban. Later a conductor.

Levant, Oscar (1906–1972), American.

Goldsand, Robert (1911–   ), American (born in Austria). One of the last in the sweeping romantic tradition of piano virtuosi. He was trained in Vienna, where he made his debut at the age of ten. His teen-age debut in New York was comparable to Josef Hofmann's some years earlier. His playing combines the superb technical equipment which is now standard among younger players with the romantic spaciousness and temperament which they find much harder to achieve.

Cherkassky, Shura (1911–   ), American (born in Russia).

Castagnetta, Grace (1912–   ), American. She gave her first full-length recital when she was eight. At the age of sixteen, and exactly five feet tall, she made her Berlin debut, which was hailed as "the sensational debut of a diminutive American pianist." She once improvised with remarkable facility on a theme suggested to her by someone in the audience; thereafter that long-dormant practice became a regular feature of all her recitals.

Mildner, Poldi (1915–   ), Austrian.

Gilels, Emil (1916–   ), Russian. This great Soviet pianist made his debut at the age of thirteen, but continued his studies, not entering the international competitions or giving concerts extensively until his early twenties. Not until the cultural exchange agreement of 1955 between the United States and the Soviet Union was this outstanding artist able to appear in this country. He made an unforgettable impression, and immediately was accepted as one of the greatest living piano virtuosi. In 1969 his nineteen-year-old daughter Elena (1950–   ) played piano on the same program with her father. His was a hard act to precede; she was adjudged far from being her father's equal, but promising, nevertheless.

Lipatti, Dinu (1917–1950), Rumanian.

Friedlander, Daniel (1918–1936), American.

List, Eugene (1919–   ), American. He made his brilliant New York debut at the age of seventeen, but he became a household word as a result of his Second World War experiences. As a sergeant in Army Special Services, he was summoned to play privately at the Potsdam Conference, for Truman, Churchill and Stalin. The lasting impression made by his playing in the grand manner resulted in many appearances at the White House, along with world-wide notoriety, and helped establish List as one of the outstanding pianists of his generation.

Kapell, William (1922–1953), American.

Larrocha, Alicia de (1923–   ), Spanish. She first appeared in public at the age of five. Perhaps the finest interpreter today of Spanish music, she wasn't permitted to play it at all until she was fifteen. Critic Harold Schonberg has called her technique "stupendous. This tiny Spanish woman is pianistically flawless, with infallible fingers, brilliant sonorities, steady rhythm, everything." In addition to her international playing career, she is head of a prominent music conservatory in Barcelona.

Pennario, Leonard (1924–   ), American. It was hearing Sergei Rachmaninoff play that determined eight-year-old Leonard to pursue a concert career. By the age of twelve he had made his debut with the Dallas Symphony Orchestra on one week's notice as an emergency replacement. His New York debut at nineteen was in Second World War Air Force uniform, and marked him as a "sensationally brilliant pianist." After several years in the armed services he resumed his career, which had suffered from the interruption. Mixed reviews that spoke of immaturity and lack of restraint gave way in time to excellent ones, so that by 1960 Pennario had gained a place among America's foremost pianists, noted for his exuberance and brilliance both in person and on his numerous recordings.

Istomin, Eugene (1925–   ), American. He won two major contests the year he was seventeen, which meant that his debut with the New York Philharmonic came just a week after he played with the Philadelphia Orchestra. In later years he became especially well-known for his work in chamber music with violinist Isaac Stern and Leonard Rose, cellist.

Janis, Byron (1928–), American.

Graffman, Gary (1928–), American. He is an example of a prodigy who was purposely withdrawn from the concert stage to ensure a normal adolescence. His impressive debut at the age of eleven led the *New York Times* music critic to say he played "with a searching style and an almost uncanny amount of musical understanding and poetry for a child of his years." Between simultaneous music study at Curtis Institute and general studies, baseball and football, his was a full life. When he made his "official" debut at nineteen that balanced background perhaps was responsible for what one critic called "a lack of platform pizzazz." That did not prevent Graffman from becoming, on quality alone, one of today's outstanding pianists.

Weissenberg, Alexis ("Sigi") (1929–), Bulgarian.

Gould, Glenn (1932–), Canadian. At the age of twelve, he was the youngest student ever to graduate from the Royal Conservatory of Music in Toronto. At fourteen he made his concert debut with the Toronto Symphony and was acclaimed as a finished, mature concert artist. It was only after several years that he played in the United States and elsewhere, becoming the first North American artist to play in the Soviet Union. Equally with his reputation as one of the greatest Bach interpreters grew his reputation as an oddball, a man very unhappy about personal concert appearances, and with hypochondriac tendencies. Success enabled him to abandon the concert stage altogether. For many years now he has confined himself to recordings which are avidly sought after by his large following.

Laszlo, Erwin (1933–), Hungarian.

Sorel, Claudette (1933–), American. At age fourteen, she was the youngest graduate (with highest honors) from the Juilliard School. She had made her New York debut at ten, appearing with the New York Philharmonic at eleven. She has had a very active and successful career, playing with over seventy-five orchestras, winning many competitions, participating in numerous festivals, and teaching extensively.

Frager, Malcolm (1935–), American. He had already made his debut at age ten, won several piano prizes, and undertaken a European concert tour by the time he graduated with honors from college (his major was languages, not music). After an interruption for military service, he resumed a brilliant career. As the *New York Times* once said, "There can be no doubt of his place among the top pianists of his generation."

Ponti, Michael (1938?–   ), American.

Bishop, Stephen (1940–   ), American, has spent most of his life in England. His first solo recital took place when he was eleven years old; at thirteen he appeared with the San Francisco Symphony. Bishop was the last student of the great English pianist Dame Myra Hess. By now he has a fine reputation on both sides of the Atlantic.

Goode, Richard (1943–   ), American.

Towlen, Gary (1943?–   ), American. A New Yorker, he made his debut at age twelve, but continued his formal education, graduating from college at twenty. He has since received many grants and decorations, and has performed abroad and in the United States from the time he was fifteen.

Ruskin, Abbott (1943–   ), American.

Fields, James (1948–   ), American.

Perahia, Murray (1948–   ), American.

Pierson, James (1948–   ), American.

Sokolov, Grigory (1950?–   ), Russian, is one of the leading young Soviet pianists. He made his debut at age ten, and won the Gold Medal in the 1966 Tschaikovsky Competition in Moscow. He has shown a particular affinity for the romantic repertoire, and has what has been cited as "an astounding technique and imagination."

Hutchinson, Karen (1952?–   ), American.

Engrum, Elaine (1959–   ), American.

Rolle, Tony (1962?–   ), American. *Ebony* Magazine dubbed this black youngster a "fledgling virtuoso." At the age of eight, he had two years of study behind him and had already appeared on television, on both the Sonny Fox and the Johnny Carson shows. Whether he will in time make his mark on the concert stage remains in the realm of speculation.

Aconcha, Leandro (1966?–   ), Spanish. He can hardly be called a prodigy yet, but may be one of the future. Son of Colombian concert pianist Roberto Aconcha, he has already displayed the exceptional ear, ability to practice with concentration, dexterity, and even showmanship—all prerequisites for a concert artist. Veteran of two television appearances and a newsreel film, he also played a full recital in Malaga when he was five-and-a-half years old.

VIOLIN

Gaviniès, Pierre (1728–1800), French.

Viotti, Giovanni (1755–1824), Italian.

Linley, Thomas (1756–1778), English.

Kreutzer, Rodolphe (1766–1831), French.

Boucher, Alexandre (1778–1861), French, was once called "that veteran violinist and conjurer." Boucher had played for the French court at the age of six, and made his concert debut at eight. By the time he was eleven he became solo violinist to King Charles IV of Spain, holding that position for almost twenty years. His sensational virtuosity was compared to Paganini's, and he was respected by such musical figures as Beethoven, Liszt, Mendelssohn, Weber and Rossini. But he was an eccentric, almost a charlatan, who traded on his remarkable resemblance to Napoleon for publicity, and resorted to violinistic tricks which marred his musicianship and eventually destroyed his considerable reputation.

Clement, Franz (1780–1842), Austrian.

Spohr, Ludwig (1784–1859), German. He began to compose for his instrument almost as soon as he learned to play it. After early tours as a traveling prodigy throughout Europe, he concentrated on teaching and composing. Some of his studies and a few works are still heard, but most of his prolific compositions have not stood the test of time. In his day he was one of the great violinists, and his autobiography gives an absorbing account of musical life in the early nineteenth century.

Mori, Nicolas (1797–1839), English.

Blagrove, Henry (1811–1872), English.

Ernst, Heinrich (1814–1865), Czech.

Sivori, Camillo (1815–1894), Italian. Paganini's only student.

Vieuxtemps, Henri (1820–1881), Belgian.

Joachim, Joseph (1831–1907), Hungarian.

Rappoldi, Edouard (1831–1903), Austrian.

Thomas, Theodore (1835–1905), American (born in Germany). Coming to the United States when he was ten, Thomas soon became one of the most important figures in American musical life. As a prodigy, he undertook the grueling tours of the makeshift clapboard "concert halls" of America of that time, noting meanwhile the desire to hear serious music as well as the showy circus-like performances that were prevalent. He became America's first important conductor, organizing numerous orchestras and concert series that did much to establish a climate for good music and a native training ground for orchestra musicians.

Sarasate, Pablo (1844–1908), Spanish.

Auer, Leopold (1845–1930), Hungarian. He began supporting his family as a touring prodigy from the time he was thirteen years old. But his greatest impact was made as a teacher. At twenty-three he was the youngest professor at the St. Petersburg Conservatory as well as being the Court soloist for the Russian Czar. The long list of his outstanding students (almost all of whom were prodigies) included Jascha Heifetz, Mischa Elman, Rafael Kubelik, Efrem Zimbalist, Toscha Seidel, Paul Stassevitch, Mischel Piastro and Max Rosen. Many of them performed together in a touching tribute to Auer in 1925, when he celebrated his eightieth birthday. He taught in New York from 1918 until his death.

Wieniawski, Henri (1835–1880), Polish.

Sauret, Emile (1852–1920), French.

Thomson, César (1857–1931), Belgian.

Hubay, Jenö (1858–1937), Hungarian.

Franko, Nahan (1861–1930), American.

Senkrah, Arma (1864–1900), American. She found it helpful, as did many American performers in the nineteenth century, to adopt an exotic foreign name. This she did by dropping the final *s* from her real name "Harkness," and spelling it backwards!

Kneisel, Franz (1865–1926), German (born in Russia).

Tua, Teresina (1867–1955), Italian.

Powell, Maud (1868–1920), American.

Burmester, Willy (1869–1933), German.

Marteau, Henry (1874–1934), French.

Huberman, Bronislaw (1882–1947), Polish. He studied under the famous Joachim, and made a successful tour of Europe when he was eleven years old. It was his playing at the Farewell Concert of the singer Adelina Patti when he was thirteen that brought him overnight fame. Soon after, Johannes Brahms, incensed at first that any mere child would undertake to play his difficult and serious violin concerto, at the actual performance made his way backstage afterwards, deeply moved, to behold and congratulate the youngster who had given such a probing, inward reading of the work. Huberman was responsible, almost singlehandedly, for the founding of the Israel Philharmonic in 1936. It is now one of the great orchestras of the world.

Kochanski, Paul (1887–1934), Russian.

Fradkin, Frederic (1892–1963), American.

Piastro, Mischel (1892–1970), American (born in Russia).

Vecsey, Franz von (1893–1935), Hungarian.

Brown, Eddy (1895–   ), American.

Mischakoff, Mischa (1895–   ), American (born in Russia). He is one of the many prodigies in that prodigious musical family, the Fishbergs, discussed earlier.

Rosen, Max (1899–1956), American (born in Rumania).

Seidel, Toscha (1899–   ), American (born in Russia).

Zimbalist, Efrem (1899–   ), American (born in Russia).

Hilsberg, Alexander (1900–1961), Polish.

Heifetz, Jascha (1901–   ), American (born in Russia). An Auer pupil, he is perhaps the greatest violinist of the twentieth century. His playing has long set the standard by which other violinists are judged. Heifetz's concert presence is austere and almost unnaturally self-composed, his playing devoid of any eccentricity or efforts at showmanship. At the age of sixteen, driven from Russia by the Revolution, he quickly became a musical idol, and was called "a modern miracle," and "the perfect violinist." After semi-retirement for several years, his appearance on television in 1970 showed him to be still the supreme master and aloof practitioner of his art.

Koutzen, Boris (1901–1966), American (born in Russia).

Rubinstein, Erna (1903–   ), Hungarian.

Milstein, Nathan (1904–   ), American (born in Russia).

Francescatti, Zino (1905–   ), French, studied with Sivori, Paganini's only pupil. At the age of ten he made his debut, playing the Beethoven Violin Concerto. At the insistence of his father he abandoned music for the study of law, not resuming his musical career until his father died, when Zino was twenty-two. With his successful debut a year later in Paris Francescatti established himself as a superb violinist with a great international reputation.

Spivakovsky, Tossy (1907–   ), American (born in Russia).

Szeryng, Henryk (1918–   ), Polish.

Stern, Isaac (1920–   ), American. Like Yehudi Menuhin and Ruggiero Ricci, Stern was brought up in San Francisco and made his debut (at the age of eleven) with that city's symphony orchestra. He is an artist of exceptional ability, one of the finest of his generation. Stern has performed and recorded at an almost frenetic pace around the globe in addition to his many other activities. In 1960 he led a campaign which succeeded in saving Carnegie Hall from demolition; he has also been an active member of the National Council on the Arts.

Travers, Patricia (1927–   ), American.

Koutzen, Nadia (1930–   ), American.

Wicks, Camilla (1934–   ), American.

Menga, Robert, (1935–   ), American.

Dubow, Marilyn (1942?–   ), American.

Tsumura, Mari (1946–   ), Japanese.

Pasquier, Regis (1946?–   ), French. He is the youngest of a long line of musicians who have made the name Pasquier famous in French musical circles. His official debut was made at the age of twelve, his

American debut at fourteen. He has already proven himself a worthy successor to his famous father, Pierre Pasquier.

Marcovici, Silvia (1952–   ), Rumanian.

VOCAL

Ferri, Baldassare (1610–1680), Italian. One of the most successful of the *castrati,* he was a very popular performer throughout Italy during his teen years.

Bordoni (Hasse), Faustina (1700–1781), Italian.

Arnould, Sophie (1740–1802), French. She entered what can only be described as a spell on sophisticated Paris. Of the throngs who fought for seats at her concerts, someone well said, "I doubt if they would take such trouble to get into Paradise." Discovered at the age of twelve in a convent by the Princess de Modena, she was sent to the King's Chapel to sing, and was signed within a year for the Opera. She made her debut at seventeen, and held center stage not only at the opera but also for many years in her famous salon (the favorite Paris haunt of Benjamin Franklin). Her unusual wit, indeed, far outlasted her voice, which she abused so much that one critic bitingly remarked on it as "the finest asthma I have ever heard." In the end it was the woman, with her beauty, grace and vivaciousness that made her immortal, rather than her voice.

Billington, Elizabeth (1765–1818), English.

Braham, John (1777–1856), English.

Lablache, Luigi (1794–1858), Italian.

Paton, Mary Anne (1802–1864), English.

Schröder-Devrient, Wilhelmine (1804–1860), German.

Sontag, Henrietta (1806–1854), German.

Grisi, Giulia (1811–1869), Italian.

Lind, Jenny (1820–1887), Swedish.

Marchisio, Barbara (1833–1919), Italian.

Lehmann, Lilli (1848–1929), German.

Hauk, Minnie (1851–1929), American.

Flagstad, Kirsten (1895–1963), Norwegian.

Supervia, Conchita (1890–1936), Spanish. She had an unusually mature voice which enabled her to make her operatic debut at the age of fourteen. At fifteen she sang Carmen at La Scala in Milan, an incredible feat for her age. She was a brilliant, florid singer, but also an excellent actress as well as an interpreter of Spanish folk songs. She eventually settled in London, specializing in the Italian repertoire. A beautiful woman, she also appeared in films up to the time of her early death.

Guilford, Nanette (1906–   ), American.

Talley, Marion (1907–   ), American.

Callas, Maria (1923–   ), Greek. She has been a "front-page" primadonna of our times. Maria had a remarkable voice but little more when she made her debut at sixteen with the National Opera in Greece. Just a year before, according to the soprano with whom she studied in Athens: "The very idea of that girl wanting to become a singer was laughable! She was tall, very fat, and wore heavy glasses. . . . Her whole being was awkward . . . not knowing what to do with her hands, she sat there quietly biting her nails while waiting her turn."

Not until she reached the age of twenty-four did Maria Callas overcome her difficulties and score her first successes. Eventually she became one of the most listened to, as well as the most talked about, of all singers—as notable for her temperament as for the authority and command of her singing of the Italian opera repertoire.

Alberghetti, Anna Maria (1936–   ), American (born in Italy). When she was six years old, her father, desperate to leave the island of Rhodes during the Second World War, hired a hundred-piece orchestra to accompany her. Her singing charmed the local government official into allowing her and her family to escape from the war-torn island on the last available plane. Her New York debut at fourteen was hailed "with incredulity and delight," as that of a real *"wunderkind."* Her appearance on television the same year elicited over four thousand telephone calls. She scored her greatest singing and acting success in the Broadway musical *Carnival* in 1961. She has since had an active career in movies, the concert stage and night clubs.

Arroyo, Martina (1936–   ), American.

NON-CLASSICAL PRODIGIES

COMPOSITION

Ellington, Edward ("Duke") (1899–   ), American, was the first jazz composer to experiment successfully with larger forms in such extended compositions as *Black, Brown and Beige,* and others. A pioneer in both composition and arranging, he began as a ragtime "stride" pianist in his native Washington, D.C., playing house parties, "parlor socials," and society and embassy affairs while in his teens. His first composition was called *Soda Fountain Rag.* From his earliest playing days he began integrating the older piano tradition, with its multi-ryhthms and displaced accents, with the style of big band music. He made jazz, both improvised and composed, acceptable to a wide audience of both races.

Monk, Thelonius (1918–   ), American. This important composer and pianist was responsible for a great change in jazz—away from the set patterns of the swing era and toward bop. The result is now called modern jazz, and he may rightly be called its father. The depth and complexity of his ideas, his choppy beat, odd accents, and surprising skips were considered weird, far out, and gained the respect and acceptance of other professionals long before public recognition. Eccentric in his stage behavior, Monk has been called both "an unpredictable sideshow," and "a pure, individual artist of undoubted integrity."

He began playing as a teen-ager in community centers, at Depression rent parties, saloons and with a traveling evangelist. In his late teens appreciative fellow musicians formed a kind of "cult" around his ideas and style. His influence has been strong on such leading figures in modern jazz as John Coltrane and Sonny Rollins, among others.

Mingus, Charles (1922–   ), American. Composer, double bass, piano, etc.

Williams, Hank (1923–1953), American, was the most popular white writer of country music. He had his own string band at the age of thirteen, and his own radio show soon after, for which he wrote a new song every week. Hank wrote quickly, carelessly, often selling his songs outright to other singers. His short hectic life was a tragic composite of early alcoholism, aimless drifting in and out of musical and other jobs, economic hardship. His recordings, more than twenty years after his early death, still sell in the millions.

Holly, Buddy (1939?–1959), American.

Cochran, Eddie (1939?–1960), American.

Valens, Richard (1940–1959), American.

Beatles, The (English). **John Lennon** (1940–   ), was seventeen and **Paul McCartney** (1942–   ), fifteen years of age when they first collaborated as songwriters. Of the over one hundred songs they wrote that first year, only one, *Love Me Do,* was recorded (six years later), and quickly became an English hit. When **George Harrison** (1943–   ) left school to join the group he was not yet sixteen. Discovery of his true age led to his deportation from Germany, where the group had been playing.

At the time when the "Beatles" name was adopted in 1959 Lennon was nineteen, McCartney seventeen and Harrison sixteen. The fourth member, Ringo Starr, joined the group later. What has been called "Beatlemania" hit the United States from their first appearance in 1964. Strongly influenced by Elvis Presley, by their skiffle-band experiences, American country music and English music-hall ballads, they revolutionized rock music as well as fashions and life-styles. Their better compositions came later in their careers, and were interpreted by all kinds of rock and jazz singers from Aretha Franklin to Peggy Lee to Ella Fitzgerald. The sound of their instrumental style also had considerable influence on other groups. After breaking up as an act, they have achieved individual success in writing and performing. Whether dabbling in art, film, religion or political opinion they have continued individually to command an enormous following.

Avalon, Frankie (1942?–   ), American.

Lymon, Frankie (1943–1967), American.

Ian, Janis (1951–   ), American. She started writing and singing her own songs about teen-age dilemmas for five dollars a night in Greenwich Village coffeehouses when she was about fourteen years old. A year later her song about interracial dating, *Society's Child,* was banned by most radio stations, but was performed by her on a Leonard Bernstein television show. It catapulted her to fame. It was a song of insight which she performed sensitively. At the time it was thought by some that she was a new musical spokesman for her generation.

Several records and a film score later Janis, still in her early twenties, has not duplicated the impact of her early hit.

FAMILY GROUPS

Brubeck family, American. The three sons of pianist-composer Dave Brubeck each displayed talent, and began playing, separately and together, very early. **Darius** (1947–   ) plays piano and guitar; **Chris** (1952–   ) plays trombone, keyboard instruments, double bass and guitar; **Daniel** (1955–   ) plays percussion. As long ago as 1964, when they were seventeen, twelve and nine years old respectively, they played as a group in a New York festival, and made a record. Since 1971 Daniel has been playing in Darius's group. Chris has formed his own group, called "New Heavenly Blue," which had been scheduled to perform at the Newport Jazz Festival, and recorded for Atlantic Records in 1972. Plans are under way for all three groups—the father's, Darius's and Chris's—to combine for a live performance and a recording in 1973.

Bender Brothers (born 1954, 1956, 1957, 1959), Virgin Islanders. These four young boys from the island of St. Kitts in the Caribbean demonstrated great skill in a concert on steel drums in 1970. Aged sixteen, fourteen, thirteen and eleven respectively, at the time, their program included arrangements of Bach works as well as more traditional Latin music. They showed undoubted musicianship on their unusual instruments.

GUITAR

Walker, Aaron ("T-bone") (1913–   ), American, is a blues singer who began making records at the age of sixteen. It is as a guitarist that he has made his greatest impact, pioneering in the use of the electric guitar for blues. An extremely skilled, dazzling performer, he has had an enormous influence on younger guitarists such as B. B. King.

Campbell, Glenn (1938–   ), American, is a virtuoso twelve-string guitarist, having played that instrument from the age of six, later adding mandolin, banjo and bass. At the age of fourteen he began to play night clubs, high-school proms, rodeos, and was soon recognized as one of the best guitarists in the Western bands. A very respected "session" (recordings and film) guitarist, he added country-flavor singing to his playing to reach great heights of popularity via television, personal appearances and recordings.

KEYBOARD (PIANO AND ORGAN)

Morton, Ferdinand ("Jelly Roll") (1885–1941), American.

Garner, Erroll (1921–   ), American. Perhaps the most commercially successful of all jazz pianists, Erroll still plays entirely by ear, since he doesn't read music. At the age of seven he played regularly on a Pittsburgh radio station. By his teens he had begun to win recognition for the individuality of his piano style. "I just hear a sound coming into my head, and hope to catch it with my hands," he has said. In 1957 he tried his hand at an extended classical composition, dictated to a fellow musician who wrote it down. But he won jazz immortality with his fine song *Misty*. He was the first jazz artist to come under classical concert management, and has brought his spontaneous style and relaxed informality to all kinds of live audiences in addition to his numerous recordings.

Loussier, Jacques (1934–   ), French.

Robinson, Frank ("Sugar-Chile") (1939?–   ), American.

Preston, Billy (1946–   ), American. Essentially an organist, Billy played the role of W. C. Handy (composer of *St. Louis Blues)* as a boy, in the movie of that name. From his earliest teens on he has supported with his fluent and dynamic organ-playing such performers as Ray Charles, The Beatles, Aretha Franklin, and the foremost gospel singing groups. In 1972 he brought his combination of infectious theatricality and spectacular musicianship to a concert benefit for Bangladesh; he thus added a new group of rock fans to his devoted gospel following.

Hundley, Craig (1953?–   ), American. The original Craig Hundley Trio played on network television and in big night clubs when its founder was fourteen and his sidemen fourteen and twelve years old. Craig began studying classical piano at the age of nine. By the time he was twelve he switched to jazz and also began a career as a child actor in films. When he made recordings (with his trio) from the age of fifteen on, he was considered a real original, able to blend classical and jazz ideas into a new sound. Still very young, he is one of the fine new pianists of the jazz world.

Peterson, "Lucky" (1956?–), American.

PERCUSSION

Williams, Tony (1947?–), American, is one of the brilliant young drummers, having played jazz-oriented rock and pure jazz incomparably since he was seventeen years old. That was the year he joined Miles Davis's group. He started drumming in his father's band when he was nine, and sat in with leading drummers whenever they came to town. He has his own group now, called "Tony Williams Lifetime," which is dominated by his original and sophisticated mastery of his instrument. He even uses amplification imaginatively to increase the range of his drum effects.

Miles, Barry (1948?–), American, started out as a jazz drummer, an eleven-year-old child wonder who led his own group of adult musicians, earning the early recognition and respect of the professional jazz world. By the time he was twenty-one and a senior at Princeton University he had switched to the piano, and wrote everything his group played except for a few standard tunes he used for his piano solos. Critic John S. Wilson admired the agile, flowing bright sound, and predicted a brilliant career for Barry. In 1971 his fourteen-year-old brother Terry Silverlight joined him on the drums and was adjudged even better than his older brother had been at the same age.

VOCAL

Rainey, Gertrude ("Ma") (1886–1939), American.

Smith, Bessie (1898–1939), American.

Turner, Joe (1911–), American. From Kansas City, he has played piano and shouted out his blues in a way that has come to be identified as the "Kansas City style." It took him a long time to succeed in New York, but he finally did, in a "Spirituals to Swing" program produced in 1938 by John Hammond. Some of his rock songs have helped make the reputation of more famous singers, and are standards in the rock field.

Johnson, Robert (1914?–1938), American, was a blues singer who died at the age of twenty-four. Even so, he managed to be an important influence, through recordings he made from the age of eighteen on, on such later groups as Cream, Led Zeppelin, Bonnie and Delaney, as well as on other blues singers such as Muddy Waters and Albert King. His singing was characterized by what one critic has called "an unusual type of tortured intensity."

Garland, Judy (1922–1969), American, was raised in the theatre; both her parents were in vaudeville and she appeared on the stage before she was three. Untrained, her voice from the time she was ten was resonant and "big," reaching out to live audiences in a way that was called "poignant and unforgettable."

From the age of fifteen on she was a movie star, with a natural flair for acting as well as singing. When she was seventeen her singing of *Over the Rainbow* in the movie *The Wizard of Oz* became a classic of popular music—few singers have dared attempt it since. The pressures of adolescent stardom were too strong for Judy. By the time she was eighteen she was already resorting to pills; her adult life was marked by five marriages, many illnesses, a suicide attempt, and numerous "comebacks" which were harrowing experiences in nostalgia for her devoted fans.

The girl who had been one of the most famous and beloved entertainment personalities by the time she was twenty died at the age of forty-seven. Something of her charisma and voice quality can be detected in the singing of her daughter, **Liza Minnelli** (1946–   ).

Short, Robert ("Bobby") (1926–   ), American. This black singer-pianist never had a music lesson and still doesn't read music. But his following, in intimate supper clubs where he establishes a close rapport with his audience, is large and devoted, including other entertainers, the jet set, visiting royalty, and musicians of all kinds. His strong brilliant voice and, especially, his artful projection of all the nuances and subtleties of the lyrics of every song he sings, have made him the greatest interpreter of Cole Porter songs, among many other genres.

Bobby began singing professionally, in white tie and tails, when he was ten, singing and accompanying himself in popular songs in local roadhouses around the Midwest and at private parties in big Chicago hotels. For three years he was on the vaudeville circuit, often billed as the "Miniature King of Swing"; at twelve, during this lonely period, he shuttled between two New York night clubs at the same time. He wisely decided to return to high school after that, since he was too young to be believable singing the kind of material he was best suited for.

Tucker, Ira (1926?–   ), American, was a headliner in the leading

New York jazz night club when he was seventeen. His roots, to which he later returned, were in gospel singing; he brought to it a new element of showmanship. His early recordings show him already to be a great stylist. His influence on such soul singers as James Brown was enormous.

Clark, Petula (1934–   ), English. She didn't become well-known in the United States until after she was thirty. She had been a child star on English radio and in films, and had had her own radio program at the age of nine. Her first recording, issued simultaneously in French and English when she was fifteen, made her an overnight star in Europe.

Penniman, Richard ("Little Richard") (1935–   ), American.

Presley, Elvis (1935–   ), American, was seventeen years old when he recorded for his private use *That's All Right,* a hillbilly country song with a rocking beat. Its primitive blues quality, once a major recording company issued it, made both the song and the singer immediately well-known. Elvis was a millionaire by the time he was twenty-one, his fortune built on a mixed bag of popular songs of little value and country songs of largely black origin to which he added a strong rhythm beat. That merger, first known as "rockabilly," later was named "rock 'n' roll." His importance lay in the fact that he was the white country singer who was most responsible for initiating the young white mass audience into black music in a form that was palatable to them and hastened the eventual acceptance of black performers.

Knight, Gladys (1944–   ), American. Like Aretha Franklin, she began as a gospel singer in a family group. She was fourteen when she joined the "Pips" to sing at local affairs. She brought the very essence of soul into her recordings of popular songs. As many as two million copies of some of her records were bought.

Lee, Brenda (1946?–   ), American.

Cassidy, David (1950–   ), American.

Dyson, Ronnie (1950–   ), American.

Wyman, Karen (1952–   ), American.

Jones, Tommy (1956?–   ), American.

Bryant, Browning (1957?–   ), American.

WOODWIND AND BRASS

Bechet, Sidney (1897–1959), American. The clarinetist and soprano saxophonist came out of the same New Orleans period as Louis Armstrong, but was of a French-speaking Creole family. He taught himself clarinet by borrowing his brother's instrument to practice on secretly. An intuitive musician, he relied almost entirely on his ear and his largely home-grown technique to begin playing professional engagements when he was ten. By the time he was fourteen he was in the renowned Bunk Johnson Band (and was brought home personally by the bandleader every night!)

When he was twenty-two Bechet discovered the soprano saxophone while in England, and thereafter became the outstanding exponent of that instrument. He spent the major part of his life in Paris, where his enormous popularity led one admirer to say that he "could be elected Mayor of Paris tomorrow if he wanted to run." One of the founders of jazz, he became a living legend in a France which, during his lifetime, was more receptive to black jazz performers than was the United States.

Shaw, Artie (1910–   ), American. Clarinetist.

James, Harry (1916–   ), American. This trumpeter began as a contortionist in the circus in which both of his parents performed; by the age of nine he was in the circus band, and by the time he was twelve he was leading it. In Texas, he won a state contest for trumpet-playing, and soon began sitting-in with dance bands all over the Southwest, going on the road from the age of fifteen on. By the time he graduated from Benny Goodman's band he was featuring a lyrical, singing trumpet style rather than the "hot" trumpet style more prevalent at the time.

His sensational appearance in New York in 1943, which caused a theater riot of mammoth proportions, marked the high point of his popularity and of the swing era of which he was an important participant.

Getz, Stan (1927–   ), American. A tenor saxophonist, while in high school in New York he played with every kind of local band, but meanwhile also played jazz after hours at all-night jam sessions. He left high school at sixteen to go on the road with Jack Teagarden's band. Later, he played with Jimmy Dorsey, Benny Goodman, Woody Herman and others, forming his first band of his own when he was twenty. But while becoming the most famous leader of the new "cool" jazz style he was also, unfortunately, becoming a heroin addict, which broke his spell of success until he was cured. In 1962 he rose to fame again on the wave of "bossa nova" (a Brazilian beat), and has since regained his appeal to a large audience.

Kirk, Andy (1932–   ), American. This alto saxophonist was a talented youth who could play any reed instrument and read anything put before him. He was considered heir to the great alto tradition of Charlie Parker, whose protegé he was. A heroin addict, he stopped playing completely at the age of twenty, but was cured and has made a comeback in recent years. He is now playing and writing for his own group.

Kloss, Eric (1950?–   ), American. A blind saxophonist who recorded his first album at the age of fifteen. He plays mostly around the Caribbean islands.

Tomasso, Enrico (1963?–   ), English. In 1971, at eight years of age, accompanied by his fourteen-year-old brother on piano, he was able to play trumpet and sing enough like Louis Armstrong and Muggsy Spanier to impress public and critics in a New York night club. He also taped a number of television appearances before returning with his family to England.

Select Bibliography

The following books were written by prodigies themselves, thus providing firsthand insights into their careers.

ARMSTRONG, LOUIS. *Satchmo: My Life in New Orleans.* Prentice-Hall, Inc., Englewood Cliffs, N.J., 1954.

AUER, LEOPOLD. *My Long Life in Music.* Frederick A. Stokes Company, New York, 1923.

BAUER, HAROLD. *Harold Bauer: His Book.* Greenwood Press, Westport, Conn., 1969. Repr. from 1948 ed.

BECHET, SIDNEY. *Treat It Gentle.* Hill and Wang, New York, 1961.

BUSCH, FRITZ. *Pages from a Musician's Life,* tr. Margaret Strachey. Hogarth Press, London, 1953.

CASALS, PABLO. *Joys and Sorrows: Reflections by Pablo Casals,* as told to Albert E. Kahn. Simon and Schuster, New York, 1970.

CHALIAPIN, FEODOR. *Chaliapin: An Autobiography, as told to Maxim Gorky.* Stein & Day, New York, 1967.

FARRAR, GERALDINE. *The Autobiography of Geraldine Farrar: Such Sweet Compulsion.* Da Capo Press 1970. Repr. from 1939 ed.

GOODMAN, BENNY and IRVING KOLODIN. *The Kingdom of Swing.* Frederick Ungar Publishing Co. New York, 1961. Repr. from 1939 ed.

GOUNOD, CHARLES. *Autobiographical Reminiscences with Family Letters and Notes on Music.* Da Capo Press, New York, 1970. Repr. of 1896 ed.

HAMBOURG, MARK. *From Piano to Forte: A Thousand and One Notes.* Cassell and Company, Ltd., London, 1931.

HAUK, MINNIE. *Memoirs of a Singer.* A. M. Philpot, Ltd., London, 1925.

HOFFMAN, RICHARD. *Some Musical Recollections of Fifty Years.* Charles Scribner's Sons, New York, 1910.

HOLIDAY, BILLIE, with WILLIAM DUFTY. *Lady Sings the Blues.* Doubleday & Company, Garden City, New York, 1956.

LEHMANN, LILLI. *My Path through Life,* tr. Alice Benedict Seligman. G. P. Putnam's Sons, New York, 1914.

LEVANT, OSCAR. *The Unimportance of Being Oscar.* G. P. Putnam's Sons, New York, 1968.

PIATIGORSKY, GREGOR. *Cellist.* Doubleday & Company, Inc., Garden City, N.Y., 1965.

RUBINSTEIN, ANTON. *Autobiography.* Haskell, 1969. Repr. from 1890 ed.

SAINT-SAËNS, CAMILLE. *Musical Memories,* tr. Edwin Gile Rich. Da Capo Press, New York 1969. Repr. from 1919 ed.

SCHNABEL, ARTUR. *My Life and Music.* St. Martin's Press, New York, 1963.

SCHUYLER, PHILIPPA. *Adventure in Black and White.* R. Speller, New York, 1960.

SHORT, BOBBY. *Black and White Baby.* Dodd, Mead & Co., New York, 1971.

SLENCZYNSKA, RUTH. *Forbidden Childhood.* Doubleday & Company, Garden City, New York, 1957.

SMITH, WILLIE THE LION, with GEORGE HOEFER. *Music on My Mind: The Memoirs of an American Pianist.* Doubleday & Company, Inc. Garden City, New York, 1964.

SPOHR, LOUIS. *Musical Journals of Louis Spohr,* tr. Henry Pleasants. University of Oklahoma Press, Norman, 1961. Repr. from 1878 ed.

SZIGETI, JOSEPH. *With Strings Attached: Reminiscences and Reflections.* Alfred A. Knopf, New York, 2nd ed., rev. & enl., 1967.

THOMAS, THEODORE. *A Musical Autobiography,* ed. George P. Upton. Da Capo Press, New York, 1964. Reprint.

WALTER, BRUNO. *Theme and Variations: An Autobiography,* tr. James Galston. Alfred A. Knopf, New York, 1946.

The following is a selection of biographies of composers and performers who were prodigies:

ARNOLD, DENIS and NIGEL FORTUNE, eds. *The Monteverdi Companion.* Faber and Faber, London, 1968.

BOWEN, CATHERIN DRINKER. *"Free Artist." The Story of Anton Rubinstein and Nicholas Rubinstein.* Random House, New York, 1939.

DANCE, STANLEY. *The World of Duke Ellington.* Charles Scribner's Sons, New York, 1970.

DAVIES, HUNTER. *The Beatles: The Authorized Biography.* McGraw-Hill Book Company, New York, 1968.

DEAN, WINTON. *Georges Bizet: His Life and Work.* J. M. Dent & Sons, Ltd., London, 1965.

DENT, EDWARD J. *Handel.* Kennikat Press, Inc., Port Washington, N.Y., 1971. Repr. from 1934 ed.

DUKE, VERNON (VLADIMIR DUKELSKY). *Passport to Paris.* Little, Brown and Company, Boston, 1955.

ELMAN, SAUL. *Memoirs of Mischa Elman's Father: S. Elman.* Privately printed, New York, 1933.

EWEN, DAVID. *George Gershwin: His Journey to Greatness.* Prentice-Hall, Englewood Cliffs, N.J., rev. ed. 1970.

FENBY, ERIC. *Menuhin's House of Music.* Praeger, New York, 1970.

FITZLYON, APRIL. *The Price of Genius: A Life of Pauline Viardot.* Appleton-Century, New York, 1964.

FLOWER, NEWMAN. *Franz Schubert & His Circle.* Dufour Editions, Inc. Chester Springs, Pa., 1949.

GAL, HANS. *Johannes Brahms: His Work and Personality,* tr. Joseph Stein. Alfred A. Knopf, New York, 1963.

GEIRINGER, KARL, with IRENE G. GEIRINGER. *Johann Sebastian Bach: The Culmination of an Era.* Oxford University Press, New York, 1966.

————. *Haydn: A Creative Life in Music.* University of California Press, rev. ed. 1968.

HALLE, C. E. and MARIE HALLE (his son and daughter), eds. *The Life and Letters of Sir Charles Hallé.* Smith, Elder & Co., London, 1896.

HARDING, BETTINA. *Concerto: The Glowing Story of Clara Schumann.* The Bobbs-Merrill Company, Inc., New York, 1961.

HARDING, JAMES. *Saint-Saëns and His Circle.* Chapman & Hall, London, 1965.

HOLST, IMOGEN. *Britten.* Thomas Y. Crowell Company, New York, 1966.

HOPKINS, JERRY. *Elvis.* Simon & Schuster, New York, 1971.

HOWARD, JOHN TASKER. *Stephen Foster: America's Troubadour.* Thomas Y. Crowell Company, New York, 1953.

JACOB, H. E. *Johann Strauss: Father and Son. A Century of Light Music,* tr. Marguerite Wolff. Halcyon House, Garden City, New York, 1939.

KIRKEBY, ED. *Ain't Misbehavin': The Story of Fats Waller.* Dodd, Mead, New York, 1966.

KIRKPATRICK, RALPH. *Domenico Scarlatti.* Princeton University Press, Princeton, N. J., 1953.

KOBALD, KARL. *Franz Schubert and His Times,* tr. Beatrice Marshall. Kennikat Press, Port Washington, N.Y., 1970. Reissued from 1928 ed.

LANG, PAUL HENRY. *George Frideric Handel.* W. W. Norton & Company, Inc., New York, 1966.

LARGE, BRIAN. *Smetana.* Duckworth, London, 1970.

LOGGINS, VERNON. *Where the Word Ends: The Life of Louis Moreau Gottschalk.* Louisiana State University Press, Baton Rouge, La., 1958.

LOMAX, ALAN. *Mister Jelly Roll: The Fortunes of Jelly Roll Morton, New Orleans Creole and "Inventor of Jazz."* Cassell & Company, Ltd., London, 1952.

MAGIDOFF, ROBERT. *Yehudi Menuhin: The Story of the Man and the Musician.* Doubleday & Company, Inc., Garden City, N.Y., 1955.

MAREK, GEORGE R. *Beethoven: Biography of a Genius.* Funk & Wagnalls, New York, 1969.

————. *Gentle Genius: The Story of Felix Mendelssohn.* Funk & Wagnalls, New York, 1972.

————. *Richard Strauss: The Life of a Non-Hero.* Simon and Schuster, New York, 1967.

OLIVER, PAUL. *Bessie Smith.* A. S. Barnes and Company, Inc., New York, 1961. Repr. from 1959 ed.

PEARCE, CHARLES E. *Sims Reeves: Fifty Years of Music in England.* Stanley Paul & Co., Ltd., London, 1924.

POUGIN, ARTHUR. *Maria Malibran: The Story of a Great Singer.* Eveleigh Nash, London, 1911.

PULVER, JEFFREY. *Paganini: The Romantic Virtuoso.* Plenum Publishing Corp., New York, 1970. Repr. from 1934 ed.

RONZE-NEVEU, M. J. *Ginette Neveu,* tr. Joyce L. Kemp. Rockliff, London, 1957.

SEROFF, VICTOR. *Franz Liszt.* The Macmillan Company, New York, 1966.

————. *Sergei Prokofiev: A Soviet Tragedy.* Funk & Wagnalls, New York, 1968.

————, with NADEJDA GALLI-SHOHAT. *Dmitri Shostakovich: The Life and Background of a Soviet Composer.* Books for Libraries Press, Freeport, New York, 1970. Reprinted from 1943 ed.

SHULTZ, GLADYS. *Jenny Lind: The Swedish Nightingale.* J. B. Lippincott, Philadelphia, 1962.

SITWELL, SACHEVERELL. *Liszt.* Cassell & Company, Ltd., London, 1955.

SMITH, MOSES. *Koussevitzky.* Allen, Towne & Heath, Inc., New York, 1947.

STEFAN, PAUL. *Anton Dvorak,* tr. Y. W. Vance. Da Capo Press, New York, 1971. Unabr. Repub. from 1948 ed.

TAUBMAN, HOWARD. *The Maestro: The Life of Arturo Toscanini.* Simon & Schuster, New York, 1951.

TORME, MEL, *The Other Side of the Rainbow, with July Garland on the Dawn Patrol.* William Morrow & Co., New York, 1970.

TURNER, W. J. *Mozart: The Man and His Works.* Tudor Publishing Co., New York, 1938.

WARRACK, JOHN. *Carl Maria von Weber.* The Macmillan Company, New York, 1968.

WEINSTOCK, HERBERT. *Chopin: The Man and His Music.* Alfred A. Knopf, New York, 1965.

————. *Rossini: A Biography.* Alfred A. Knopf, New York, 1968.

WILLIAMS, ROGER. *Sing a Sad Song: The Life of Hank Williams.* Doubleday and Company, Garden City, New York, 1970.

ZIMMERMAN, FRANKLIN B. *Henry Purcell, 1659–1695: His Life and Times.* St. Martin's Press, New York, 1967.

Index of Names

Aconcha, Leandro, 216–217
Albeniz, Isaac, 50–51
Alberghetti, Anna Maria, 222
Albert, Eugen d', 210
Alfidi, Joseph, 200
Alkan, Henri, 182
Anka, Paul, 147
Armstrong, Louis, 135, 137–142
Arnould, Sophie, 221
Arrau, Claudio, 166, 187
Arriaga, Juan, 110
Arriola, Pepito, 212
Arroyo, Martina, 222
Ashkenazy, Vladimir, 188
Aspull, George, 110
Auber, Daniel, 71, 182
Auer, Leopold, 171, 218
Avalon, Frankie, 224
Bach, Johann Christian, 19
Bach, Johann Sebastian, 15–16
Backhaus, Wilhelm, 211
Barber, Samuel, 180
Barbosa-Lima, Antonio-Carlos, 202
Barenboim, Daniel, 112, 189
Barnett, John, 209
Bauer, Harold, 112, 205
Beach, Amy ("Mrs. H.H.A."), 210
Beatles, the, 224
Bechet, Sidney, 230
Beethoven, Ludwig Van, 208
Behrend, Louise, 191
Belleville-Oury, Anne, 176, 209
Bender Brothers, 225
Bennett, William Sterndale, 204
Benzi, Robert, 88
Billington, Elizabeth, 221
Bishop, Stephen, 216
Bizet, Georges, 198–199
Björling, Jussi, 163
Blagrove, Henry, 217
Blahetka, Leopoldine, 209
Blind Tom, 69–72

Bochsa, Robert, 202
Bohrer, Sophie, 209
Bordoni (Hasse), Faustina, 221
Borge, Victor, 111
Boucher, Alexander, 217
Braham, John, 221
Brahms, Johannes, 40, 205
Brain, Dennis, 202
Bream, Julian, 108, 201
Bridgetower, George, 37
Bronsart, Ingeborg von, 205
Brott, Boris, 200
Brown, Eddy, 219
Brubeck family, 225
Bryant, Browning, 229
Bülow, Hans von, 47, 209
Burco, Ferruccio, 87–88
Burke, Joseph, 81
Burmester, Willy, 219
Busoni, Ferruccio, 187
Buswell, James Oliver, IV, 128
Callas, Maria, 222
Campbell, Glenn, 225–226
Carreño, Teresa, 48, 176
Casadesus, Robert, 212
Casals, Pablo, 105–106
Cassadó, Gaspar, 196
Cassidy, David, 229
Castagnetta, Grace, 213
Castleman, Charles, 172, 183
Chaliapin, Feodor, 12, 59–60
Charles, Ray, 157–158
Cherkassky, Shura, 213
Cherniavsky family, 201
Cherubini, Luigi, 30–31
Chopin, Frédéric, 23, 204
Christian, Charles, 148–150
Clark, Petula, 229
Clauss-Szarvady, Wilhelmine, 209
Clement, Franz, 217
Clementi, Muzio, 203
Cochran, Eddie, 224

Cohen, Harriet, 212
Cooke, Thomas, 203
Cooper, George, 208
Couperin, François ("le Grand"), 207
Cowen, Frederic, 199
Cramer, Johann, 208
Crotch, William, 203
Curzon, Clifford, 174
Czerny, Carl, 43, 181
Daquin, Louis, 207
David (Biblical), 110
Dengremont, Maurice, 111
Dohnanyi, Ernst von, 206
Domb, Daniel, 197
Donizetti, Gaetano, 198
Dragonetti, Domenico, 200
Dubow, Marilyn, 220
Duke (Dukelsky), Vernon, 113-114
DuPré, Jacqueline, 112
Dupré, Marcel, 208
Dyson, Ronnie, 229
Echaniz, José, 213
Ellington, Edward ("Duke"), 223
Elman, Mischa, 171, 186
Enesco, Georges, 172
Engrum, Elaine, 216
Ernst, Heinrich, 217
Eto, Toshiya, 191
Farinelli (Carlo Broschi), 57-58
Farrar, Geraldine, 66-68
Feliciano, José, 159-160
Ferri, Baldassare, 221
Feuermann, Emanuel, 196
Field, John, 187
Fields, James, 216
Filtsch, Karl, 110
Fitzgerald, Ella, 151-152
Flagstad, Kirsten, 222
Fleisher, Leon, 172, 186
Forqueray, Antoine, 196
Foss, Lukas, 206
Foster, Lawrence, 130
Foster, Stephen, 198
Fradkin, Frederic, 219
Frager, Malcolm, 215-216
Francescatti, Zino, 220
Franklin, Aretha, 153-154
Franko, Nahan, 218
Friedheim, Arthur, 210
Friedlander, Daniel, 214
Friedman, Erick, 172
Friedman, Ignaz, 211
Galamian, Ivan, 172
Gamba, Pierino, 87
Gampel, Lilit, 191-192
Ganz, Rudolph, 206
Garbusova, Raya, 196
García, Manuel, 61
Garland, Judy, 228
Garner, Erroll, 226

Gaviniès, Pierre, 217
Gérardy, Jean, 196
Gershwin, George, 199-200
Getz, Stan, 230-231
Gilels, Emil, 213
Goddard, Arabella, 176, 209
Godowsky, Leopold, 182, 183
Goethe, Johann Wolfgang von, 27-29
Goldsand, Robert, 213
Goode, Richard, 216
Goodman, Benny David, 142-145
Gottschalk, Louis, 22-24
Gould, Glenn, 215
Gould, Morton, 206
Graffman, Gary, 215
Grandjany, Marcel, 202
Grétry, Lucile, 176
Grisi, Giulia, 221
Guilford, Nanette, 222
Gulda, Friedrich (Fred), 113
Hallé, Sir Charles, 71, 209
Hambourg, Mark, 211
Hancock, Herbie, 113
Handel, George Frideric, 16-17
Harris, Margaret, 114
Hauk, Minnie, 221
Haydn, Franz Joseph, 17-18
Hegner, Otto, 211
Heifetz, Jascha, 171, 172, 219-220
Heller, Stephen, 204
Henselt, Adolf, 182
Herschel, William, 111
Hess, Myra, 211
Hiller, Ferdinand, 29, 204
Hilsberg, Alexander, 219
Hilsberg, Ignaz, 211
Hoffman, Richard, 209
Hofmann, Josef, 54, 173
Holiday, Billie, 152-153
Hollander, Lorin, 131-133
Holmes, Alfred, 201
Holly, Buddy, 224
Holmès, Augusta, 210
Holmes, Henry, 201
Horowitz, Vladimir, 212-213
Horszowski, Mieczyslaw, 211
Hubay, Jenö, 218
Huberman, Bronislaw, 171, 219
Hummel, Johann, 209
Hundley, Craig, 226
Hutchinson, Karen, 216
Hyllested, August, 210
Ian, Janis, 224-225
Istomin, Eugene, 214-215
Iturbi, Ampara, 176
James, Harry, 230
Janis, Byron, 172, 190, 215
Janotha, Natalie, 210
Joachim, Joseph, 218
Johnson, Robert, 227-228

Jones, Tommy, 229
Kalkbrenner, Friedrich, 209
Kapell, William, 214
Kentmer, Louis, 213
Kirk, Andy, 231
Kirk, Roland ("Rahsaan"), 159
Kloss, Eric, 231
Kneisel, Franz, 218
Knight, Gladys, 229
Knussen, Oliver, 89
Kochanski, Paul, 219
Korngold, Erich, 199
Koussevitsky, Serge, 107
Koutzen, Boris, 220
Koutzen, Nadia, 220
Krebs, Marie, 210
Kreisler, Fritz, 184
Kreutzer, Rodolphe, 217
Kriens, Christian, 206
Kubelik, Jan, 164, 171
Kubelik, Rafael, 165
La Guerre, Elizabeth de, 176
La Marchina, Robert, 196
Lablache, Luigi, 221
Laredo, Jaime, 172, 187
Larrocha, Alicia de, 214
Laszlo, Erwin, 215
Lecuona, Ernesto, 199
Lee, Brenda, 229
Lefébure-Wély, Louis, 208
Leginska (Liggins), Ethel, 211
Lehmann, Lilli, 67, 221
Leschetitzky, Theodor, 209
Levant, Oscar, 213
Levitzki, Mischa, 212
Lewis, Henry, 207
Lhevinne, Josef, 211
Lind, Jenny, 60-61, 221
Linley, Thomas, 217
Lipatti, Dinu, 214
List, Eugene, 214
Liszt, Franz, 23, 41, 43-46, 49
Loussier, Jacques, 226
Lully, Jean-Baptiste, 35
Lyman, Frankie, 224
Maazel, Lorin, 85-87
Maehashi, Teiko, 129
Malibran (Garcia), Maria, 61
Mara, Gertrude, 36, 176
Marchisio, Barbara, 221
Marco, Gianella de, 88-89
Marcovici, Silvia, 221
Marteau, Henry, 219
Martinez, Marianne de, 203
Mattheson, Johann, 203
Mendelssohn, Fanny, 26, 29, 176
Mendelssohn, Felix, 25-34
Menga, Robert, 220
Menter, Sophie, 176, 210
Menuhin, Yehudi, 92-98, 176, 190

Merö, Yolanda, 211
Meyerbeer, Giacomo, 203
Milanollo sisters, 176
Mildner, Poldi, 213
Miles, Barry, 227
Milstein, Nathan, 220
Mingus, Charles, 223
Mischakoff, Mischa, 219
Monk, Thelonius, 223
Monteverdi, Claudio, 197
Montoya, Carlos, 108-110
Moore, Kermit, 196
Mori, Nicolas, 217
Morini, Erica, 177
Morton, Ferdinand ("Jelly Roll"), 226
Moscheles, Ignaz, 29-30, 71, 209
Mozart, Marianne ("Nannerl"), 176
Mozart, Wolfgang Amadeus, 18-20, 180
Munsel, Patrice, 172-173
Napoleon (Napoleão), Arthur, 82, 210
Nat, Yves, 206
Nelsova, Zara, 196
Neruda, Wilma, 163
Novaës, Guiomar, 181, 211-212
Nyro, Laura, 155
Oistrakh, David, 188
Paganini, Niccolò, 37-41
Parisot, Aldo, 196
Parkenning, Christopher, 129-130
Pasquier, Regis, 220-221
Paton, Mary Anne, 221
Patti, Adelina, 62-66
Pennario, Leonard, 174, 214
Penniman, Richard ("Little Richard"), 229
Perahia, Murray, 216
Perlman, Itzhak, 128, 189
Persinger, Louis, 91
Peterson, "Lucky," 227
Philidor, André, 110
Piastro, Mischel, 219
Piatigorsky, Gregor, 106-107
Pierson, James, 216
Planté, François, 209
Ponti, Michael, 216
Potter, Cipriani, 204
Powell, Maud, 219
Presley, Elvis, 229
Preston, Billy, 226
Previn, André, 114
Prokofiev, Sergei, 199
Purcell, Henry, 197
Putterman, David, 58-59
Rabin, Michael, 172
Rachmaninoff, Sergei, 53
Rainey, Gertrude ("Ma"), 227
Ran, Shulamit, 207
Randalls (Randles), Elizabeth, 209

Rappoldi, Edouard, 218
Reeves, Sims, 204
Rheinberger, Josef, 205
Ricci, Ruggiero, 98–103
Richter, Sviatoslav, 188
Rivé-King, Julie, 210
Robinson, Frank ("Sugar-Chile"), 226
Rodgers, Richard, 200
Rolle, Tony, 216
Romero family, 201
Rosen, Max, 219
Rosenthal, Moritz, 210
Rossini, Gioacchino, 40, 64, 197
Rostropovich, Mstislav, 188, 196
Rubinstein, Anton, 46–48
Rubinstein, Artur, 48, 170, 180, 181
Rubinstein, Beryl, 212
Rubinstein, Erna, 220
Ruskin, Abbott, 216
Saint-Saëns, Camille, 47
Saperton, David, 211
Sarasate, Pablo, 218
Sauret, Emile, 218
Scarlatti, Domenico, 203
Schauroth, Delphine, 209
Schnabel, Artur, 10, 211
Schnabel, Karl Ulrich, 211
Schröder-Devrient, Wilhelmine, 221
Schubert, Franz, 20–21
Schuller, Gunther, 207
Schumann (Wieck), Clara, 48–50, 176
Schumann, Robert, 48
Schuyler, Philippa, 72–79
Scott, Hazel, 112–113
Segovia, Andrés, 13, 108
Seidel, Toscha, 219
Senior, John, 202
Senkrah, Arma, 218
Serebrier, José, 200
Serkin, Peter, 164
Serkin, Rudolf, 164, 180
Sgambati, Giovanni, 209
Shaw, Artie, 230
Shearing, George, 156
Sherwood, Arabella Parepa, 205
Short, Robert ("Bobby"), 228
Shostakovitch, Dmitri, 200
Sivori, Camillo, 217
Slenczynska, Ruth, 51–55
Smetana, Bedrich, 204
Smith, Bessie, 227
Sokolov, Grigory, 216
Soldat, Marie, 210
Sontag, Henrietta, 221
Sorel, Claudette, 215
Spivakovsky, Tossy, 220
Spohr, Ludwig, 217
Stainer, John, 208

Stanley, John, 208
Starker, Janos, 196
Stassevitch, Paul, 206
Stern, Isaac, 185, 193, 220
Strauss, Johann (the Younger), 198
Strauss, Richard, 199
Strungk, Nicolaus, 207
Supervia, Conchita, 222
Suzuki, Shinichi, 190–191
Szell, George, 83–84
Szeryng, Henryk, 220
Szigeti, Josef, 170, 172, 188
Talley, Marion, 222
Tatum, Art, 156–157
Tausig, Karl, 210
Telemann, Georg, 197
Templeton, Alec, 155–156
Thalberg, Sigismond, 209
Thomas, Theodore, 64, 218
Thomson, César, 218
Tomasso, Enrico, 231
Tong-il Han, 130
Toscanini, Arturo, 82–83, 96
Towlen, Gary, 216
Travers, Patricia, 220
Tsumura, Mari, 220
Tua, Teresina, 218
Tucker, Ira, 228–229
Turner, Joe, 227
Urso, Camilla, 176
Ushioda, Masuko, 129
Valens, Richie, 224
Vecsey, Franz von, 219
Viardot-Garcia, Pauline, 61–62
Vieuxtemps, Henri, 217
Viotti, Giovanni, 217
Walker, Aaron ("T-bone"), 225
Waller, Thomas ("Fats"), 150–151
Walter, Bruno, 12, 84
Watts, André, 130–131, 182, 183
Webb, Jim, 154
Weissenberg, Alexis ("Sigi"), 215
Wesley brothers, 203
Wicks, Camilla, 220
Wieniawski, Henri, 218
Williams, Hank, 223–224
Williams, Tony, 227
Wilson, Eric, 197
Winwood, Stevie, 154
Wonder (Judkins), Stevie, 160–161
Wyman, Karen, 229
Yong Uck Kim, 129
Zabaletor, Nicanor, 202
Zeisler (Bloomfield), Fanny, 210
Zimbalist, Efrem, 171, 186, 219
Zukerman, Pinchas, 172, 189
Zukofsky, Paul, 127